Library of Congress Cataloging-in-Publication Data
Feltenberger, Gregory S.
Gans, David N.
MGMA (Association); publisher.
EGZ Publications; production.
Benchmarking Success: The Essential Guide for Medical Practice Managers
  p ; cm
Includes bibliographical references.

Description: 1st. | Englewood, CO : Medical Group Management Association,
  Gregory S. Feltenberger,
  David N. Gans.
  c2017. | Includes bibliographical references.

Subjects: 1. Medical care-U.S. 2. Medicine-Practice-U.S.-Management
[DNLM 1. Management of Health Services-Methods-U.S. 2. Practice Management, Medical-U.S.]

MGMA Product ID 8913

PRINT ISBN 978-1-56829-483-4

Printed in the United States of America

10 9 8 7 6 5 4 3 2 1

BENCHMARKING
SUCCESS:

The Essential Guide For
Medical Practice Managers

Gregory S. Feltenberger, PhD, MBA, FACMPE, FACHE
David N. Gans, MHSA, FACMPE

BENCHMARKING SUCCESS:

The Essential Guide For Medical Practice Managers

GREGORY S. FELTENBERGER

DAVID N. GANS

This book is dedicated to my children,

Brittany, Aaron, and Taylor for always making

me proud. To my mother, Linda, for her strength and inspiration,

to my father, Ron, for his drive and focus, and to the love of my life,
Rachel.

And finally, to all the outstanding members of the

Air Force Medical Service Corps and the physicians and staff of

the Idaho Urologic Institute & Surgery Center of Idaho.

— Greg

This book is dedicated to my parents,

Hope and Harry, who instilled a love of learning,

and to my spouse, Joan,

who encouraged me to pursue my dreams.

— David

ACKNOWLEDGEMENTS

We would like to thank Craig Wilberg and the staff at the MGMA for their patience, support, and invaluable guidance. In addition, we would like to thank several people for support, review, and chapter development in the 1st edition: Lee Ann Webster, CPA, FACMPE, Ronald L. Stoudt, Senior Vice President, and Greg Staab, Area Banking Executive, both of Key Bank, and Colonel Ted Woolley (retired) of the Air Force Medical Service Corps. And we would like to thank Marcia Brauchler, MPH, FACMPE, CPC, COC, CPC-I, CPHO for writing Chapter 12, Bencharmking Resources, and Owen J. Dahl, MBA, FACHE, LSSMBB for writing Chapter 14, Using Lean Six-Sigma to Improve Operations. Finally, we would like to thank the many people who provided support for this edition.

TABLE OF CONTENTS

PREFACE

Benchmarking and the use of medical practice data have become a necessity in today's health care environment. To lead a successful practice, administrators and physician-owners must ask (and answer) several questions. For instance, how does my practice compare with others and what metrics should I use? And how profitable and productive is my practice and what performance metrics should I look at? This book will answer these and many other questions. Also, many of the calculations are presented with a goal (for example, "higher the better" or "lower the better"). In general, the goals presented are typical across all practices; however, and in most cases, practice-specific factors (context) will determine the right goal for your practice.

The idea for this book originated from the need for a user-friendly "how-to" guide for medical practice benchmarking complete with standardized medical practice terms, ratios, and formulas. The examples used in this book were developed to illustrate and explain benchmarking methods and are not representative of actual medical practices. In addition, as you read through and use this book, if you have suggestions for improving the content or you know of (or use) other formulas, ratios, or methods of measurement that should be included, the authors would greatly appreciate the input.

Users of medical practice data should pay careful attention to the first few chapters since the true value of benchmarking can only be realized by understanding the process and interpreting and communicating the findings. Also, the implications of improperly using data or making decisions based on erroneous interpretations can result in serious and costly mistakes—perhaps your job or the practice's financial health.

To help users with many of the benchmarking tools presented in this book, most of the practice factors presented can be associated with line items from a sample accounts receivable (A/R) aging report, operational report, balance sheet, or income statement (profit & loss) found in Appendix I, "Example Practice: Description, Reports, and Financial Statements."

Chapter 1: Why Benchmark?

This chapter answers the question, "why benchmark?" It also addresses the reasons for benchmarking or "if you don't measure it, you can't manage it" and "if you don't value it, you won't change it."

Chapter 2: Benchmarking Fundamentals

This chapter explains the importance of and need for standards and describes techniques for determining baseline and current status of a practice. In addition, this chapter presents factors that can be changed to improve a practice. And finally, this chapter describes similarities and differences of small and solo practices in comparison to larger practices.

Chapter 3: Measurement and Benchmarking

This chapter defines measurement, associated terms, the art and science of benchmarking, and several benchmarking methods. In addition, this chapter describes common mistakes to avoid when interpreting measurements and benchmarks.

Chapter 4: Management by the Numbers

This chapter presents methods of describing and presenting data in meaningful ways, changing it into information, and using it to help make management decisions.

Chapter 5: How to Show the Bank a Credit-Worthy Practice

This chapter explains differences in medical practice financial accounting, what financial indicators banks want to see, and how to demonstrate practice credit-worthiness.

Chapter 6: Key Performance Indicators

This chapter identifies several very important metrics that could be used to establish a core metric set for a practice.

Chapter 7: Benchmarking Ancillaries, Scribes, and Support Staff

This chapter describes metrics to assess anciallary services, the use of scribes, and productivity of support staff.

Chapter 8: Measuring Quality

This chapter explores different metrics used to measure clinical quality to include measures developed by the insurance industry and the government.

Chapter 9: Measuring Practice Operations

This chapter provides serveral techniques for measuring practice operations at the patient, provider, and staffing levels.

Chapter 10: Tools for Measuring Practice Finances

This chapter identifies serveral metrics associated with financial activities.

Chapter 11: Hospital and Inpatient Metrics

This chapter presents common hospital and inpatient metrics for determining market share, occupancy rate, length-of-stay, average daily census, payer mix, expense and revenue per discharge, full-time equivalents per bed and other measures.

Chapter 12: Benchmarking Resources

This chapter explores free online resources for assessing E&M coding and fee schedule for benchmarking provider and practice factors.

Chapter 13: Talking Numbers to Physicians

This chapter describes methods for communicating with physicians using executive summaries, presentations, graphs, charts, and tables. It also presents considerations regarding audience, formatting, and writing style.

Chapter 14: Using Lean Six Sigma to Improve Operations

This chapter provides an overview of concepts to include a general foundation to increase effectiveness and efficiency of operations using Lean Six Sigma.

Chapter 15: Performance and Practices of Sucessful Medical Groups

This chapter presents all the key metrics used by MGMA to assess Performance and Practices of Successful Medical Groups.

Conclusion and Future Implications

This section summarizes, highlights, and presents possible future implications and uses of benchmarking in health care.

Appendices:

I. Example Practice: Description, Reports, and Financial Statements

This section presents a description, an A/R aging and operational report, a balance sheet, and an income statement (profit & loss) for a sample practice. Many of the factors presented in the formulas and ratios throughout this book can be referenced in this section to assist users with finding numbers and performing calculations.

II. Predicting Demand

This is a reprint of an article by Murray J. Cote and Stephen J. Tucker that presents four methods of forecasting, the pros and cons of each method, and an explanation of how to apply each method.

III. Patient Satisfaction

This section presents several reprints from MGMA identifying techniques and information related to patient satisfaction and patient perceptions.

IV. Advanced Access (Open Access)

This section includes four reprints related to advanced access to include lessons learned from practices that have implemented open access.

V. Benchmarking Guidance

This section contains two articles from the MGMA Connection on advanced benchmarking.

VI. Value-Based Care

This section includes four articles on value-based care at the organizational and physician compensation levels.

VII. Profitability and Operating Costs

This section contains two articles from the MGMA Connection with a focus on profitability and control of costs.

VIII. Productivity, Capacity, and Staffing

This section contains four articles from the MGMA Connections related to cost efficiencies, provider compensation, and rightsizing staff.

IX. Accounts Receivable and Collections

This section contains data and articles from the MGMA Connections and MGMA Performance and Practices of Successful Medical Groups reports on accounts receivable and collections.

X. Operations

This section includes three articles from the MGMA Connection related to practice operations.

Glossary

This section provides terms and definitions used throughout this book.

Acronyms and Geographic Sections

This section provides many common acronyms and geographic sections used throughout this book and in MGMA surveys and other publications.

Physician Categories

This section presents most of the typical physician categories (specialties) used throughout this book and in MGMA surveys and other publications.

Index

CHAPTER 1

WHY
BENCHMARK?

"When you're finished changing, you're finished."
- Benjamin Franklin
"Insanity: Doing the same thing over and over again and expecting different results."
- Albert Einstein

Why benchmark? There are many reasons to benchmark (compare a selected set of criteria against a given standard) in any medical practice. For example, a practice may want to determine how the billing office performance or physician productivity compares to other practices. Practices use benchmarking to gain a deeper understanding of where they are, where they want to go, and how to they will get there. The complexity of healthcare dictates practices use more sophisticated and accurate methods of measurement, analysis, comparison, and improvement. Since a practice's long-term success is directly related to its ability to identify, predict, and adjust for changes, benchmarking, when used properly, is the best tool for overcoming these challenges.

This book is meant to be a desktop reference for medical practice benchmarking. It hopes to "set the standard" by eliminating ambiguity in healthcare measurement.

Two key principles of benchmarking are

1.   If you don't measure it, you can't manage it and
2.   If you don't value it, you won't change it.

These principles have been applied to other industries for many years and are ideally suited for use in healthcare. It has been said that healthcare is the only service industry that doesn't treat itself like one. The healthcare industry may appear separate from other business sectors, but there are more similarities than differences. In the classroom, students are taught that managers manage processes and leaders lead people. The same can be said of the healthcare field—there are processes to be managed and people to be led. Like other service industries providing customers with services, healthcare too has customers (patients) who expect services (procedures and treatments).

If You Don't Measure It, You Can't Manage It

To manage something, it is necessary to know *what* it is, *where* it is in relation other things, and *describe* how it got there. This can be accomplished through measurement and benchmarking (see Exhibit 1.1). Proper practice management requires the use of subjective and objective measurement, analysis, comparison, and improvement.

For example, if you want to reduce a given set of supply costs, you would first identify and define these costs. In this case, supply costs are defined as any disposable medical item used to provide clinical services to patients. Supply cost can then be calculated using a formula for average daily cost of supplies used per provider and per patient. Comparing this to historical data, it is possible to determine whether costs are increasing and to what degree. If costs are increasing, it would then be necessary to explore the context surrounding this increase—increase cost of items in question, increase in number of patients treated, etc.

EXHIBIT 1.1 QUESTIONS TO HELP ANSWER, "HOW IT GOT THERE?"

HOW IMPORTANT ARE THE SUPPLIES TO THE PROVIDERS?

HOW LONG HAS THE PRACTICE DONE BUSINESS WITH THE SUPPLY COMPANY?

HOW COMPETITIVE IS THE LOCAL SUPPLY MARKET?

HOW WAS THE PRACTICE'S BUSINESS ARRANGEMENT WITH THE SUPPLY COMPANY SETUP?

DOES THE PRACTICE HAVE A CONTRACTUAL AGREEMENT WITH THE SUPPLY COMPANY? IF YES, WHEN DOES IT EXPIRE?

WHAT INTERNAL CONTROLS ARE IN-PLACE TO MANAGE COSTS FOR PURCHASING AND INVENTORY FUNCTIONS?

WHAT FACTORS COULD BE CAUSING HIGH SUPPLY COSTS (E.G., THEFT, WASTE, DISORGANIZATION, SPOILAGE [PHARMACEUTICAL INVENTORY], OBSOLESCENCE, OR KICKBACKS BETWEEN THE SUPPLY COMPANY AND CLINIC PERSONNEL)?

If You Don't Value It, You Won't Change It

Driving change in a practice will affect every member of the organization and many will resist; therefore, the value of instituting a change must outweigh the status quo. Measurement and benchmarking are not the final step in the process—they simply enable the process to evolve toward action. Measuring and benchmarking is an activity performed in vain if something isn't done with the findings. Ideally, the results should be used to support change; however, they can be used to validate past changes or support the current status quo. Once the benchmarking process is finished, the practice can select the areas to focus its efforts, create buy-in, and start the process of improvement—or repeat the entire benchmarking exercise in the process of continuous improvement.

What can be done with the findings? Options include:

1. Drive and/or support change,
2. educate staff,
3. gain credibility with your physicians,
4. validate the past,
5. build buy-in with the staff,
6. conduct performance reviews, and
7. plan for the future.

When using the key benchmarking principles— "if you don't measure it, you can't manage it" and "if you don't value it, you won't change it," it is imperative to understand interrelationships (see Exhibit 1.2). First, proper management requires some degree of measurement to ensure the thing you're interested in measuring is well understood (for example, is an FTE clearly defined as working 40 hours/week or only 32?). Second, once measurement is taken, management must decide whether the value of pursuing change is worth disrupting the practice's normal routine in the quest for improvement. And third, if management feels value can be realized by making a change, it is important that a sense of value be instilled with physicians and staff—without their commitment, the change will never be fully realized.

This is key. Processes can easily be changed, but it is only with the support and buy-in of physicians and staff that real improvement can be achieved. It is an old U.S. Army saying that, "If you take care of your people, your people will take care of you." Conversely, if you don't take care of your people, your people won't take care of you.

EXHIBIT 1.2 RELATIONSHIP BETWEEN KEY BENCHMARKING PRINCIPLES

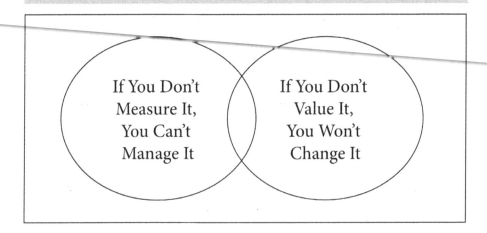

People naturally resist change and there are several reasons for this. They may fear a loss of control or discomfort from uncertainty.[1] If the change comes as a surprise to the staff, they will likely resist and/or seek to undermine any changes.[1] Some staff might be emotionally invested in a current process or may consider change a threat to their abilities or competence.[1] Change can often be interpreted as a disruption that will create more work.[1]

Organizational commitment is necessary to drive change (see Exhibit 1.3). That is, the organization must feel strongly that change is needed, be focused on discovering what it wants or needs to change, and has developed a vision and expectations for the organization's future.[2] Acceptance of the change's benefits, ability of the organization to change, and a commitment to improve can be demonstrated best by showing disbelievers an organization that has already implemented the proposed change—via a field trip, for example.[2]

EXHIBIT 1.3 METHODS OF FACILITATING CHANGE[1]

INVOLVE PROVIDERS AND STAFF IN THE PROCESS

COMMUNICATE, COMMUNICATE, COMMUNICATE

COMMUNICATE EARLY AND REGULARLY

EXPLAIN PURPOSE

ESTABLISH EXPECTATIONS

ASK FOR COMMENTS, SUGGESTIONS, AND INVOLVEMENT IN PROCESS

DISSECT AND IMPLEMENT CHANGE INTO MANAGEABLE PARTS

BE PATIENT

IDENTIFY "STAR PERFORMERS" AND RECOGNIZE THEM PUBLICLY

ENSURE RESOURCES AND TRAINING IS AVAILABLE TO ACHIEVE GOAL

REMAIN FLEXIBLE

FOCUS ON THE FUTURE; DON'T DWELL ON THE PAST

The importance of creating buy-in and facilitating change must be seriously considered and built into the change process. For instance, the change driver (typically an administrator) must understand staff will have strong emotional reactions toward change and will often perceive it as a threat.[1] Therefore, the administrator must fully explore the underlying feelings and perceptions of providers and staff.[1] To maximize acceptance, the administrator should

- Solicit providers and staff for feedback and suggestions,
- explain the reasons behind the need for change, and
- involve all members in the process as much as is reasonable based on the planned timeline.[1]

---

1 D. Balestracci and J. Barlow, Quality Improvement, Practical Applications for Medical Group Practice, 2nd ed. (Englewood, CO: Center for Research in Ambulatory Health Care Administration, 1998).

2 R. Camp, "Best Practice Benchmarking: The Path to Excellence." CMA Magazine, 72, no. 6 (1998): 10.

CHAPTER 2

BENCHMARKING FUNDAMENTALS

"To compare is to improve."
- Unknown

Medical practice benchmarking is a systematic, logical, and common-sense approach to measurement, analysis, comparison, and improvement (see Exhibit 2.1). Benchmarking improves understanding of processes and clinical and administrative characteristics whether measured at a single point in time or over span of time,[3] and whether you're measuring and comparing performance internally to determine changes between the practice a year ago, and now, or externally, comparing your practice to a practice that demonstrates superiority in a given quality. Benchmarking also helps determine how the "best in class" practices achieve their performance levels. This consists of analyzing and comparing those "best" practices to uncover what they did, how they did it, and what must be done to adopt those changes into your practice.[1]

EXHIBIT 2.1 WHAT IS BENCHMARKING?

A SYSTEMATIC, LOGICAL, AND COMMON-SENSE APPROACH TO MEASUREMENT, COMPARISON, AND IMPROVEMENT

COPYING THE BEST, CLOSING GAPS/DIFFERENCES, AND ACHIEVING SUPERIORITY[2]

"A POSITIVE, PROACTIVE PROCESS TO CHANGE OPERATIONS IN A STRUCTURED FASHION TO ACHIEVE SUPERIOR PERFORMANCE. THE PURPOSE IS TO GAIN A COMPETITIVE ADVANTAGE."[1]

COMPARING ORGANIZATIONAL PERFORMANCE TO THE PERFORMANCE OF OTHER ORGANIZATIONS[3]

CONTINUOUS PROCESS OF COMPARISON WITH THE BEST[5] OR "THE TOUGHEST COMPETITORS OR COMPANIES RENOWNED AS LEADERS"[3]

A METHOD FOR IDENTIFYING PROCESSES TO NEW GOALS WITH FULL SUPPORT OF MANAGEMENT[5]

Who Set the Standard?

The importance of having a standard is to establish a common understanding and ensure consistency and continuity over time. To date, a true standard has not been set for medical practice benchmarking. Therefore, this book is an attempt to fill this void. In addition, the MGMA has a long history of surveying and providing medical practices with valuable benchmarking information. Therefore, survey reports and DataDive from MGMA are excellent standard-setting tools since they have amassed several decades of medical practice data and have provided the foundation for building true standards.

Reasons for Benchmarking[1]

There are many reasons for benchmarking. The benefits[4] include

1. Increase understanding of practice operations,
2. learn about industry leaders, competitors, and best practices,
3. incorporate best practices,
4. gain or maintain a competitive advantage and industry superiority,
5. adopt best practices from any industry into organizational processes (learn and compare against others),
6. breakdown reluctance to change,
7. uncover new concepts, ideas, and technologies,
8. objectively evaluate performance and understand organization's strengths and weaknesses[6],
9. observe where you have been, and predict where you are going[6],
10. analyze what others do, to learn from their experiences[6],
11. determine how the best in class achieve their performance levels so you can implement their processes[6],
12. and convince internal audiences of the need for change[6].

THE VALUE OF BENCHMARKING

Proper benchmarking is more than the comparison of two or more numbers. Its true value lies in using the data collected to better understand the current state of the practice, to calculate a difference between the current state and a new value or benchmark, to develop the context and background of the practice values when interpreting the results, to decide on a course of action and goal, and to determine when the goal is achieved. Consider a comparison of an average number of procedures per patient visit per physician to a known benchmark—numerically it provides an accurate analysis. However, what if one physician in the practice has been focusing on patients with simple medical issues, ones that don't generate procedures? The numbers alone would indicate this physician is underperforming; whereas, when the background, the context, is considered, a more useful analysis is possible. Perhaps this physician's focus is on acute care services and his/her average number of patient encounters per day is almost twice that of other physicians in the practice.

SOURCES OF BENCHMARKS

Benchmarks are available from many sources. The most common source is from averages (means) or medians of healthcare performance measures derived from surveys, reports, or data files. For example, the *MGMA Physician Compensation and Production Survey* and *MGMA Cost Survey for Single-Specialty and Multispecialty Practices* are excellent sources for benchmarks. Another source is measures and processes from better performing practices. These are modeled on organizations that have achieved a particular goal or attained a certain level of success or performance. The *MGMA Performance and Practices of Successful Medical* Groups is an ideal source for better performing practice benchmarks. Benchmarks from "best in industry" practices are also excellent sources for measures and processes. These benchmarks are taken from organizations inside and outside healthcare. Of note, benchmarks from outside the healthcare industry are excellent sources that are often overlooked. For example, the Disney Corporation is an excellent resource for customer service and Wal-Mart is ideal for supply chain management and cost containment.

How to Benchmark[4]

There are several methods of benchmarking. A simple 10-step process might consist of the following:

- Determine what is critical to your organization's success
- Identify metrics that measure the critical factors
- Find a source for internal and external benchmarking data
- Measure your practice's performance
- Compare your practice's performance to the benchmark
- Determine if action is necessary based on the comparison
- If action is needed, identify the best practice and process used to implement it
- Adapt the process used by other in the context of your practice
- Implement new process, reassess objectives, evaluate benchmarking standards, and recalibrate measures
- Do it again—benchmarking is an ongoing process and tracking over time allows for continuous improvement

Standardizing Data for Comparison[4]

Since the primary purpose of benchmarking is comparison, it is necessary to standardize data so organizations of different sizes can be compared. A common method for standardizing data is to convert measures to percentages, per unit of input, or per unit of output. For example, per unit of input can be presented as per full-time equivalent (FTE) physician, per FTE provider, or per square foot; whereas, per unit of output can be presented on a per patient, per RBRVS unit (or wRVU), or per procedure level.

What's Our Baseline?

Benchmarking, like any activity involving comparison, requires an understanding of where you are. This is known as your baseline (see Exhibit 2.2). The baseline represents where you are today or where you've been and provides a point of origin or starting point. In addition, a baseline is an initial state that forms a logical basis for comparison.[5] For example, to determine whether physicians have increased the average number of procedures per patient visit, two measurements are required: the old baseline value and the new value. To calculate the delta (or difference) between the two values, a simple formula can be used: new value minus old value. Without the baseline, it would not be possible to perform this or many other calculations like percent change.

How Are We Doing?

This question can be answered by asking the question, "what is the difference between a baseline and the practice's current state?" The baseline can be an internal benchmark (historical measure) from inside the practice, a benchmark from similar practices (from an MGMA survey report), or a benchmark from outside the industry like Disney or Wal-Mart. Additional insights can also be assessed by calculating the difference between current state and an established benchmark or industry average or median. To determine the difference there are several methods and statistical tools. For instance, the mathematical difference or delta consists of subtracting the baseline value from the current value. Whereas, percent change (new value minus old value then divide by old value) assesses changes over time or the proportion of one value in comparison to another. In addition to these methods, there are more statistically intense methods to determine difference that can be generalized across a group (see Exhibit 2.2).

EXHIBIT 2.2 WHAT IS THE DIFFERENCE?

MATHEMATICAL DIFFERENCE (DELTA)

NEW VALUE MINUS OLD VALUE

CURRENT STATE MINUS INITIAL STATE

BENCHMARK/INDUSTRY VALUE MINUS CURRENT STATE

PERCENT CHANGE

INFERENTIAL STATISTICAL METHODS

INDEPENDENT T-TEST

DIFFERENCE BETWEEN TWO INDEPENDENT AVERAGES

MANN-WHITNEY U-TEST

DIFFERENCE BETWEEN TWO INDEPENDENT MEDIANS

PAIRED T-TEST

DIFFERENCE BETWEEN TWO AVERAGES

COMPARES A CASE AND MATCHED CONTROL OR REPEATED MEASURES

WILCOXON MATCHED PAIRS TEST

DIFFERENCE BETWEEN TWO MEDIANS

COMPARES A CASE AND MATCHED CONTROL OR REPEATED MEASURES

ONE-WAY ANOVA

DIFFERENCE BETWEEN THREE OR MORE AVERAGE

KRUSKAL-WALLIS H-TEST

DIFFERENCE BETWEEN THREE OR MORE MEDIANS

More complex inferential methods are available to determine the statistical significance of the difference between two or more averages or medians: Independent T-test, Mann-Whitney U-test, Paired T-test, Wilcoxon Matched Pairs Test, One-Way ANOVA, and Kruskal-Wallis H-test. However, these methods require greater understanding of the use, limitations, requirements, analysis, and interpretation and are outside the scope of this book. For information on these methods, see Exhibit 2.3 for a short list of resources.

MEASUREMENT

EXHIBIT 2.3 SOURCES OF STATISTICS INFORMATION

BLUMAN, A. G., *ELEMENTARY STATISTICS: A STEP BY STEP APPROACH* (9TH EDITION). BOSTON: McGRAW-HILL HIGHER EDUCATION; 2014.

DANIEL, W. W. & CROSS., C. *BIOSTATISTICS: A FOUNDATION FOR ANALYSIS IN THE HEALTH SCIENCES* (10TH EDITION). NEW YORK: JOHN WILEY & SONS, INC.; 2013.

HYPERSTAT ONLINE, HTTP://DAVIDMLANE.COM/HYPERSTAT/

KELLEY, L. D., *MEASUREMENT MADE ACCESSIBLE: A RESEARCH APPROACH USING QUALITATIVE, QUANTITATIVE, AND QUALITY IMPROVEMENT METHODS.* THOUSAND OAKS: SAGE PUBLICATIONS; 1999.

ONLINE STATISTICS BOOK, HTTP://ONLINESTATBOOK.COM/

ROSNER, B., *FUNDAMENTALS OF BIOSTATISTICS* (7TH EDITION). CENGAGE LEARNING; 2010.

ROTHSTEIN, J. M. & ECHTERNACH, J. L., *PRIMER ON MEASUREMENT: AN INTRODUCTORY GUIDE TO MEASUREMENT ISSUES.* ALEXANDRIA: AMERICAN PHYSICAL THERAPY ASSOCIATION; 1993.

TABACHNICK, B. G. & FIDELL, L. S., *USING MULTIVARIATE STATISTICS* (4TH EDITION). BOSTON: ALLYN AND BACON; 2001

Interpretation of the difference is dependent on the method used. When using the delta, the difference will be a raw number, since the method consists of simple subtraction. Determining whether the difference is good or bad depends on the context, background, and what the values represent. For example, if medical revenue after operating cost per FTE family practice physician is $145,000 and the MGMA benchmark indicates a median of $214,377, then the delta is $69,377 ($214,377 - $145,000). A delta of $69,377 may suggest poor practice performance, reduced physician productivity, a capital investment, or other practice deficiencies or large expenses. Whereas, the percent change method indicates this practice is only generating 67% of the median for similar types of practices (see Exhibit 2.4). Therefore, the result is different between delta and percent change and the interpretation may also be different.

Exhibit 2.4 Difference between Delta and Percent Change		
Is the result positive or negative?	Delta	Percent Change
Positive value	New value (or benchmark) is *greater* than the old value. For example, $214,377 minus $145,000 equals a delta of $69,377	New value has *increased*. For example, $145,000 divided by $214,377 equals 0.67. This when multiplied by 100 equals 67%.
Negative value	New value is *less*.	New value has *decreased*

Getting from Here to There

Once the difference between baseline and current state or current state and benchmark is known, the next step is to determine whether there is a desire to change and what factors (practice measures) can be influenced in the preferred direction. Therefore, it is imperative a desire to change be established throughout the organization. In addition, this desire should be grown and nurtured by involving physicians and staff in the entire process.

Best Practices and Lessons Learned

Knowing the best method for completing a task and mistakes to avoid would result in quicker and less costly improvements. Lessons learned are suggested techniques or efficiencies for overcoming errors or avoiding mistakes. They can be tips, tricks, or cautions from those who've already tried and succeeded (or failed). And best practices are specific characteristics, measures, or processes considered to be best in class (see Exhibit 2.5). And best practices are specific characteristics, measures, or processes considered to be best in class by subjective (personal opinion) or objective criteria (for example, a measure at or above the 90th percentile).

EXHIBIT 2.5 BEST PRACTICES AND LESSONS LEARNED RESOURCES	
REQUIRE MGMA MEMBERSHIP: MGMA's EBSCO (ELTON B. STEPHENS COMPANY) DATABASE MGMA MEMBERSHIP FORUMS	HARVARD BUSINESS REVIEW (WWW. HBR.ORG) THE MCKINSEY QUARTERLY (WWW. MCKINSEYQUARTERLY.COM) SIX SIGMA (WWW,ISIXSIGMA.COM)

METHODS AND CHECKLISTS

Failing to plan, it has been said, is planning to fail. Therefore, an integral component of the benchmarking process is the proper use of systematic methods, checklists, scales, and comparable measures. Systematic methods consist of formulas and ratios as found in this book. Checklists are a planning tool to ensure all variables and methods are used and considered—checklists ensure attention to detail and minimize the chance of missing steps in a process (see Exhibit 2.6). Scales provide the measuring stick—meaning they indicate whether your measures are high or low, good or bad, or where they are in comparison to others. And comparable measures are key to the heart and soul of benchmarking and provide a means for determining how your practice compares to others.

EXHIBIT 2.6 EXAMPLE CHECKLIST[6]

THE FOLLOWING CHECKLIST ITEMS CAN BE USED TO INCREASE THE LIKELIHOOD THAT A CLAIM WILL BE PROCESSED AND PAID WHEN FIRST SUBMITTED:

- PATIENT INFORMATION IS COMPLETE.
- PATIENT'S NAME AND ADDRESS MATCHES THE INSURER'S RECORDS.
- PATIENT'S GROUP NUMBER AND/OR SUBSCRIBER NUMBER IS CORRECT.
- PHYSICIAN'S SOCIAL SECURITY NUMBER, PROVIDER NUMBER OR TAX IDENTIFICATION NUMBER IS COMPLETED AND CORRECT.
- CLAIM IS SIGNED BY THE PHYSICIAN.
- ALL NECESSARY DATES ARE COMPLETED.

- DATES FOR CARE GIVEN ARE CHRONOLOGICAL AND CORRECT—FOR EXAMPLE IS THE DISCHARGE DATE LISTED AS BEFORE THE ADMISSION DATE?

- DATES FOR CARE GIVEN CONCUR WITH THE CLAIMS INFORMATION FROM OTHER PROVIDERS SUCH AS THE HOSPITAL, ETC.

- DIAGNOSIS IS COMPLETE.

- DIAGNOSIS IS CORRECT FOR THE SERVICES OR PROCEDURES PROVIDED.

- DIAGNOSTIC CODES ARE CORRECT FOR THE SERVICES OR PROCEDURES PROVIDED.

- CPT AND ICD-10 CODES ARE ACCURATE.

- DIAGNOSIS IS CODED USING ICD-10-CM TO THE HIGHEST LEVEL OF SPECIFICITY.

- FEE COLUMN IS ITEMIZED AND TOTALED.

- ALL NECESSARY INFORMATION ABOUT PRESCRIPTION DRUGS OR DURABLE MEDICAL EQUIPMENT PRESCRIBED BY THE PHYSICIAN IS INCLUDED.

- THE CLAIM IS LEGIBLE.

SMALL AND SOLO PRACTICE BENCHMARKING

Small and solo practices share many similarities with their larger counterparts; however, the benefits and risks associated with the differences can have significant impact on a small practice's longevity and financial success.

SIMILARITIES WITH LARGER PRACTICES

There are many similarities small and solo practices share with larger organizations. For instance, all medical practices must operate in the same healthcare environment and deal with the same healthcare legislation, malpractice insurance, payers, collection challenges, patient needs and expectations, delivery/standards of care, and processes—just to name a few.

Also, the benchmarking methods used by large organizations are identical to those used by small and solo practices (see Exhibit 2.7). And the use of normalized metrics permits comparison regardless of organizational size. Common examples available in most benchmarking datasets consist of measures per FTE physician/provider, per square foot, per patient, per procedure, and per RVU.[6]

EXHIBIT 2.7 SIMILARITIES REGARDLESS OF SIZE OR TYPE[7]

LEGISLATION CAN CHANGE PAYMENT (FOR EXAMPLE, MEDICARE/MEDICAID REIMBURSEMENT RATES ARE DETERMINED THROUGH LEGISLATION)

COSTS ARE INCREASING GREATER THAN INFLATION (FOR EXAMPLE, MEDICAL SUPPLIES AND EQUIPMENT COSTS ARE INCREASING AT A GREATER PERCENTAGE THAN REIMBURSEMENT RATES)

EXPENSES CHANGE

INCREASES IN PHYSICIAN COMPENSATION ARE FROM PRODUCTION (FOR EXAMPLE, MUCH OF PHYSICIAN COMPENSATION IS BASED ON PHYSICIAN PRODUCTION OR THE NUMBER OF PATIENTS SEEN AND THE PROCEDURES PERFORMED)

HEALTH SAVINGS ACCOUNTS WILL CHANGE PATIENT BEHAVIOR (FOR EXAMPLE, PATIENTS WILL TREAT MEDICAL CARE MORE LIKE A PRODUCT OR SERVICE THEY PAY FOR USING THE FUNDS IN THEIR ACCOUNT)

HOSPITALS ARE PURCHASING PHYSICIAN PRACTICES (AGAIN)

ADVANCES IN MEDICAL CARE ARE CHANGING CARE DELIVERY

PHYSICIANS ARE PUBLICLY RATED FOR QUALITY AND OUTCOMES

PHYSICIANS ARE PUBLICLY RATED FOR PATIENT SATISFACTION

WHAT'S THE DIFFERENCE?

Small and solo practices are different from larger groups in several ways, some of which a beneficial, while others are not. For instance, smaller organizations are generally more flexible, can adapt/change quickly, and in general, tend to be more efficient. However, small and solo practices are more sensitive to the risks associated with costly mistakes, lack of alternative revenue generating methods, and the absence of (or antiquated condition of) robust information systems. For example, with only one or two physicians in a practice, what impact would a poor decision or loss of a physician (due to sickness or some other unforeseen event) have on the practice? Can a small practice afford to retain adequate earnings for contingencies? Does the existing information system compliment and add to the efficiency of the practice? And does it interface with the information systems used by payers, hospitals, and other medical practices like referring practices/physicians?

Ultimately, the goals of smaller practices mirror those of larger groups—to have more satisfied patients, more fulfilling work environments for physicians and staff, and better economic outcomes.[5] However, the additional sensitivities of small and solo practices must be considered to ensure surprise events don't adversely impact the practice.

---

[1] R. Camp, "Benchmarking: The Search for Best Practices that Lead to Superior Performance, Part 1." *Quality Progress*, 22, no. 1 (1989): 61.

[2] D. Gans, "Benchmarking Successful Medical Groups to Improve Your Practice Performance." Presentation at MGMA Conference, Ohio, September 2006.

[3] R. Camp, "Best Practice Benchmarking: The Path to Excellence." *CMA Magazine*, 72, no. 6 (1998): 10.

[4] R. Camp, "A Bible for Benchmarking by Xerox." *Financial Executive*, July/August, 9, 4, (1993): 23.

[5] D. Gans and G. Feltenberger, "Benchmarking Military Performance Using Civilian Metrics." Presentation at American College of Healthcare Executives Annual Conference, March 2007.

[6] Wikipedia, "Baseline (configuration management)," http://en.wikipedia.org (2006).

[7] M. Zairi and J. Whymark, "The Transfer of Best Practices: How to Build a Culture of Benchmarking and Continuous Learning, Part 2." *Benchmarking*, 7, no. 2 (2000): 146.

CHAPTER 3

MEASUREMENT AND BENCHMARKING

"There are two possible outcomes: If the result confirms the hypothesis, then you've made a measurement. If the result is contrary to the hypothesis, then you've made a discovery."

- Enrico Fermi

Measurement is the collection and organization of data. In many cases, measurement is a method of converting an array, group, list, or set of data into a single variable that describes the entire dataset. A mean or average is a calculation that summarizes the central tendency or mathematical center of many data points, provided all data is of the same unit of measurement. An average is the most common calculation used to analyze and compare data. It is the most common since most people understand the concept of an average and how to calculate it.

For example, if we count the number of patients seen per month for the last 10 months for an eight-provider family medical practice located in the suburbs, we have an array of data with 10 data points—one data point for each month (see Exhibit 3.1). If we also have a list with the number of patients seen per month for the last 10 months for an eight-provider family medical practice located in a rural community, how can we easily compare these two practices? We can line up and organize the data points in chronological order, but what does this tell us? We might conclude the suburban practice sees a greater number of patients per month, but we can't accurately describe the difference or make a comparison. All we've done so far is arrange the data and guessed there was a difference by looking at or "eyeballing" the data—not the most accurate method. However, by calculating the average number of patients seen per month for the last 10 months for each practice, a single and accurate measure can be used to describe and compare the two groups.

EXHIBIT 3.1 EXAMPLE OF MEASUREMENT: NUMBER OF PATIENTS SEEN
PER MONTH

MONTH	SUBURBAN PRACTICE	RURAL PRACTICE
JANUARY	2,620	2,650
FEBRUARY	2,231	2,660
MARCH	2,264	2,266
APRIL	2,650	2,067
MAY	2,657	1,687
JUNE	2,670	3,690
JULY	3,067	3,070
AUGUST	2,690	2,071
SEPTEMBER	3,171	2,731
OCTOBER	3,710	3,730
SUM OF NUMBER OF PATIENTS SEEN PER MONTH	27,730	26,622
NUMBER OF DATA POINTS (MONTHS)	10	10
AVERAGE (SUM DIVIDED BY NUMBER OF MONTHS)	2,773	2,662

Comparing these practices, the suburban practice, on average, sees more
patients per month than the rural practice: 111 more (average number of
patients seen per month in the suburban practice minus average number of
patients seen per month in the rural practice).

ART AND SCIENCE OF BENCHMARKING

Benchmarking is the art and science of comparison. The "science" is the
systematic and logical process of analysis, whereas the "art" occurs during
the data gathering and interpretation phases and requires some common
sense. Once interpretation and analysis have occurred, data can be used for
comparison and decision-making. Exhibit 3.2 represents several examples of
metrics and associated benchmarks.

Exhibit 3.2 Examples of Benchmarks[1]

Encounters per FTE* physician	Mean	3,006	4,759	5,891	7,612	9,159
Procedures per FTE physician (Total)	6,341	3,006	4,759	5,891	7,612	9,159
Physician work RVUs** per FTE physician	4,751	4,412	7,506	5,123	5,622	6,809
Physician compensation	4,751	1,426	3,684	5,123	5,622	6,809

Other areas associated with benchmarking are

• Continuous improvement and
• evaluation and assessment.[5]

Continuous improvement refers to the need for repeated analysis using the same measures over time (trend). Evaluation and assessment describes the ways in which values are interpreted. An evaluation is a subjective, personal judgment of the value of something; whereas, an assessment is objective and quantifiable.[2]

Benchmarking Methods

Effective benchmarking requires a systematic process; therefore, several methods have been developed to ensure the process is handled efficiently (see Exhibit 3.3).

Exhibit 3.3 Common Benchmarking Methods

Transfer Model[3]	Five Stages of Benchmarking[4]	Five Steps of Benchmarking[5]	10 Steps to Benchmarking[6]
1. Identification and documentation of best practices.	1. Planning, selecting the processes to benchmark, and identification of customer expectations and critical success factors.	1. Planning what to benchmark and what organization to benchmark against.	1. Determine what is critical to your organization's success.
2. Validation and consensus of what to focus on and what are true best practices.			2. Identify metrics that measure the critical factors.
		2. Analyze performance gaps and project future performance.	3. Identify a source for internal and external benchmarking data.
3. Transfer and develop buy-in; sell ideas to management and get commitment to performance assessments, identification of priorities, and establishment of a plan.	2. Form the benchmarking team from across the organization.		
	3. Collect the data from best practice organizations and identify own processes.	3. Set targets for change and communicate to all levels.	4. Measure your practice's performance.
		4. Develop action plans, implement plans, and adjust as necessary.	5. Compare your practice's performance to the benchmark.
4. Implementation using team champions, selection of critical practices to support strategic initiatives.	4. Analyze data for gaps.	5. Achieve a state of maturity by integrating best practices into organization.	6. Determine if action is necessary based on the comparison. .
	5. Take action, identify what needs to be done to match best practice, and implement change.		

EXHIBIT 3.3 COMMON BENCHMARKING METHODS (CONT'D)

TRANSFER MODEL[3]	FIVE STAGES OF BENCHMARKING[4]	FIVE STEPS OF BENCHMARKING[5]	10 STEPS TO BENCHMARKING[6]
			7. IF ACTION IS NEEDED, IDENTIFY THE BEST PRACTICE AND PROCESS USED TO IMPLEMENT IT.
			8. ADAPT THE PROCESS USED BY OTHERS IN THE CONTEXT OF YOUR PRACTICE.
			9. IMPLEMENT NEW PROCESS, REASSESS OBJECTIVES, EVALUATE BENCHMARKING STANDARDS, AND RECALIBRATE MEASURES
			10. DO IT AGAIN, BENCHMARKING IS AN ONGOING PROCESS AND TRACKING OVER TIME ALLOWS FOR CONTINUOUS IMPROVEMENT.

Proper measurement begins with selecting the right practice attribute, characteristic, property, dimension, or variable to be assessed. In other words, what do we want to measure? Encounters per FTE physician, total procedures per FTE physician, and physician work RVUs per FTE physician are common examples of benchmarks and practice measures (see Exhibit 3.2). This book presents many practice attributes that have been operationally defined, that is, the attribute and measurement process have been clearly described in practice and literature as generally accepted. However, there may be practice attributes that are not typically measured or found in the literature. In these cases, it would be necessary to fully explore the characteristic before moving to the next step—this would be considered a "homegrown" attribute. Homegrown attributes are likely not needed, however, as the healthcare management field is sufficiently mature to have identified most, if not all, key practice characteristics.

Once a practice variable is selected, the next step is to decide on the appropriate method of measurement and the intended purpose. There are two general categories of metrics:

1. Informational and
2. actionable.

Informational metrics provide a simple description and unlike actionable metrics, they don't clearly suggest ways of affecting change. For example, if we decide to measure the average number of patients seen per month in a suburban practice as a metric to describe monthly practice productivity, then this metric simply tells us the arithmetic mean; it doesn't suggest anything more; whereas, actionable metrics are usually more complex, require an understanding of the context, and are compared to a benchmark or baseline. For instance, the formula to calculate average number of patients seen per month for the last 10 months per provider for an eight-provider family medical practice is the sum of the number of patients seen per month for the last 10 months divided by the number of months divided by the number of providers (see Exhibit 3.1). If we use this formula as a metric to assess monthly practice productivity per provider and we want to improve productivity per provider, then this metric used in this context suggests, for example, we can affect change by working with individual providers whose average is below the

practice's overall average to increase the number of patients seen per month
by the provider of interest.

Several questions should be asked as part of preliminary measurement steps.
For instance, what do you want to measure? Is the measurement a generally
accepted practice characteristic or is it a "homegrown" practice attribute? What
metric should be used? What is the appropriate method for measurement?
And finally, what type of metric do you want to use and what is your intended
purpose?

INTERPRETATION PITFALLS

Reliability is defined as repeatability and consistency. If given the same data
set and using the same measure, someone else should be able to calculate,
describe, and compare the data in the same way. For instance, if given the
number of patients seen per month for the last 10 months in a suburban and
rural practice and asked for the average number of patients seen per month for
both practices, you should find the same average with the same comparison for
each practice. Note that the same unit of measurement must be used (number
of patients, in the above example). Reliability cannot be achieved if the unit of
measurement varies in any of the data used. You cannot calculate an average
using patients between January and July and appointments booked in August
without first changing appointments booked to the number of patients seen
in August.

Validity is meaningfulness within a generally accepted theoretical basis (see
Exhibit 3.4.) To put it another way, does a measurement really mean what it
is expected to mean or is it being interpreted accurately? How you interpret
your data are as important as ensuring you have used a highly reliable method.
Understanding what a particular measure is meant to describe is paramount
to using data properly. For instance, an average, or mean, represents the
mathematical center of an array of data or central tendency; whereas, the
median represents the center-point of the array. In some cases, the mean and
median can be the same, but oftentimes they are different. Therefore, knowing
how a measure is used, collected, and calculated results in a more valid and
meaningful analysis, and thus supports better decisions. This is particularly

important when presenting your findings to others since the better you understand the measures, why you selected them, and how to explain them to others, the more credible will be your recommendations and/or decisions.

FIGURE 3.4 EXAMPLE OF MEANINGFULNESS

UNDERSTAND THE FORMULAS USED FOR MEASUREMENT AND HOW THE MEASUREMENT IS COLLECTED AND CALCULATED.

USING THE DATA ARRAY FROM THE PREVIOUS EXAMPLE OF NUMBER OF PATIENTS SEEN PER MONTH (SUBURBAN PRACTICE):

2620 (JAN), 2231 (FEB), 2264 (MAR), 2650 (APR), 2657 (MAY), 2670 (JUN), 3067 (JUL), 2690 (AUG), 3171 (SEP), 3710 (OCT)

MEAN = SUM OF ALL DATA DIVIDED BY THE NUMBER OF DATA POINTS

SUM OF ALL DATA = 2620 + 2231 + 2264 + 2650 + 2657 + 2670 + 3067 + 2690 + 3171 + 3710 = 2773

NUMBER OF DATA POINTS = 10

MEAN = 2773

MEDIAN = THE DATA POINT IN THE CENTER OF THE ARRAY (WHEN ARRANGED IN ORDER)

DATA ARRAY = 2231, 2264, 2620, 2650, 2657, 2670, 2690, 3067, 3171, 3710

CENTER OF ARRAY ARE TWO DATA POINTS = 2657 & 2670

MEDIAN = 2657 + 2670 DIVIDED BY 2 = 2664

NOTE: IF THE DATA ARRAY CONSISTED OF AN ODD NUMBER OF POINTS, THE MEDIAN WOULD BE THAT NUMBER THAT LAY HALFWAY BETWEEN THE HIGHEST AND LOWEST RANGE OF NUMBERS IN THE ARRAY.

Another common pitfall to avoid is averaging averages. Since any array of data points can be averaged, it is important to understand the limitations or implications of measuring previously measured data points. The validity of the interpretation may be suspect (see Exhibit 3.5).

EXHIBIT 3.5 EXAMPLE OF AVERAGING AVERAGES PROBLEM

MONTH	NO. OF PATIENTS		
	FAMILY PRACTICE 1	FAMILY PRACTICE 2	FAMILY PRACTICE 3
JANUARY	2,231	1,687	2,159
FEBRUARY	2,264	2,067	2,353
March	2,620	2,071	2,520
April	2,650	2,266	2,564
May	2,657	2,650	2,660
June	2,670	2,660	2,961
JULY	2,690	2,731	3,162
AUGUST	3,067	3,070	3,259
SEPTEMBER	3,171	3,690	3,359
OCTOBER	3,710	3,730	3,763
AVERAGE (MEAN)	2,773 (NORMAL PRODUCTIVITY PRACTICE)	2,662 (LOW PRODUCTIVITY PRACTICE)	2,876 (HIGH PRODUCTIVITY PRACTICE)
AVERAGE OF THE AVERAGES FOR PRACTICES 1, 2, AND 3 = 2,770			

The extremely low and high values in all the practices are minimized or diluted (their effect is almost eliminated). The effects of the low productivity and high productivity practices almost eliminate one another, which is why the average of the averages is near the average of the more balanced array (Family Practice 1).

Strength is related to validity and is the power, magnitude, or accuracy of your interpretation or how confident you are in your interpretation. For instance, to describe the number of patients seen per month for three months (2231, 2264, and 2620), an average is an ideal descriptive statistic (average = 2372). This figure is descriptive of the lower months of 2231 and 2264, but a 2372 average is not descriptive of the higher months when 2620 patients were seen. Therefore, your confidence in an average of 2372 patients seen per month provides a less accurate description of the average number of patients seen per month. However, if this array consisted of a larger number of months, that is, a large dataset with many data points, the accuracy of this metric and your confidence in the descriptive power of the average should be much higher.

A final interpretation issue is related to the mutually exclusive and exhaustive nature of data. Mutually exclusive refers to a data point fitting into only one category.[5] For example, we decide months with 3,600 or more patients are categorized as high productivity, months with between 2,401 and 3,599 patients are medium or normal, and months with 2,400 or less patients are low. Therefore, each month fits into only one category—that's mutually exclusive—a single month cannot be categorized as both "high" and "medium." If a single month could be assigned to multiple categories, it would be difficult to accurately describe each month or interpret your findings. Exhaustive refers to the description of the attribute, that is, does the definition encompass all collected attributes? For example, since all the measurements taken consisted of the number of patients seen per month, this attribute was defined to be actual patient encounters with a provider and all collected measures were based on this definition. Patients seen only by a nurse were not included since these encounters didn't fit the definition or criteria.

1 MGMA, Cost Survey for Single-Specialty Practices: 2005 Report Based on 2004 Datta and Physician Compensation and Production Survey: 2005 Report Based on 2004 Data (Englewood, CO: Medical Group Management Association, 2005).

2 J. Rothstein and J. Echternach, Primer on Measurement: An Introductory Guide to Measurement Issues (Alexandria, VA: American Physical Therapy Association, 1993).

3 M. Zairi and J. Whymark, "The Transfer of Best Practices: How to Build a Culture of Benchmarking and Continuous Learning, Part 2." Benchmarking, 7, no. 2 (2000): 146.

4 D. Elmuti and Y. Kathawala, "An Overview of Benchmarking Process: A Tool for Continuous Improvement and Competitive Advantage." Benchmarking for Quality Management & Technology, 4, no. 4 (1997): 229.

5 R. Camp, "Benchmarking: The Search for Best Practices that Lead to Superior Performance, Part 1." Quality Progress, 22, no. 2 (1989): 70.

6 D. Gans, "Benchmarking Successful Medical Groups to Improve Your Practice Performance," Presentation at Medical Group Management Association Conference, Ohio, September 2006.

CHAPTER 4

MANAGEMENT BY THE NUMBERS

"If I had to sum up in one word what makes a good manager, I'd say decisiveness. You can use the fanciest computers to gather the numbers, but in the end you have to set a timetable and act."

- Lee Iacocca

M anagement can use numbers to diagnose and treat practice deficiencies, plan improvements, and examine practice activities and processes. And because numbers are less susceptible to the effects of human variations such as feelings and emotions, they are more appropriate for decision-making. The beauty of numbers comes from their brevity, clarity, and precision. For example, using the example array of no-shows (see Exhibit 4.3) which illustrates the number of no-shows per day from last month, it is possible to quickly summarize the week or the entire month regarding no-show activity. These averages and totals provide a brief, clear, and precise picture describing no-show activity during each week or the entire month. There's little room for misinterpretation or confusion, provided a no-show is clearly and consistently defined (a no-show being defined as a patient who fails to show up within 15 minutes of an appointment rather than someone who fails to cancel 24 hours prior to his/her appointment.)

Organizing numbers is the cornerstone in the benchmarking process. An array or group of numbers only become valuable once they are arranged allowing for statistical methods and proper interpretation of the findings necessary to uncover the useful information behind the numbers. It is necessary to approach this systematically, through the use of averages (means), medians, standard deviations, percentiles, quartiles, and percent change (see Exhibit 4.1). These techniques can be used to measure and benchmark all practice attributes. In addition, these methods are easy to use, understand, and communicate as most people are familiar with at least some of the methods.

EXHIBIT 4.1 MEASUREMENT AND BENCHMARKING STATISTICS

AVERAGE (MEAN)	QUARTILE
MEDIAN	STANDARD DEVIATION
PERCENTILE	PERCENT CHANGE

TYPES OF DATA

There are four categories for classifying data (see Exhibit 4.2). Nominal data is defined as data that is mutually exclusive and exhaustive in which no order or ranking can be assigned, they can be regarded and labels or names, hence the term nominal.[1] Ordinal data can be ranked but without quantifiable or numerical differences between data; for example, by using a Likert scale (small, medium, large; never, sometimes, usually, always; and poor, fair, good, very good, excellent).[2] Interval data is rank ordered with quantifiable differences between data but without a meaningful zero point.[2] And ratio data is equal to interval data but with a true zero.[2]

EXHIBIT 4.2 TYPES OF DATA AND EXAMPLES

NOMINAL	INTERVAL
GENDER, MARITAL STATUS, ETHNICITY/ RACE, BLOOD TYPE	TEMPERATURE (CELSIUS), SAT SCORE, IQ SCORE
ORDINAL (CATEGORICAL)	RATIO
LIKERT SCALE SCORE (SMALL, MEDIUM, OR LARGE)	PULSE RATE, WHITE BLOOD CELL COUNT, HEIGHT, WEIGHT, AGE

ORGANIZING DATA

In order to describe and interpret a data array, it must be organized. The most common method of organizing data is to build a frequency distribution. A frequency distribution is defined as data organized into table form by category or group with frequencies and percentages (see Exhibit 4.5).[2]

When constructing a frequency distribution, it is important to follow these guidelines: (1) each group remains equal in width (see Exhibit 4.4), (2) employ 12 or fewer categories or groups in any given array, (3) data points contained within categories or groups are mutually exclusive, and (4) all categories or groups themselves are all inclusive.[2] Mutually exclusive means each data point cannot occupy two categories or groups simultaneously; whereas, inclusive means each data point is included in a category or group.[4]

EXHIBIT 4.3 EXAMPLE DATA ARRAY

NUMBER OF NO-SHOWS PER DAY LAST WEEK:						
MONDAY	TUESDAY	WEDNESDAY	THURSDAY	FRIDAY	WEEKLY AVERAGE	WEEKLY TOTAL
2	1	3	6	4	3.2	16
4	0	1	5	3	2.6	13
2	3	2	2	3	2.4	12
1	2	2	4	5	2.8	14
MONTHLY TOTAL = 55 MONTHLY AVERAGE = 2.75						

The type of data will dictate whether it should be categorized or grouped. Nominal and ordinal data and should be categorized; whereas, interval and ratio data should be grouped. For example, using the data in Exhibit 4.3, which is ratio level data, that should be organized into groups. The formula in Exhibit 4.4 can be used to adhere to the guidelines mentioned above and group the data.[4]

EXHIBIT 4.4 GROUPING DATA

FORMULA FOR GROUPING DATA = [(MAXIMUM VALUE +1) – (MINIMUM VALUE)] / (NUMBER OF GROUPS DESIRED)

EXAMPLE:

MAXIMUM VALUE = 6

MINIMUM VALUE = 0

NUMBER OF GROUPS DESIRED = 4

[(6 + 1) – (0)] / 4 = 1.75

ROUNDED UP = 2

THEREFORE, THE GROUPS ARE:

0 – 2 NO-SHOWS (GROUP #1)

3 – 4 NO-SHOWS (GROUP #2)

5 – 6 NO-SHOWS (GROUP #3)

REMINDER: WHEN CONSTRUCTING A FREQUENCY DISTRIBUTION, IT IS IMPORTANT TO FOLLOW THESE GUIDELINES:[2]

EACH GROUP IS EQUAL IN WIDTH (I.E., THERE ARE AN EQUAL NUMBER OF VALUES/VARIABLES PER CATEGORY OR GROUP)

EMPLOY 12 OR FEWER CATEGORIES OR GROUPS; THIS IS LESS OF A REQUIREMENT, THAN A GOOD-RULE-OF-THUMB TO KEEP THE FREQUENCY DISTRIBUTION TABLES AND ANY CHARTS/GRAPHS FROM GETTING TOO LENGTHY OR BUSY (FEWER CATEGORIES OR GROUPS RESULT IN MORE CONCISE TABLES AND ILLUSTRATIONS, THOUGH TOO FEW CATEGORIES OR GROUPS WILL RESULT IN LOSS OF DETAIL)

DATA POINTS WITHIN CATEGORIES OR GROUPS ARE MUTUALLY EXCLUSIVE

ALL CATEGORIES OR GROUPS THEMSELVES ARE ALL INCLUSIVE (EXHAUSTIVE)

Once the group size is determined, a frequency table, like Exhibit 4.5, can be constructed and loaded with data from the array. Frequency (the number "n") represents the tally or number of occurrences within each group; whereas, relative frequency is indicative of the percentage each group relative to the total. And cumulative frequency is represented as the sum of present and previous relative frequencies per group.

EXHIBIT 4.5 EXAMPLE FREQUENCY DISTRIBUTION

GROUPS (GROUP #)	FREQUENCY (N)	RELATIVE FREQUENCY (%)	CUMULATIVE FREQUENCY (%)
0 – 2 (1)	13	54%	54%
3 – 4 (2)	8	33%	87%
5 – 6 (3)	3	13%	100%

Another method of organizing data is through graphing. Graphs, much like frequency tables, can be used to summarize, identify patterns, and visually display large amounts of data.[4] For example, the average number of patient encounters per physician per month are ideally suited for display using a bar chart (see Exhibit 4.6).

EXHIBIT 4.6 EXAMPLE BAR CHART (AVERAGE NUMBER OF PATIENT ENCOUNTERS PER PHYSICIAN PER MONTH)

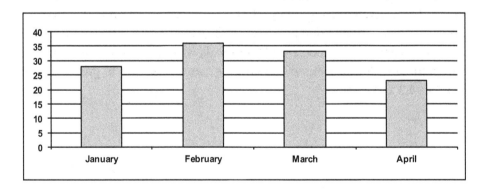

Continuous data is ideally suited for display in a histogram.[7] For example, the distribution or list of patient ages are perfect for display using a histogram (see Exhibit 4.7).

EXHIBIT 4.7 EXAMPLE HISTOGRAM WITH NORMAL CURVE (DISTRIBUTION OF PATIENT AGES)

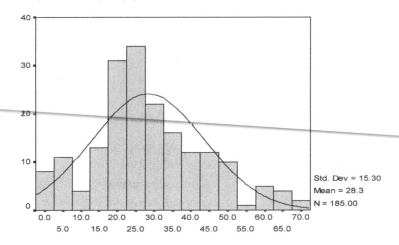

Age of Patient

Relative frequency is perfectly suited for display in a pie chart. For example, the no-show groupings (Exhibit 4.8) displays groups of no-shows from one month (data derived from Exhibit 4.3). That is, group #1 consists of 0 to 2 no-shows, group #2 of 3 or 4 no-shows, and group #3 of 5 or 6 no-shows. The chart and legend below indicate 54% of the days per month were in group #1 with 0 to 2 no-shows, 33% were in group #2, and 13% were in group #3 (see Exhibits 4.3 and 4.5).

EXHIBIT 4.8 EXAMPLE PIE CHART (RELATIVE FREQUENCY DATA FROM
EXHIBIT 4.5)

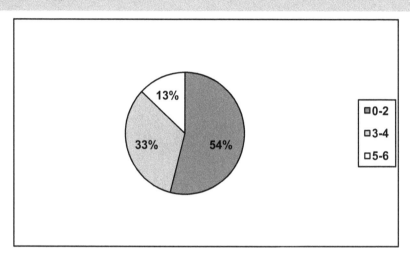

Continuous data showing trends can be graphed using a line chart (see Exhibit
4.9).[4]

EXHIBIT 4.9 EXAMPLE LINE CHART (NUMBER OF RVUS PER PROVIDER
PER MONTH)

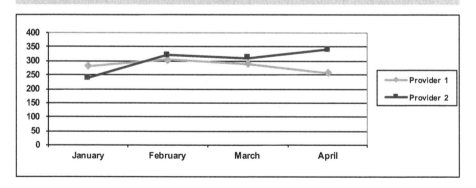

A scatter plot is the best format to show relationships between two variables
located on the x-axis and y-axis (see Exhibit 4.10).[4]

EXHIBIT 4.10 EXAMPLE SCATTER PLOT

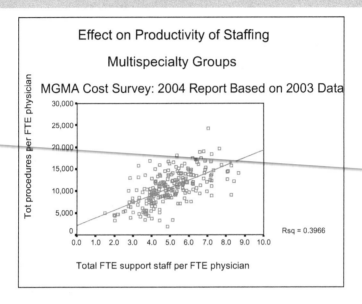

Averages (means) and Medians

Averages (means) and medians are measures of central tendency. That is, they represent the intermediate or middle point of all the data[3] and are a single value that is descriptive of the dataset.[4] The average is calculated by adding all data points and dividing by the number of data points (see Exhibit 4.11).

EXHIBIT 4.11 FORMULA FOR CALCULATING THE AVERAGE (MEAN)

AVERAGE (MEAN)

- AVERAGE (MEAN) = SUM OF ALL DATA POINTS / NUMBER OF DATA POINTS
- EXAMPLE
  - DATA POINTS = 101, 145, 167, 189, 192, 201
  - NUMBER OF DATA POINTS = 6
    - (101 + 145 + 167 + 189 + 192 + 201) / 6
    - AVERAGE (MEAN) = 995 / 6 = 165.8

The median is the data point in the true center of the dataset. An equal number of data points should exist above the median as below it. However, if the number of data points in the dataset is an even number, the median is the average of the two data points in the center (see Exhibit 4.12).

EXHIBIT 4.12 FORMULA FOR CALCULATING THE MEDIAN

MEDIAN

- IF ODD NUMBER OF DATA POINTS
    - MEDIAN = CENTER DATA POINT
    - THE DATA POINT LOCATED AT THE CENTER POSITION IN THE DATASET WHEN PLACED IN ASCENDING ORDER; LOCATED AT = [(NUMBER OF DATA POINTS + 1) / 2]
    - EXAMPLE
        - DATA POINTS = 101, 145, 167, 189, 192, 201, 213
        - NUMBER OF DATA POINTS = 7
        - LOCATION OF MEDIAN = [(7 + 1) / 2] = 4TH POSITION
        - MEDIAN = 189
        - IF EVEN NUMBER OF DATA POINTS
        - MEDIAN = (TWO CENTER DATA POINTS) / 2
    - THE TWO DATA POINTS LOCATED AT THE CENTER POSITIONS IN THE DATASET WHEN PLACED IN ASCENDING ORDER; LOCATED AT = (NUMBER OF DATA POINTS / 2) AND [(NUMBER OF DATA POINTS / 2) + 1]
    - EXAMPLE
        - DATA POINTS = 101, 145, 167, 189, 192, 201
        - NUMBER OF DATA POINTS = 6
        - LOCATION OF MEDIAN, POINT #1 = (6 / 2) = 3RD POSITION
        - LOCATION OF MEDIAN, POINT #2 = [(6 / 2) +1] = 4TH POSITION
        - MEDIAN = (167 + 189) / 2 = 178

Special care should be taken when rounding averages and should be reserved for calculations.[2] If rounding is performed prior to the final calculation of the average or median, the difference between the calculated answer and the true answer may be significant and accuracy will be lessened. In addition, and when possible, the average or median should be rounded to one more decimal place than is found in the dataset.[2] For instance, if the values in the dataset are in whole numbers (for example, 1, 2, 3, 4, and 6), the average or median should be shown to the tenth decimal place, that is, the average is 3.2 and the median is 3.0.

STANDARD DEVIATION

Standard deviation is a measure of variation or dispersion of a data set. That is, it represents the spread of the data around the mean—does the data cluster or spread out from the average? Exhibit 4.13 represents the probabilities associated with the standard distribution for a normally distributed array of data—a normally distributed array of data follows the bell-curve when graphed as a histogram (see Exhibit 4.7). However, there is a theorem that generally holds true and states 95% or more of data will fall within two standard deviations of the mean regardless of the distribution (normal or not normal) of the data.[2]

EXHIBIT 4.13 DISTRIBUTION OF DATA BY STANDARD DEVIATION

- 68% OF DATA FALL WITHIN +/- 1 STANDARD DEVIATION

- 95% OF DATA FALL WITHIN +/- 2 STANDARD DEVIATIONS

- 99.7% OF DATA FALL WITHIN +/- 3 STANDARD DEVIATIONS

- 99.99% OF DATA FALL WITHIN +/- 4 STANDARD DEVIATIONS

- 99.9999% OF DATA FALL WITHIN +/- 5 STANDARD DEVIATIONS

For example, a data set containing all the ages of every established and new patient seen for the past year can be graphed using a histogram. In Exhibit 4.7, it is possible to see the distribution of the ages in relation to the normal curve. In addition, since the bars of this histogram approximately match the normal curve line, the data can be considered normally distributed – this is the "art" of measurement and benchmarking. Since this data is normally distributed, the probabilities from Exhibit 4.13 can be applied to draw conclusions from the data. Since the distribution is normally distributed and the average age is 28.3 years and the standard deviation is 15.3 years, using the probabilities from Exhibit 4.13 it is possible to conclude that 68% of the practice's patients are between the ages of 13 and 44 and 96% of patients are between the ages of 0 and 59 (see Exhibit 4.14).

EXHIBIT 4.14 STANDARD DEVIATION EXAMPLE

- AVERAGE = 28.3 YEARS
- STANDARD DEVIATION = 15.3 YEARS
  - □ 68% = +/- 1 STANDARD DEVIATION
    - 28.3 + 15.3 = 44 YEARS
    - 28.3 – 15.3 = 13 YEARS
  - □ 96% = +/- 2 STANDARD DEVIATIONS
    - 28.3 + (15.3 * 2) = 59 YEARS
    - 28.3 - (15.3 * 2) = -2.3 = 0 YEARS

PERCENTILES AND QUARTILES

Percentiles and quartiles provide some indication of the relative position with respect to the other data points. A percentile is a value indicating the percent of values less than or equal to the percentile (see example in Exhibit 4.15).[2] Quartiles are simply the 25th (25%), 50th (50% or median), and 75th (75%) percentiles.[2]

EXHIBIT 4.15 FORMULA FOR CALCULATING PERCENTILE

PERCENTILE

- PERCENTILE = [(NUMBER OF VALUES BELOW A SPECIFIC VALUE) + 0.5] / TOTAL NUMBER OF VALUES * 100%

- EXAMPLE

  □ AN ADMINISTRATOR COLLECTS THE NUMBER OF ESTABLISHED PATIENTS SEEN PER MONTH FOR THE PAST 12 MONTHS. WHAT IS THE PERCENTILE RANK OF SEEING 265 PATIENTS?

  □ DATA POINTS = 201, 211, 245, 251, 265, 267, 273, 275, 289, 292, 301, 313

  □ PERCENTILE = [(4) + 0.5] / 12 * 100% = 38TH PERCENTILE

  □ THEREFORE, ANY MONTH WHERE 265 ESTABLISHED PATIENTS WERE SEEN WAS 38% BETTER THAN ALL THE MONTHS CONSIDERED.

PERCENT CHANGE

Percent change is a valuable method for assessing changes over time since it compares a new value with an old value (see Exhibit 4.16). To calculate percent change, use the following formula:

EXHIBIT 4.16 PERCENT CHANGE

- PERCENT CHANGE = (NEW VALUE - OLD VALUE) / OLD VALUE

  □ EXAMPLE: WHAT IS THE PERCENT CHANGE IN THE NUMBER OF NO-SHOWS FROM LAST MONTH TO THIS MONTH?

    - NEW VALUE (# OF NO-SHOWS THIS MONTH) = 18

    - OLD VALUE (# OF NO-SHOWS LAST MONTH) = 26

    - (18 - 26) / 26 = -31%

    - THEREFORE, WE CAN CONCLUDE FROM THIS ANALYSIS THAT NO-SHOWS HAVE DROPPED BY 30% THIS MONTH VERSUS LAST MONTH.

Averages (means), medians, percentiles, quartiles, standard deviations, and percent change are tools needed to thoroughly assess, measure, and benchmark a practice. These methods, when used properly, are very powerful since they are easy to calculate, communicate, and understand – the strength of these methods lies in their simplicity.

---

[1] Bluman, A. G., *Elementary Statistics: A Step by Step Approach* (9th edition). Boston: McGraw-Hill Higher Education; 2014.

[2] D. L. Kelley, *Measurement Made Accessible, A Research Approach Using Qualitative, Quantitative, and Quality Improvement Methods* (Thousand Oaks, CA: SAGE Publications, 1999).

[3] Daniel, W. W. & Cross., C. *Biostatistics: A Foundation for Analysis in the Health Sciences* (10th edition). New York: John Wiley & Sons, Inc.; 2013.

[4] Rosner, B., *Fundamentals of Biostatistics* (7th edition). Cengage Learning; 2010.

CHAPTER 5

HOW TO SHOW THE BANK A CREDIT-WORTHY PRACTICE

"Capital as such is not evil; it is its wrong use that is evil. Capital in some form or other will always be needed."
—*Mahatma Gandhi*

It is bound to happen sooner or later—your practice will need to go to the bank for a loan. And the more you know about what the bank will be looking for, the better the chances of successfully borrowing needed capital. Benchmarking can play a key part in showing the financial, operational, and clinical health of the practice. In addition, the more the bank knows about your practice—the type and nature of work, the local market, and its management, leadership and operations—the better your relationship with the bank will be and the fewer unanticipated and unwanted surprises will occur.

When approaching a bank, ask questions and educate them on your practice and the healthcare environment. Discover how well they understand the challenges facing medical practices. Determine how much they know about nature and speed of the changes in the medical practice industry. And don't underestimate the importance of examining the bank as closely as they will be examining your practice.

The right banking partner will be the one that not only cares about your practice's success, but actively works to help you achieve it. With so many banks to choose from, be certain to choose the most informed and most sincere and caring.

DIFFERENCES IN MEDICAL PRACTICE FINANCIAL ACCOUNTING

Today, the majority of medical groups are legally organized as Limited Liability Companies (LLCs) or Professional Corporations (PCs). As members or partners, the physicians are not personally liable for the entity's debts and obligations.

The bank's review of an LLC's (or PC's) operating agreement is important because the operating agreement may allocate respective rights, obligations, funding requirements, tax liabilities, and other matters to LLC (or PC) members in different ways. Reimbursements may be affected by government regulation and by the practice's financial reporting.

WHAT BANKS WANT TO SEE

The bank will look primarily for amount of risk the loan represents—the healthier the practice, the less risky a loan and thus the more likely that it will be granted.

QUALITIES OF A SUCCESSFUL MEDICAL PRACTICE

The bank will assess the overall condition of the practice and not just its finances. The list below will help when assessing the current state of the practice before the bank. A lender may not be familiar with every type of practice measure, but a bank that will work as a partner in the practice's success should be asking questions that help the bank (and the practice) determine how well the practice is planning for its future. A successful practice performs well against these critical measurements:

- The practice manages operating costs with detailed cost accounting.
- Revenue and physician ratios are higher and cost and procedure ratios are lower.
- The practice performs timely billing and collections. Claims are submitted within 48 hours of a patient visit, filed electronically, and coded thoroughly, promptly, and accurately.
- Quality standards are established and adhered to and quality is measured regularly.
- The practice uses an excellent medical information system from a reputable vendor that is updated regularly. Business office procedures for patient records and coding is ideally centralized and automated to enhance the day-to-day productivity of the practice.

- The practice understands its competition and community demographics. The practice management team regularly conducts demographic studies to identify any changes such as age of local population, household size, income levels, employments trends, insurance companies in the area, and practice competition. The business plan includes a section to monitor and analyze this information.

- The practice has good relationships with the provider community.

- A low debt ratio, demonstrating a strong financial position.

- The practice delivers streamlined service by staffing at appropriate levels, designed to cater to patient's perception of convenience, waiting time, staff friendliness and professionalism.

- The practice understands and adapts to the changing health care environment.

- The practice employs experienced administration that knows how to assess and negotiate with managed care companies. Administration must determine the financial impact of entering into managed care contracts to limit financial risk by fully understanding the terms of the contract.

- The practice's physicians are leaders in the community. To help shape the image of the practice in the community, physician involvement might include participation in speakers' bureaus, sponsorship of community events, wellness and prevention seminars, and charity events.

- The practice attracts, retains, and appropriately compensates a mix of physicians. Physician compensation should reward both efficiency and effectiveness. In doing so, the practice does not run the risk of turnover and retaining underperforming physicians.

AREAS THE BANK WILL FOCUS ON

Once a specific bank is selected and an application for a loan is submitted, the practice will find its operations are under a microscope. The bank will carefully examine five broad areas:

1. The way your business is legally organized,
2. financial controls and reporting,
3. practice management,
4. market position, and
5. credit worthiness.

BUSINESS ORGANIZATION

Each type of business organization has advantages and disadvantages that may affect the risks of lending. A loan to one type of business organization may be structured differently from a loan in the same amount to a different type of business organization.

FINANCIAL CONTROLS AND REPORTING

The bank will be interested in the practice's contractual agreements with various other payers. These contractual agreements often specify allowances for certain types of patient care. In addition, these agreements are typically negotiated or the practice accepts the allowances "as-is." Adjustments to the contract generally result from the payer reimbursing the practice for less than what was billed. In particular, the bank will want to see:

- Automated operational functions: particularly billing, accounts receivable, monitoring, collections, and financial reporting.
- The practice collecting at least 95% of gross billings after any contractual adjustments. This is important because cash flow from operations is the primary source of repayment for a loan.
- Reimbursement rates based on contractual allowances from third-party payers that are predictable and incorporated into the management for the practice's finances. If this is not the case, collections for receivables may be overstated.
- The practice collecting from a diverse mix of payers. A practice that relies too heavily on one payer for reimbursement is considered riskier than a practice with several payers.

- Accounts receivable information that is accurate and complete—this is critical, as A/R are the practice's largest asset. A/R, sorted by payer, should be reported net of contractual allowance (such as Medicare, Medicaid, Managed Care and Commercial Insurance, and bad debts). The bank will use the accounts receivable figure to determine an appropriate amount for working capital loans. And this information helps the bank select the right loan for the practice.

- A/R more than 90 days past due—this compares favorably to industry standards.

- Medicare and Medicaid receivables representing less than 50% of total A/R. The practice's A/R mix should be diverse.

- A plan in place to mitigate the impact of potential financial commitments, such as obligations to buy-out retiring or withdrawing partners so they will not create undue financial stress on the practice.

- Co-pays that are collected at the time of service.

PRACTICE MANAGEMENT

The bank will assess the management and market position of the practice. Due diligence by the bank's credit officer will include an analysis of the practice's strategic plans, management capabilities, service areas, competition, and negotiations of third-party contracts. The credit officer must be comfortable with the results of all analyses and the findings from performing due diligence.

In addition, the bank will look closely at the day-to-day management of the practice. So, if the practice is managed internally, the management team must be financially astute. Some practices choose an external management option, contracting with a Physician Practice Management (PPM) company or an Independent Practice Association (IPA) to handle all non-medical-related business. This is done for efficiency and is an acceptable alternative to managing these functions internally.

The bank will want to see that each physician in the practice is financially responsible. The physician's personal leverage and cash flows should fall within acceptable ranges. These ranges may vary slightly from bank to bank. And this may be necessary whether or not the physicians have pledged guarantees on the loan. The physicians in the practice should not be financially overextended. The practice and physicians should not be contingently liable for financial obligations outside of the practice or its related entities. Contingent liability is an obligation of a person who signs a promissory note as an accommodation endorser, co-maker, or guarantor, becoming liable for payment in the event the original borrower defaults. If they are contingently liable, the bank will want assurances the liability will not damage the practice if recourse were sought. If there are contingent liabilities, it is crucial the physicians fully understand the extent of their liability and how it might affect the practice. The bank will thoroughly assess this risk as part of the credit underwriting process. However, medical malpractice claims against the practice should be inconsequential. In addition, the practice must demonstrate all required licensing to practice medicine and dispense prescriptions has been maintained continually and is current. And the practice must show that every physician in the practice carries adequate malpractice, life, and disability insurance.

MARKET POSITION

The bank will want to see that the practice is part of a successful hospital network or has long-term or ongoing contracts with several hospitals or managed care companies. These include Health Maintenance Organizations (HMOs) and Preferred Provider Organizations (PPOs). The practice should have a strong reputation and demonstrated market power to withstand competition.

DEMONSTRATING CREDIT-WORTHINESS

When banks consider lending, they follow established criteria for granting credit. Four guidelines, or "core factors," are considered when the bank is deciding whether to approve a loan request. These guidelines are as follows:

- *Debt Service Coverage (Operating Cash Flow to Fixed Charges):* This is an examination of the borrower's operating cash flow to cover debt service requirements. The effect of any new debt is included in the calculation.

- *Leverage (Total Liabilities to Tangible Net Worth):* Leverage ratios are used to help determine a practice's level of debt relative to equity. Goodwill, other intangibles, and A/R from officers, owners, and affiliates must be excluded from tangible net worth. Debt that is fully subordinated to the bank may be deducted from total liabilities and added to tangible net worth.

- *Profitability:* Profitability ratios reveal whether the practice has adequate earnings and how effectively the practice is being managed. The bank will want to see positive earnings before taxes for two of the three prior fiscal years, excluding extraordinary items, with the most recent year being profitable.

- *Liquidity (Current Assets divided by Current Liabilities):* Equivalent to the Current Ratio, liquidity is used to assess the availability of cash, or near cash resources, for meeting the practice's obligations. Other liquidity ratios include a Quick Ratio and A/R Turnover ratio.

- In addition, the bank may also consider other Credit Granting Guidelines such as Collateral Coverage Guidelines and Guarantor's Strength.

FINANCIAL COVENANTS

Financial covenants are contracts attached to a formal debt agreement, promising certain activities will or will not be carried out. The purpose of a covenant is to give the lender more security. In general, covenants are required to control debt service coverage, liquidity, and leverage for long-term credit facilities. Covenants will require the practice to keep these core factors within acceptable ranges. These ranges may vary slightly from bank to bank. Short-term working capital lines of credit do not typically have financial covenants. Expect term loans or leases for equipment, leaseholds, or real estate acquisitions will, at a minimum, include the following covenants:

- Cash flow after shareholder distributions and physician bonuses to debt service should have minimum 1.0 x coverage. This assures adequate cash flow is retained for debt service coverage.

- A certain amount of equity in the practice by establishing Minimum Tangible Net Worth and Earnings Retention Requirements.

- No applying for or accepting additional loans from other sources without approval from the bank.

Types of Loans and How They are Used

Medical professional groups typically look for financing such as short-term working capital lines of credit, permanent working capital loans, term loans, and mortgages for owner-occupied medical office buildings. It is a plus if the practice can show affiliation with a strong hospital, large medical groups, or a managed care sponsor.

- *Short-term working capital financing* is generally used for lump sum expenses such as bonuses, tax planning strategies, or malpractice insurance premiums. Because the purpose of this type of debt is only for short-term needs, the bank will require a 30-day clearance of the balance during the fiscal year.

- *Permanent working capital financing* is typically used to fund A/R when a practice is establishing a new location by adding physicians, or merging with or acquiring another practice. These loans generally require personal guarantees. More rapid payout is encouraged when cash flow permits.

- *Term loans (or leases)* are used to purchase medical and office equipment, make leasehold improvements to office space, purchase real estate, or for practice buy-in or buy-out. The bank will be very cautious, as should the practice, when considering financing for Magnetic Resonance Imaging (MRI), Computed Tomography (CAT), or other high-tech radiology equipment without alternative sources of repayment, collateral, or guarantees. The loan amortization should not exceed the useful life of the asset.

- *Owner-occupied mortgage loans* are granted for medical office buildings. Given the rapid and ongoing changes in the health care industry, the bank will prefer the practice have hospital alliances and be located close to hospitals.

Collateral

When collateral is required, the bank generally places blanket liens on all types of collateral such as: health care insurance receivables, inventory, equipment, software, and general intangibles of the practice. A blanket lien is a security interest covering nearly all assets owned by the debtor. And the bank will follow recommended guidelines for advance rates:

- *A/R advance rate of 70 percent* of eligible A/R. Eligible A/R are receivables net of bad debts and contractual allowances from third-party payers including Medicare, Medicaid, managed care, and some commercial insurance. When Medicare/Medicaid receivables represent more than 50% of total receivables, expect the advance rate to drop below 70%, oftentimes it may drop to 60% or less. In general, the bank may require A/R aging monthly that provides a breakdown by payer and excludes or identifies anything more than 90 days past due for secured lines of credit.

- *Inventory advance rate of 50%*

- *Equipment advance rate for new equipment is 80%* of invoice or fair market value. Recommended guidelines for used equipment are 50% of invoice or fair market value. Upward deviations are based on above-average quality, age, and liquidation value of the specific collateral.

GUARANTEES

In the case of loans to smaller medical practices, expect the bank to require all stockholders of the operating entity guarantee the obligation. In larger groups, limited guarantees may be required. The bank will first conduct an overall financial evaluation of the practice and only then will it determine a requirement, if any, for full or limited guarantees. With a full guarantee, the guarantor is responsible for the full amount of the debt obligations to the lender. Whereas, with a limited guarantee, the guarantor is only responsible for a predetermined portion of the debtor obligations to the lender.

When the practice is a partnership or has an expense-sharing arrangement, the bank will require a copy of the agreement. This agreement should describe how assets and liabilities are allocated among the parties, particularly in the event the practice should dissolve.

As in most professional service organizations, the success of a medical practice depends on the principals. The bank will consider whether existing life and disability insurance policies would cover outstanding obligations if a principal were to die or become disabled.

OTHER ELEMENTS

The bank will also examine the following:

- *Subordination:* For term debt, Shareholder Notes or Notes Payable to physicians should be subordinated to the bank's lien. Subordination is the priority of interests in the ownership of property or placement of liens.

- *Trend Analysis of Total Physician Compensation:* Because most professional groups do not require capital to be maintained in the business, total physician compensation and dividends normally produce debt service coverage of 1:1. The bank will analyze trends in income streams of physicians to determine the success of the practice. A rapidly declining trend or income relative to the physician's personal leverage above 40%, are warning signs. Debt service coverage is a ratio used in determining sufficient personal income to service personal debt. Ideally, this ratio should be below 40-45%. That would mean the individual is generating sufficient income to pay debt obligations.

- *Capitation:* The bank will determine the managed care position of the practice by completing an analysis of capitation contracts. This is of concern because under managed care and financial risk is shifted from the patient and the payer to the practice. The bank will want to see the practice actively managing capitation and managed care pricing. Capitation is a fixed payment remitted at regular intervals to a medical provider by a managed care organization for an enrolled patient.

- *Employment Contracts:* The bank will analyze all employment contracts and physician contracts. In general, physicians should not be allowed to exit the practice without one or more of the following penalties:
    1. A/R stay with the practice.
    2. The physician has restrictions on practicing within a particular geographic area, to limit patient loss.
    3. Financial penalty.

These penalties should not be used if the physician is a guarantor, provided the guarantee is not released when the physician leaves.

- *Personal Leverage:* The bank will perform an analysis and verification of all guarantors, owners, or significant revenue generators by running credit checks and examining three years of federal income tax returns.
- *Malpractice Insurance:* The bank will verify amounts with insurance carriers to determine if any material liabilities are outstanding.
- *Disability Insurance:* The bank will verify amounts with insurance carriers to determine if the practice is adequately covered.
- *A/R:* The bank may require aging reports, certified by an officer of the practice, at least quarterly.

CONCLUSION

The types of intense financial scrutiny cited in this chapter can be daunting. However, the right banking partner will conduct them in such a way that the practice will gain a clear picture of its current health and, if needed, a prescription to help strengthen its condition. The bank wants to minimize risk to itself—and to the practice since it is in the bank's best interest, as well as the practice, for the practice to be successful. And finally, consider the bank's scrutiny a tool to use for long-term growth and success.

CHAPTER 6

KEY PERFORMANCE INDICATORS

"An organization's ability to learn, and translate that learning into action rapidly, is the ultimate competitive advantage."

- Jack Welch

For most organizations, there are far too many measures to monitor on a routine basis. However, in keeping with the Pareto Principle of 80% of effects come from 20% of causes, a small subset of key measures should be monitored regularly. Among this set of measures, several should be selected as the primary measures for display and/or presentation at monthly board meetings. These measures can be used to gauge the health of an organization.

At a minimum, these measures should be reviewed as "trends," such as a moving twelve-month run, a month versus same month five-year trend, and a complete year versus year five-year trend. The periods of time are incidental; however, to truly see a trend, several data points are needed. Therefore, the operational and physician-specific measures that follow are ideally suited for trending.

REVENUE CYCLE MEASURES

These measures are specific to the process of collecting payments for services and assessing performance of the front and back office functions.

Total net collections

Definition: Indicates how much of a given charge is collected.

Goal: Higher the better

Net fee-for-service revenue + Capitation revenue – Provision for bad debt
──
Gross (unadjusted) collection ratio

Total net collections

Total gross charges

Note: The goal of this measure is "higher the better"; however, this metric will vary significantly depending on the fee schedule (master charge schedule) of the practice. For instance, a practice with a high fee schedule will have a lower gross collection ratio than a practice with a low fee schedule (setting a fee schedule too low can have a negative effect on net revenue). This metric is often used to measure billing office performance.

Gross collection ratio

Definition: Indicates a ratio of the amount of fee-for-service (FFS) revenue collected over the amount charged.

Goal: Higher the better

$$\frac{\text{Net FFS revenue or collections}}{\text{Gross FFS charges}}$$

Adjusted (net) collection ratio[1]

Definition: Indicates how much of what is being charged (gross FFS charges) is collected after total adjustments to charges; does not include funds the practice should not receive (e.g., contractual allowances) and funds it will not receive (e.g., bad debt).

Goal: Higher the better

$$\frac{\text{Net FFS collections}}{\text{Net FFS charges}}$$

Average adjusted collections (revenue) per day

Definition: Indicates the average amount of revenue generated per business day.

Goal: Higher the better

$$\text{Adjusted charges for the last three (or x number) months}$$

Number of business days for the same time period

Note: The period used needn't be three months; rather, but a recent period of time like the previous quarter is optimal.

Days revenue outstanding

Definition: Indicates how long it takes before claims/charges are paid.

Goal: Lower the better

Step 1: Calculate day's revenue

Step 2: Calculate day's revenue outstanding

$$\frac{\text{Outstanding net A/R}}{\text{Day's revenue}}$$

Total revenue for the last three months

Number of business days in the last three months.

Days in A/R

Definition: Indicates how long it takes before claims/charges are paid.

Goal: A net collection ratio (NCR) of 96% – 99% and 40 – 50 days in A/R (days in A/R of 45 or less is ideal) indicate your practice is functioning efficiently and doing very well. If NCR is 93% - 95% and 50 – 60 days in A/R, there is some (little) room for improvement. And if 92% or less and 70 or more days in A/R, there is significant room for improvement in billing operations.

Outstanding A/R

Average monthly charges / 30

Note: Include the last three months

Days in A/R (alternate calculation)

Definition: Indicates how long it takes before claims/charges are paid.

Goal: Lower the better

$$\frac{\text{Outstanding net A/R}}{\text{Average adjusted revenue per day}}$$

Months revenue in A/R

Definition: Indicates the average number of months that charges are outstanding for collection.

Goal: Lower the better

$$\frac{\text{Total A/R}}{\text{Annual adjusted FFS charges} * 1/12}$$

Aged Trial Balance (Aged A/R)[1]

Definition: Identifies the age of receivables in 30-day increments (0-30, 31-60, 61-90, 91-120, and 121+) and most billing software can generate this metric.

Goal: 12% to 15% at greater than 90 days

Note: This measure should be assessed using the total A/R, insurance, and patient responsibility categories.

Collections rate by payer

Definition: Indicates different rates of reimbursement by payer.

Goal: Depends on many practice factors; should be proportional to the percentage of patients covered by each payer.

$$\frac{\text{Net collections by payer}}{\text{Total gross charges by payer}}$$

Note: Reimbursement received from a payer is based on the specific fee schedule established with a payer and is on a per procedure basis. Net collections is the sum of all reimbursement received from a payer; whereas, gross charges is what the practice billed the payer.

Financial Measures

These measures assess revenue and expense (costs) relationships and are related to revenue cycle measures.

Expense to earnings (operating expense ratio)

Definition: Indicates the ratio of overhead (expenses) to revenue (collections).

Goal: Lower the better

$$\frac{\text{Total operating expenses}}{\text{Total collections}}$$

Average revenue per patient

Definition: Indicates the average amount of revenue generated per patient seen. In addition, it can be used to determine the number of patients that must be treated to receive a predetermined amount of revenue (collections).

Goal: Higher the better

$$\frac{\text{Total monthly collections for last month}}{\text{Total patient visits last month}}$$

Average cost per patient

Definition: Indicates the average cost of providing treatment per patient visit.

Goal: Lower the better

$$\frac{\text{Total operating expenses}}{\text{Total patient visits}}$$

Departmental or service ratio

Definition: Indicates the expenses to revenues ratio for a specific department or service.

Goal: Lower the better

$$\frac{\text{Total expenses for ancillary service for the last three months}}{\text{Total net charges for all CPT codes related to ancillary service}}$$

Reimbursement (revenue) by service line

$$\frac{\text{Revenue (collections) by service line}}{\text{Total practice revenue (collections)}}$$

Surgical yield

Definition: Indicates relative contribution of revenue generated from surgical or procedural workload to total practice revenue.

Goal: Depends on many practice factors; in most cases, volume should be directly related to revenue generated by service line.

$$\frac{\text{Revenue derived from surgeries or procedures}}{\text{Total practice revenue}}$$

Reimbursement per procedure code

Definition: Indicates average amount of revenue generated from procedures provided to patients.

Goal: Depends on many practice factors; in general, it will be higher if the procedures provided to patients are higher RVU procedures.

$$\frac{\text{Net collections}}{\text{Total number of procedures}}$$

Note: This metric can be adapted to show average reimbursement per procedure by payer using net collections by payer divided by total number of procedures charged to a payer.

Operational Measures

These measures assess practice operations related to payer mix, E&M coding, number of patients seen (volume), and operating room utilization. The payer mix is the percent of patients seen with a specific insurance (see Chapter 9). And E&M coding (see Chapter 9) is the percent distribution of new patient E&M codes (99201 thru 99205) and established patient codes (99211 thru 99215).

Volume and reimbursement by service line

Definition: Indicates workload volume or number of patients by service line; provides a method for identifying the relative contribution of each service line.

Goal: Depends on many practice factors; in most cases, volume should be directly related to revenue generated by service line.

Volume by service line

Volume measurement (encounters/visits, RVUs, etc.) by service line

Volume measurement for total practice

Operating room utilization (if an ambulatory surgery center/ASC)

Definition: Indicates average percentage of available surgical time used (or the percentage of time available).

Goal: Higher the better

$$\frac{\text{Total time from surgical start to end time to include setup/turnover time for 30 days}}{\text{Total available time (e.g., 8 hours of block time/day) for 30 days}}$$

Note: This should not be the only metric to assess OR efficiency and this metric is extremely dependent on efficiency of surgical pre/post-operative processes, workflows to include room setup/turnover and staffing, and surgeon on-time start rates (late start) and good surgical time estimates. In addition, the 30 days used above can be any time period (e.g., previous quarter, previous 12-months).

Physician-Specific Measures

The physician is typically the primary revenue generating unit for a practice. Therefore, gross charges, net revenue, operating costs, medical revenue after operating costs, and gross collections at the per FTE physician level provide much insight into the general performance of all FTE physicians in a practice. Also, 'gross collection ratio' is an excellent performance indicator (see Key Financial Indicators).

Total gross charges per FTE physician

Definition: The average gross charges per FTE physician; indicates financial productivity of all physicians in the practice.

Goal: Higher the better

Add the following:

$$\frac{\text{Gross fee-for-service charges} + \text{Gross charges for patients covered by capitation contracts}}{\text{Total FTE physicians}}$$

Total net revenue per FTE physician

Definition: The average medical revenue per FTE physician to include all revenues from medical activities. Indicates financial stability and can be used to compare productivity and profitability among practices.

Goal: Higher the better

$$\frac{\text{Total net revenue}}{\text{Total FTE physicians}}$$

Total operating costs per FTE physician

Definition: Indicates amount of operating costs used to provide patient care per FTE physician.

Goal: Lower the better

$$\frac{\text{Total operating costs}}{\text{Total FTE physicians}}$$

Note: Rightsizing, treating a higher volume of patients, and lowering costs can help to optimize and lower this measure.

Total medical revenue after operating costs per FTE physician

Definition: Indicates the amount per FTE physician of remaining revenue available for physician compensation, as retained earnings, or for reinvestment (measure of profitability).

Goal: Higher the better

$$\frac{\text{Total medical revenue} - \text{Total operating costs}}{\text{Total FTE physicians}}$$

Additional key measures are operational in nature (included in Chapter 9). For instance, average physician work RVUs per visit (or per appointment type or type of patient/new & established), and comparisons with other physicians.

Ideally, to ensure metrics have meaning, they must be benchmarked (compared). Therefore, key indicators should be used in relation to other like-sized and like-specialty practices and to other physicians and if possible to national standards as presented in Chapter 12. There's much value in presenting physician/provider-specific metrics compared to the average of all other providers in the organization (or using MGMA specialty-specific benchmarks)—for many providers, competition equals increased motivation.

---

[1] Keegan, D.W. & Woodcock, E. (2016). *The Physician Billing Process*, 3rd edition. Englewood: Medical Group Management Association.

CHAPTER 7

BENCHMARKING ANCILLARIES AND SCRIBES

"Strive not to be a success, but rather to be of value."
- Albert Einstein

Generally, measures for ancillary services and scribes take the form of staffing metrics per physician or per FTE provider. While these metrics are valuable from a comparison and rightsizing standpoint, they can be insufficient regarding performance analyses. Ancillaries can be assessed using many of the same formulas used for physicians since they are revenue centers. Scribes, however, are more difficult to associate with an increase in revenue or profit (that is, the return on investment can be more challenging to determine).

Typically, two benchmarking options can be used. First, a reoccurring assessment (month-by-month and year-by-year) for trending and benchmarking against external practices. In addition, when implementing a significant change or addition (such as hiring a scribe), a pre- and post-analysis will validate the improvement. And second, a business case analysis should be used to evaluate and plan for a change, particularly when the impact on the practice could be significant.

The following section is focused primarily on radiology and laboratory as ancillaries. However, any other ancillaries (for example, retail or cash-pay pharmaceuticals) can all be assessed using the same methods. In general, profitability is the key factor in determining the value of an ancillary service.

RADIOLOGY & LABORATORY MEASURES

The number of procedures or tests can be collected by most EHRs. And EHRs can identify the number of specific types of procedures or tests, offering greater granularity and specificity. There are also several descriptive measures for ancillary services. For instance, the number of procedures/tests per month can be compared to previous month's. Or the total number of tests for the year can be compared to previous years and/or to compared against

MGMA benchmarks. However, when trending data over multiple months, it is important to take in to consideration context items like seasonal and environmental fluctuations. The month-to-month measures should also be evaluated in the light of a year-to-year measure, since monthly ranges and/or seasonal fluctuations can be deceiving.

Number of radiology procedures/laboratory tests

This is a measure of workload or volume and refers to the number of procedures or tests or the number of procedures or tests per period (per month or per year). This measure can be further divided to assess the average number of test/procedures performed per day, which can shed light on daily capacity if the average length of time was known. For example, if the average number of non-contrast CTs performed is five per day and it takes a total of 30 minutes for a CT from the time the patient enters the CT area until they leave plus turnaround time, that would result in 2.5 hours of workload in each 8-hour day, revealing 5.5 hours of capacity that could be filled with additional CTs or other radiology procedures. This calculation would need to be adjusted for room prep between patients and some required cool downs times of some CT units; a time-motion study could be used to fine tune this assessment's accuracy.

Average revenue (collections) per patient

What is the average collected (payer and patient responsibility) per patient? The components of this measure—total collections and total patients seen over the same time period—are available from your EHR, practice management, or billing software. Use this analysis with care, however, as the potentially broad range in the procedures and tests performed and the associated collections tend not to reconcile quickly. Short periods of time (e.g.: weekly averages) are more likely to show large differences in the data. A revenue center that does not at least break even with its expenses should be assessed further to determine its value and longevity. Some ancillaries might be regarded as acceptable as a breakeven if the board feels the value to their practice or the patient warrants the financial position (the center is somewhat minimal but provides physicians and patients with a relevant benefit).

Total expenses (ancillary)

This amount should be an all-inclusive number that reflects the total cost to the practice for a given ancillary. The emphasis on all-inclusive is key: staffing costs, supplies, equipment, service contracts, leases, facilities (rent allocation and utilities), and general maintenance and sustainment should all be included.

Business case analysis/financial viability

Periodically re-assessing the benefit of an ancillary on a practice is useful and valuable. If it is already in the practice, then it is clear time and effort have already been sunk into it; however, a re-assessment can help validate its need from a cost-benefit standpoint.

A business case analysis can help decide if you want to add the revenue center and a financial viability assessment can be used to decide whether to keep a given revenue center or outsource. For the assessment, if the total revenue for a period minus the total expense for the same period equal a positive number, the revenue center is generating income for the practice. If the result is zero, the revenue center is operating at a breakeven point. If it is a negative number, however, the center is operating at a loss and should be evaluated more thoroughly since long-term losses can seriously impact the practice. Even a breakeven result should be of concern since the slightest change could push it into a loss. Assessing ancillary profitability with other like practices (via benchmarking) is key to know where you are and where you want to be.

SCRIBE MEASURES

The use of medical scribes continues to rise as the demands on providers grow to input increasingly more information into an EHR. Many providers are spending more time typing than interacting with patients. The benefits of a scribe are many. And providers are finding they can spend more time focused on the patient and less time on data input since this function can easily be delegated. Some providers have found they are spending less time after clinic hours documenting so their quality of life has improved using scribes. In addition, EHRs have become extremely complex, so a scribe is ideally suited to become a typing, point-n-click, and EHR expert.

Several metrics could be used to assess a scribe directly. Many of these metrics would require time-and-motion studies or supplemental software to collect the number of point-n-clicks, characters typed, errors, and time spent per chart. The time needed to manage these metrics is probably cost prohibitive for most practice managers. A proxy measure for scribe "value," such as patient survey results associated with patient perception of time spend with the provider or quality of time spent with the provider, is liable to be better. This measure is apt be higher with a scribe versus without, due to the expected stronger patient-provider relationship that would be the result of more patient-centric interaction.

Other measures can be used and calculated more efficiently that are a strong proxy for scribe value to the practice. The following is a list of proxy measures that should be trended or compared with an average pre-scribe versus post-scribe.

Patient count

Many practices that was employed a scribe have realized an increase of one or two additional patients per day since the provider can focus on patients more documentation less. If we assume there are 260 work days in a year, that's an increase of between 260 and 520 patients annually. Apply the average revenue per patient to this increase and the financial benefit of a scribe becomes clear.

EXHIBIT 7.1 SCRIBE ASSESSMENT (EXAMPLE)

1. INCREASE OF 260 MORE PATIENTS IN YEAR 1 OF A SCRIBE VERSUS A PRE-SCRIBE YEAR

2. AVERAGE REVENUE PER PATIENT = $200

3. ESTIMATED REVENUE INCREASE = $52,000 (260 PATIENTS X $200)

4. TOTAL COMPENSATION OF A SCRIBE (SALARY, TAXES, AND BENEFITS) = $30,000

5. NET INCOME = $22,000 ($52,000 MINUS $30,000)

Number of days from date of service until the provider finalizes the chart

Since a scribe will remove the bulk of typing and pointing-n-clicking from the provider, the remaining task for the provider is to thoroughly review, add, edit the chart, and then finalize (sign). Therefore, the amount of time between the date of service and finalization is a valid proxy measure.

Most EHRs can produce reports identifying the date of service (DOS) and date the chart was finalized by the provider, by the patient, by all patients within a given period, and by provider. For EHRs that do not have this function, most can download this data into a comma-separated value (CSV) or Microsoft Excel file for consolidation and analysis.

This measure would only provide value if providers are not signing their charts on the day of service (unless the EHR also provides a time stamp). The expectation of this assessment is to see a reduction in time between DOS and date signed. In addition, the days in A/R metric is also a proxy if DOS (and not date signed) is used in the formula.

Error rate or number of missed charges

This is a more difficult measure since it requires an EHR with advanced error algorithms or a billing department that performs quality control and tracks findings. Categorizing errors, if not automated, can add a layer of difficulty in data collection. Therefore, the easiest method of data collection in this case is to simply identify the number of errors in total as a monthly trend or do a similar comparison pre-scribe versus post-scribe. Like the other measures, this formula is also a proxy.

E&M distribution or average wRVUs per patient

If the assumption that a scribe will capture and document more than a provider since it is his/her core competency, then it is an appropriate assumption the E&M distribution will shift to the right (i.e., the number of higher level codes should increase—perhaps only slightly since it is dependent on what the provider does). Similarly, if the E&M distribution shifts (increases toward higher codes), then the average wRVUs per patient will also increase.

Therefore, a comparison of E&M distribution percentages pre/post-scribe by month (January versus January) or year will provide an appropriate comparison. Further, for average wRVUs per patient, a trend or 12-month pre/post-scribe analysis should provide a good comparison.

Financial improvements

There are many factors affecting practice finances, so it is reasonable to expect the addition of a scribe would result in an increased patient count, an E&M distribution that shifts to the right, and increased average wRVUs per patient. All these metric improvements ultimately drive an increase in collections (practice revenue).

Many of the metrics within this book can be used for a pre/post-scribe analysis provided practice context is understood and that a cause-effect relationship does not necessarily exist with a scribe. That is, there could be a correlation/association (when we add a scribe, revenue increases) but not a true cause-effect (we cannot be 100% certain the addition of a scribe is the reason revenue increased).

Goodwill

Another benefit to having a scribe that is far more challenging to quantify is patient goodwill (that is, the perceived value and loyalty given to the practice by its patients). A scribe allows a provider to focus more on the patient, resulting in a greatly enhanced patient-provider relationship (and better compliance and outcomes). A happy patient is also likely to tell others about the practice. In effect, these patients are doing free marketing for your practice. The providers will likewise enjoy greater job satisfaction since they will finally able to focus on the patient versus a computer screen.

CHAPTER 8

MEASURING QUALITY

CHAPTER 8

MEASURING

"If you don't drive your business, you will be driven out of business."
- B. C. Forbes

OPERATIONS

There has been a push for many years in medical billing to establish metrics to assess quality of care and tie them to reimbursement or incentive payments. Several quality-based initiatives have been established and some are more visible than others. For instance, the Centers for Medicare & Medicaid Services (CMS) have developed the Hospital Inpatient Quality Reporting (IQR) Program, Hospital Outpatient Quality Reporting (OQR) Program, and the Physician Quality Reporting System (PQRS). And, according to the CMS, "quality measures are tools that help us measure or quantify healthcare processes, outcomes, patient perceptions, and organizational structure and/or systems that are associated with the ability to provide high-quality health care and/or that relate to one or more quality goals for health care."[1]

In 2015, PQRS was replaced by the Medicare Access and CHIP Reauthorization Act (MACRA) which includes a Quality Payment Program (QPP) with two options: (1) the Merit-based Incentive Payment System (MIPS) and (2) Advanced Alternative Payment Models (APMs).[2] MACRA and QPP are still evolving with changes projected in 2018, so regular visits to the CMS website (https://qpp.cms.gov/) are necessary to ensure the most up-to-date information is applied to your practice. In addition, the National Committee for Quality Assurance (NCQA) developed the Healthcare Effectiveness Data and Information Set (HEDIS) to measure care and services for health plans.[3] There is also a movement among payers and networks to establish risk-based or value-based contracts with service providers/physician practices.

Merit-Based Incentive Payment System (MIPS)

This QPP track provides an opportunity to earn a performance-based payment adjustment in 2019 if 2017 data is submitted by the end of March 2018.[2] And based on the data submitted, Medicare payments can go up, down, or remain the same.[2] If no data is submitted for 2017, however, then a 4% negative payment adjustment will result in 2019,[2] so its optimal to submit a full year of 2017 data to potentially receive the maximum positive payment adjustment.[2] For 2017, three categories of data are necessary and include quality (replaces PQRS), improvement activities, and advancing care information (replaces meaningful use).[2] In 2018, a cost category will be added to replace the value-based modifier.[2]

Advanced Alternative Payment Models (APMs)

This QPP track includes subcategories specific to a clinical condition, care episode, or population.[2] It provides an opportunity to earn a 5% incentive payment in 2019 if 2017 data is submitted by the end of March 2018 and 20% of Medicare patients are seen through an APM (or 25% of your Medicare Part B payments are through an APM).[2] To join an APM, a practice chooses an available option from a list, and submits an application. The APM must be appropriate for the practice speciality.[2]

Healthcare Effectiveness Data and Information Set (HEDIS)

According to the NCQA, HEDIS "is a tool used by more than 90 percent of America's health plans to measure performance on important dimensions of care and service. Altogether, HEDIS consists of 81 measures across five domains of care. Because so many plans collect HEDIS data, and because the measures are so specifically defined, HEDIS makes it possible to compare the performance of health plans on an 'apples-to-apples' basis."[3] HEDIS includes measures for asthma, breast cancer screening, cervical cancer screening, childhood immunizations, diabetic care by A1C screening, diabetic care by A1C control, and colorectal cancer screening (see Exhibit A.4).[3] According to the NCQA, HEDIS are a standardized set of clinical performance measures and the measures are related to several public health issues. For more information, visit the NCQA HEDIS website at http://www.ncqa.org/Programs/HEDIS/index.htm.

Exhibit 8.1 Clinical Question and Performance Thresholds for HEDIS Measures[3]

Asthma: What percentage of beneficiaries 5 to 56 years of age with persistent asthma are prescribed medications acceptable as primary therapy for the long-term control of asthma in accordance with HEDIS?

Sub-standard (54% or less)

Marginal (greater than 55% to less than or equal to 59%)

Above standard (60% or more)

Breast Cancer Screening: What percentage of women 52 to 69 years of age continuously enrolled have completed breast cancer screening in accordance with HEDIS and the minimum screening recommendations from the American Academy of Family Physicians and the US Preventive Services Task Force?

Sub-standard (73% or less)

Marginal (greater than 73% to less than 81%)

Above standard (81% or more)

Cervical Cancer Screening: What percentage of women 21 to 64 years of age continuously enrolled have completed cervical cancer screening in accordance with HEDIS and the minimum screening recommendations from the American Academy of Family Physicians and the US Preventive Services Task Force?

Sub-standard (less than 81%)

Marginal (81% to less than 87%)

Above standard (87% or more)

Childhood Immunizations: What percentage of children 24 to 35 months of age continuously enrolled to Air Force medical treatment facilities (hospitals) completed four DPT/DTaP, three IPV/OPV,

ONE MMR, THREE HEPATITIS B, THREE HIB, ONE VZV, AND FOUR PCV VACCINATIONS IN ACCORDANCE WITH HEDIS AND THE CENTERS FOR DISEASE CONTROL AND PREVENTION, THE AMERICAN ACADEMY OF PEDIATRICS, AMERICAN ACADEMY OF FAMILY PHYSICIANS, AND THE ADVISORY COMMITTEE ON IMMUNIZATION PRACTICES?

SUB-STANDARD (LESS THAN 30%)

MARGINAL (30% TO LESS THAN 55%)

ABOVE STANDARD (55% OR MORE)

DIABETIC CARE BY A1C SCREENING: WHAT PERCENTAGE OF ENROLLEES WITH DIABETES (TYPE 1 OR 2) AGED 18 TO 75 YEARS OF AGE CONTINUOUSLY ENROLLED WHO HAD A A1C TEST IN THE PAST 12 MONTHS IN ACCORDANCE WITH HEDIS AND THE MINIMUM SCREENING RECOMMENDATIONS FROM THE DIABETES QUALITY IMPROVEMENT PROJECT (DQIP) AND THE US PREVENTIVE SERVICES TASK FORCE?

SUB-STANDARD (LESS THAN 86%)

MARGINAL (86% TO LESS THAN 92%)

ABOVE STANDARD (92% OR MORE)

DIABETIC CARE BY A1C CONTROL: WHAT PERCENTAGE OF ENROLLEES WITH DIABETES (TYPE 1 OR 2) AGED 18 TO 75 YEARS OF AGE CONTINUOUSLY ENROLLED WHOSE MOST RECENT A1C TEST DURING THE PAST 12 MONTHS WAS LESS THAN OR EQUAL TO 9.0 IN ACCORDANCE WITH HEDIS?

SUB-STANDARD (LESS THAN 70%)

MARGINAL (70% TO LESS THAN 79%)

ABOVE STANDARD (79% OR MORE)

COLORECTAL CANCER SCREENING: WHAT PERCENTAGE OF MEN AND WOMEN 51 TO 80 YEARS OF AGE CONTINUOUSLY ENROLLED WHO HAVE AT RECEIVED AT LEAST ONE COLON CANCER SCREENING PROCEDURE IN ACCORDANCE WITH HEDIS AND THE MINIMUM SCREENING RECOMMENDATIONS FROM THE US PREVENTIVE SERVICES TASK FORCE?

SUB-STANDARD (LESS THAN 49%)

MARGINAL (49% TO LESS THAN 61%)

ABOVE STANDARD (61% OR MORE)

NOTES:

THERE ARE SEVERAL NOTES AND SPECIAL CRITERIA, NOT INCLUDED HERE

Risk-based/value-based contracts

Traditional fee-for-service payer contracts continue to fade away as a result of the payment evolution that included HMOs, PPOs, Patient-Centered Medical Home (PCMH), bundled payments, and CMS initiatives (MACRA). It will become more common for contracts and networks to be focused on risk-based or value-based contracts. The methodologies behind these contracts and the associated networks are still developing. However, it is likely many will follow suit with CMS by using the same or similar categories found in MIPS and APMs. And gainsharing (often found in most bundled payment programs) will also be a key component where physicians are paid a contracted rate and additional dollars are pooled and shared if a savings is achieved.[4]

---

[1] https://www.cms.gov/medicare/quality-initiatives-patient-assessment-instruments/value-based-programs/macra-mips-and-apms/macra-mips-and-apms.html (June 2017)

[2] https://qpp.cms.gov/ (June 2017)

[3] http://www.ncqa.org/hedis-quality-measurement (June 2017)

[4] Gosfield, A. (2015). "Understanding risk-based payer contracts" *Medical Economics* (16 March 2015).

CHAPTER 9

MEASURING
PRACTICE
OPERATIONS

"Until you can measure something and express it in numbers, you have only the beginning of understanding."

- Lord Kelvin

P ractice operations are as important to the practice as quality patient care—without both activities, the practice would not exist. Therefore, this chapter will provide several techniques for measuring medical practice operations at the patient, provider, and staffing levels.

PATIENT DEMOGRAPHICS

Demographics are statistical population characteristics and can be used to help understand and prepare for patient needs and expectations (see Exhibit 9.1). Age and gender are the primary demographics most practices should measure to identify the distribution of established patients and predict the characteristics of new patients. However, as noted in Exhibit 9.1., several demographic factors that can and should be assessed to maximum an understanding of the types of patients served. This assessment provides a foundation and a context for patient needs and behaviors related to care seeking

EXHIBIT 9.1 TYPES OF DEMOGRAPHICS

• AGE	• EDUCATION
• GENDER	• FAMILY SIZE
• RACE	• MARITAL STATUS
• SOCIOECONOMIC STATUS (SES)	• OWNERSHIP (HOME, CAR, PET,
• RELIGION	ETC.)
• NATIONALITY	• LANGUAGE
• OCCUPATION	• MOBILITY

Charting patient ages and genders provide a method for describing the types of patients seen in a practice. And age and gender distributions at the practice level provide some insight. But at the provider level, the data may uncover significant differences between providers. In addition, when the data is sorted by new and established patients, greater differences may appear.

In most cases, the type (or specialty) of the practice will determine the "shape" of the patient age distribution (see Exhibits 9.2 thru 9.4). That is, a histogram chart will quickly identify the most common patient ages or age ranges. Each bar represents an age range of patients at the practice level starting at 0-10, 11-20, etc. The profile of patient ages in practice #1 (see Exhibit 9.2) could be from a family practice clinic since the greatest proportion of patients tends to be between 21 to 40 years of age (50%). Obviously, this distribution would not be expected from an internal medicine or cardiology practice since patients seen in these types of practices tend to be older. If this chart was representative of an internal medicine practice's patient population, it might suggest the need for further investigation.

EXHIBIT 9.2 PROFILE OF PATIENT AGES FOR PRACTICE #1

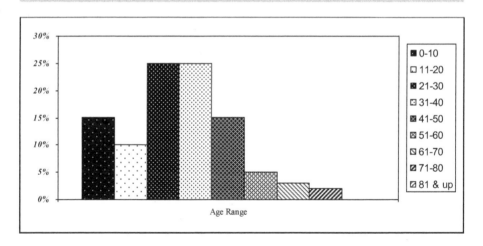

The profile of patient ages in practice #2 (see Exhibit 9.3) is probably from a pediatric practice since the greatest proportion of its patients are under 20 years of age (95%).

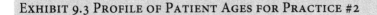

EXHIBIT 9.3 PROFILE OF PATIENT AGES FOR PRACTICE #2

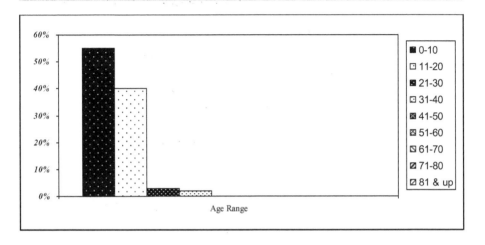

The profile of patient ages in practice #3 (see Exhibit 9.4) is probably from an internal medicine practice since the greatest proportion of its patients are 51 years of age or older (65%).

EXHIBIT 9.4 PROFILE OF PATIENT AGES FOR PRACTICE #3

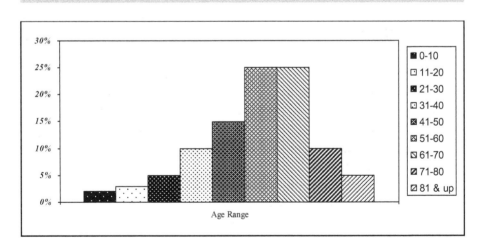

Based on the distribution in Exhibit 9.5, what type of practice might this be? If you thought OB/GYN, you would probably be right. Since 100% of patients seen in this practice are female, the distribution certainly points to an entirely female-oriented practice type or specialty.

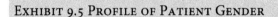

EXHIBIT 9.5 PROFILE OF PATIENT GENDER

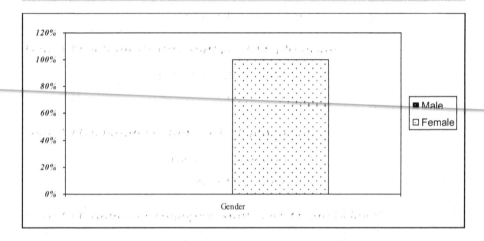

PATIENT SATISFACTION

In general, the purpose of surveying patients is to uncover how patients feel about or perceive the practice. The importance of patient satisfaction was rated very high (mean of 4.61 on a scale with 5 being "extremely important") by practices identified as successful medical groups. And patient satisfaction is typically assessed using some type of survey instrument. Survey questions should be simple and easy to understand. Questions should be focused on one specific item and should never be two questions in one (for example, do you feel your appointment time was appropriate and should it have been longer or shorter?). Simple and standard questions are easier to interpret and provide more consistency among patients. There are many sources of survey questions that have been thoroughly tested for consistency and validity, so there's usually no reason to create new questions.

There can be much value in using the same questions over time to uncover trends or changes. The same questions also provide value when used before, during, and after a change in the practice to provide insights into the effect of a change. The types of questions used must also be carefully selected since qualitative questions tend to provide greater opportunity and flexibility for patients to explain their feelings; whereas, quantitative questions are better for focusing of specific topics (see Exhibit 9.6). The strength of qualitative questions lie in their ability to let patients elaborate in their own words on aspects of the practice. However, it is somewhat difficult to organize qualitative question responses given their unstructured nature. The strength behind quantitative questions lies in their simplicity, specificity and measurability—this makes analysis much easier. These types of questions provide patients with a list of preset answers to choose from (for example, circle "1" for poor, "2" for good, or "3" for excellent).

EXHIBIT 9.6 QUALITATIVE VERSUS QUANTITATIVE SURVEY QUESTIONS

QUALITATIVE	QUANTITATIVE
HOW SATISFIED WERE YOU WITH THE CARE YOU RECEIVED TODAY? WHAT COULD THIS PRACTICE DO TO IMPROVE THE CARE YOU RECEIVED TODAY?	USING THE CHOICES BELOW, HOW WOULD YOU RATE THE EASE OF MAKING TODAY'S APPOINTMENT BY PHONE? (CIRCLE "1" FOR POOR, "2" FOR GOOD, OR "3" FOR EXCELLENT.)
WHAT BROUGHT YOU INTO THE PRACTICE TODAY?	USING THE CHOICES BELOW, HOW MANY TIMES DID YOU OR SOMEONE ELSE TRY TO SCHEDULE TODAY'S APPOINTMENT? (CIRCLE "1" FOR ONE TIME, "2" FOR TWO OR THREE TIMES, OR "3" FOR FOUR OR MORE TIMES.)
HOW WOULD YOU DESCRIBE WHAT YOU'RE FEELING?	
HOW SATISFIED WERE YOU WITH THE CARE YOU RECEIVED TODAY?	
WHAT COULD THIS PRACTICE DO TO IMPROVE THE CARE YOU RECEIVED TODAY?	

PROVIDER PROFILES

Profiles display data by provider for most any measure. They typically consist of information related to each provider matched to selected benchmarks. Profiling can be used for many purposes. For instance, some practices use profiles as part of their physician compensation methodology. But, in many cases, profiling is used to provide individual providers with a summary of their unique measures in relation to the overall practice.

For example, a typical use of profiling is to portray the E&M coding distribution by provider for new and established patients compared to the overall practice distribution. Exhibit 9.7 illustrates a percent distribution of E&M codes for established patients seen by an individual provider (Dr. Smith) versus the distribution for the entire practice. These profiles (see Exhibit 9.7) suggest Dr. Smith has a slightly different patient population than other providers in the practice; however, it might also suggest Dr. Smith may benefit from additional coding training.

EXHIBIT 9.7 PROFILES OF DR. SMITH'S E&M ESTABLISHED VERSUS THE OVERALL PRACTICE

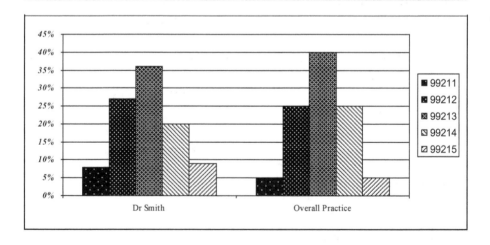

COST OF NON-CLINICAL SERVICES

For the most part, practice revenue and physician compensation are directly related to the number and type of clinical services provided to patients. When physicians spend time at meetings, making phone calls, answering telephone consults, and corresponding with patients, revenue is not being generated, though overhead costs continue to accrue. Since every practice will require some provider involvement in non-clinical activities, it is possible to approximate the cost (or lost revenue) in response to the performance of these types of activities using an estimation of the physician's hourly rate. For instance, the following formula can be used to assess cost (or lost revenue): number of hours spent performing non-clinical activities multiplied by physician's hourly rate. The number of hours spent is probably an easier to determine, possibly by counting those hours using the physician's past schedule and personal schedule. However, establishing the hourly rate can be trickier, since most physicians are under varying compensation methodologies that range from a purely "eat what you kill" model to base-plus-production-plus-quality bonuses. Therefore, a more valid approach might consist of taking total annual compensation over a few years to reach an average and use 2,080 hours as an equivalent for an FTE. This isn't a perfect approach given physicians typically are not a standard FTE, but it will provide a ballpark for the question being asked—approximately how much does it cost to have a physician perform non-clinical or non-direct care activities?

PAYER MIX

Payer mix typically consists of Medicare fee-for-service, Medicare managed care fee-for-service, Medicare capitation, commercial fee-for-service, commercial managed care fee-for-service, commercial capitation, workers' compensation, charity care and professional courtesy, self-pay, and other federal government payers.

Payer mix ratio 2,3

Definition: Indicates the sources of payment as a percentage or the relative value of a specific health insurance plan to the bottom line.

Version #1:2

$$\frac{\text{Gross charges by payer}}{\text{Total gross charges}}$$

Version #2:3

$$\frac{\text{Each payer's net charges}}{\text{Total net charges}}$$

Total percentage distribution of payers

% Medicare fee-for-service + %Medicare managed care fee-for-service + % Medicare capitation + + % commercial fee-for-service + % commercial managed care fee-for-service + % commercial capitation + % workers' compensation + % charity care and professional courtesy + % self-pay + % other federal government payers = 100%

PROVIDERS, PHYSICIANS, AND STAFF FTES

The following support staffing formulas are from the MGMA Cost Surveys (FTE support staff should be calculated to the nearest tenth FTE).

FTE provider staffing[2]

Add the following:

$$\text{FTE non-physician providers +FTE physicians}$$

Total FTE physicians[2]

Add the following:

FTE primary care physicians +FTE nonsurgical specialty physicians +FTE surgical specialty physicians

FTE providers[2]

Add the following:

Total FTE non-physician providers +Total FTE physicians

Total business operations FTE support staff[4]

Take the following:

Number of general administration FTE support staff (administrator, CFO, medical director, human resources, marketing) +Number of patient accounting FTE support staff (billing, collection) =Number of general accounting FTE support staff (controller, account manager, accounts payable, and budget) +Number of managed care administration FTE support staff (contract administration and utilization review) +Number of information technology FTE support staff (data processing, programming, telecommunications) +Number of housekeeping, maintenance, and security FTE support staff

Total front office FTE support staff[4]

Add the following:

Number of medical receptionist FTE support staff +Number of medical secretaries and transcriber FTE support staff +Number of medical records staff FTE support staff +Number of other administrative support staff FTE support staff

Total clinical FTE support staff[4]

Add the following:

Number of registered nurse FTE support staff +Number of licensed practical nurse FTE support staff +Number of medical assistant and nurse's aide FTE support staff

Total ancillary full-time equivalent (FTE) support staff[4]

Add the following:

Number of clinical laboratory FTE support staff +Number of radiology and imaging FTE support staff +Number of other ancillary medical support services FTE support staff

Total employed FTE support staff[4]

Add the following:

Total number of business operations support FTE support staff +Total number of front office support FTE support staff +Total number of clinical support FTE support staff +Total number of ancillary support FTE support staff

Total FTE support staff[4]

Add the following:

Total employed FTE support staff +Total contracted and temporary FTE support staff

Staffing ratio[3]

$$\frac{\text{Total number of FTE employees}}{\text{Total number of FTE providers or physicians}}$$

Total FTE medical support staff per FTE physician[5]

$$\frac{\text{Total FTE medical support staff}}{\text{Total FTE physicians}}$$

Total FTE administrative staff per FTE physician[5]

$$\frac{\text{Total FTE administrative staff}}{\text{Total FTE physicians}}$$

Total FTE laboratory staff per FTE physician[5]

$$\frac{\text{Total FTE laboratory staff}}{\text{Total FTE physicians}}$$

Total FTE radiology (imaging) staff per FTE physician[5]

$$\frac{\text{Total FTE radiology (imaging) staff}}{\text{Total FTE physicians}}$$

RELATIVE VALUE UNITS

A Relative Value Unit (RVU) is a measure of resources/work performed based on coding documentation of E&M and CPT codes and each code is associated with a specific number of RVUs. For example, in family practice the average RVUs per patient will typically vary around one (1) RVU. The CMS publishes RVU tables every year in an itemized format consisting of malpractice, facility, and professional components. These components can be added to arrive at a total RVU per E&M or CPT code. In addition, the professional component can be used to determine Total Physician Work RVUs. In many practices, Physician Work RVUs are used to assess physician (provider) productivity and they are often used in compensation methodologies as the pay-for-performance (P4P) component.

Physician work relative value units per visit (for a single visit)

Add the following:

Sum of RVUs by E&M codes +Sum of RVUs by CPT codes

Note: A more valuable measure is to calculate the mean (average) RVUs per visit across a user-defined timeframe.

Average physician work relative value units per visit

Add the following:

$$\frac{\text{Sum of Work RVUs by all E\&M codes} + \text{Sum of Work RVUs by all CPT codes}}{\text{Total number of visits}}$$

Note: An adjustment must be made when calculating this measure across multiple calendar years since CMS publishes new RVU Exhibits/values every year for E&M and CPT codes

Other Operational Measures

Operational measures related to supply (physician availability), access to care, and utilization of space also provide a basis for benchmarking standard operations of the practice.

Ambulatory/Outpatient patient encounters (visits/appointments) per FTE physician[5]

$$\frac{\text{Physician ambulatory patient encounters}}{\text{Total FTE physicians}}$$

Hospital admissions per FTE physician[5]

$$\frac{\text{Hospital inpatient admissions}}{\text{Total FTE physicians}}$$

New patient registrations per FTE physician[5]

$$\frac{\text{New patient registrations}}{\text{Total FTE physicians}}$$

Physician weeks worked per year

Total number of weeks worked per year per physician

Half-days worked per month

Total number of half-days worked per month per physician

Note: A half-day standard definition is needed to ensure consistency (for example, if a physician has a template/schedule to provide direct-care for three hours or more, then it counts as a half-day); to convert this to a percent for comparing month-to-month, divide the number of half-days by the total number of half work days per month

Clinical service hours worked per week

Total number of clinical service hours worked per week per physician

Appointment duration (average) in minutes

$$\frac{\text{Total number of clinical service hours worked per week per physician} * 60}{\text{Number of total scheduled appointments per physician}}$$

Note: From a practical standpoint, there can be data quality issues with this measure since appointment duration is typically driven by the template and most practices do not change the schedule based on "actual" appointment duration; therefore, this measure can provide an average based on the template only (not "actual" appointment duration); to arrive at an actual appointment duration figure it would be necessary to perform a "time and motion" study through direct observation

Appointment type mix

$$\frac{\text{Number of each appointment type}}{\text{Number of total scheduled appointments}}$$

Note: Some practices use different types of appointments to ensure patient needs (chief complaint) is allocated an appropriate amount of time with the physician.

Appointment availability[2]

Number of days to next available new or established patient appointment

No-show rate[2]

$$\frac{\text{Number of appointment no-shows}}{\text{Number of total scheduled appointments}}$$

Cancellation conversion rate[2]

$$\frac{\text{Number of cancellations converted to appointments}}{\text{Total cancellations}}$$

New patient appointments as a percentage of total appointments[2]

$$\frac{\text{Number of new patient appointments}}{\text{Number of total scheduled appointments}}$$

Productivity by space (RVUs per square foot)[2]

$$\frac{\text{Total RVUs}}{\text{Total square footage}}$$

In addition to the previous formulas and ratios, there a several other operational metrics that, if possible, should be collected, monitored, and communicated to all practice personnel (see Exhibit 9.8).[3]

EXHIBIT 9.8 OTHER OPERATIONAL METRICS[3]

- AMOUNT OF WAIT TIME PER VISIT
- WAIT TIME ON THE TELEPHONE
- ACCESS WAIT TIME BY APPOINTMENT TYPE
- NUMBER OF NO-SHOWS
- TRANSCRIPTION TURNAROUND TIME
- ACCOUNTS WORKED PER BILLING CLERK/COLLECTOR FTE PER DAY
- WORDS OR LINES TRANSCRIBED PER DAY
- AUTHORIZATION TURNAROUND TIME
- RETURN TELEPHONE CALL WAIT TIME

[1] Wikipedia. Search for "Demographics" at www.wikipedia.com; 2017.

[2] Woodcock, Elizabeth W. Practice Benchmarking, Chapter 11 of Physician Practice Management edited by Lawrence F. Wolper. Boston: Jones and Bartlett Publishers, 2012.

[3] The Coker Group. Physician Ancillary Services: Evaluation, Implementation, and Management of New Practice Opportunities. Boston: Jones and Bartlett Publishers, 2006.

[4] MGMA. Cost Survey Questionnaire, Englewood, CO.

[5] Pavlock, E. J. Financial Management for Medical Groups, 2nd edition. Englewood: MGMA, 2000.

CHAPTER 10

TOOLS FOR MEASURING PRACTICE FINANCES

"Innovation has nothing to do with how many R&D dollars you have. When Apple came up with the Mac, IBM was spending at least 100 times more on R&D. It's not about the money. It's about the people you have, how you're led, and how much you get it."

- Steve Jobs

There are several financial performance indicators used by most practices to manage financial operations. Many of these formulas are presented in this chapter as a comprehensive "starter set" of performance indicators and financial metrics for benchmarking.

FEE-FOR-SERVICE (FFS) ACTIVITIES

FFS activities consist of gross FFS charges (not including capitation charges), adjustments to FFS charges (value of services performed for which payment is not expected; that is, bad debts or noncontractual write-offs), adjusted FFS charges (contractual write-offs), bad debts due to FFS activity (accounts assigned to collection agencies), and net FFS collections/revenue.

Adjusted FFS charges

Take the following:

> Gross FFS charges (not including capitation charges) –Adjustments to FFS charges (value of services performed for which payment is not expected)

Capitation activity

Capitation activity consists of gross charges for patients covered by capitation contracts, gross capitation revenue (per member per month capitation payments and capitation patient co-payments), purchased services for capitation patients, and net capitation revenue.

Net capitation revenue

Gross capitation revenue (per member per month capitation payments and capitation patient co-payments) – Purchased services for capitation patients

OTHER MEDICAL ACTIVITIES

Other medical activities consist of other medical revenue (research contract revenue, honoraria, and teaching income), revenue from the sale of medical goods and services, gross revenue from other medical activities (flat-rate contract services or professional services agreements/PSAs), cost of sales and/ or cost of other medical activities (retail or cash-only), and net other medical revenue.

Gross revenue from other medical activities

Add the following:

> Other medical revenue (research contract revenue, honoraria, and teaching income) +Revenue from the sale of medical goods and services

Net other medical activities revenue

Take the following:

> Gross revenue from other medical activities –Cost of sales and/or cost of other medical activities

OPERATING COSTS INDICATORS[3]

Costs associated with operating the practice, also referred to as overhead, typically consist of employee salaries and benefits, equipment and supplies, professional insurance, and facility expenses. However, the definition of overhead is dependent on its use. For instance, when computing profitability in a practice, physicians are typically not included; whereas, when calculating costs for contracting purposes, physician costs are included. This highlights the importance of understanding and ensuring clarity in the definition of overhead, particularly when comparing with external benchmarks, that is, how does the external organization or external benchmark define overhead?

Total operating cost as a percent of total medical revenue

Definition: Indicates overhead in relation to total revenue.

Goal: Lower the better

$$\frac{\text{Total operating costs} \times 100}{\text{Total medical revenue}}$$

Total support staff salary expenses per FTE physician

Definition: Indicates average cost of support staff salary per FTE physician.

Goal: Depends on many practice factors; in general, lower the better. However, it has been found that too few staff (too low support staff expense) results in poor productivity; therefore, rightsizing is imperative.

$$\frac{\text{Total support staff salary expenses}}{\text{Total FTE physicians}}$$

Total medical and surgical supply expenses per FTE physician

Definition: Indicates supply expenses per FTE physician.

Goal: Depends on many practice factors; in general, lower the better. However, since supply expenses are a variable cost, the more productive providers will have greater medical and surgical supply expense due to their higher volume.

$$\frac{\text{Total medical and surgical supply expenses}}{\text{Total FTE physicians}}$$

Total general and administrative expenses per FTE physicians

Definition: Indicates average cost of general and administrative costs per FTE physician.

Goal: Lower the better

$$\frac{\text{Total general and administrative expenses}}{\text{Total FTE physicians}}$$

Note: Rightsizing and attention to productivity issues can help to optimize and lower this measure.

ACCOUNTS RECEIVABLE (A/R) INDICATORS[3]

A/R consist of bills to patients, third-party payers, and other sources of revenue. Several aspects of A/R can be monitored at per FTE physician, adjustments, bad debts, adjusted collections, and months revenue in A/R levels. Typically, A/R aging categories include receivables that are current to 30 days, 31 to 60 days, 61 to 90 days, 91 to 120 days, and over 120 days. In addition, A/R that has been turned over to a collection agency should also be considered (that is, it can be included or excluded from A/R totals/categories). Also, 'gross/net/ adjusted collection ratio', 'days in A/R', 'adjustments as a percent of gross FFS charges', 'months revenue in A/R' are excellent performance indicator.

Total A/R

Add the following:

Current to 30 days +31 to 60 days +61 to 90 days +91 to 120 days +Over 120 days

Adjustment ratio[3]

Definition: Indicates the percentage of gross FFS charges that will not be collected.

Goal: The adjustment ratio should be consistent over 12, 18, 24 months. If your adjustment ratio doesn't show large fluctuations over time, it indicates a steady revenue cycle that is functioning properly.[1] In most cases, lower the better.

$$\frac{\text{Adjustments (write-offs)}}{\text{Gross FFS charges}}$$

A/R per FTE physician

Definition: Indicates the average charges outstanding per FTE physician.

Goal: Depends on many practice factors; in general, higher the better. However, there are two main drivers associated with this metric: (1) higher charges result in higher A/R and (2) slow collections.

$$\frac{\text{Total A/R}}{\text{Total FTE physicians}}$$

Bad debts due to FFS activity as a percent of gross FFS charges

Definition: Indicates the percentage of gross FFS charges that will not be collected.

Goal: Lower the better

$$\frac{\text{Bad debts due to FFS activity} * 100}{\text{Gross FFS charges}}$$

Prepaid Services Indicators[3]

Prepaid services are generally synonymous with capitation payments for members enrolled in a prepayment plan (HMO or PPO). To monitor increases or decreases in revenue and charges, the following measures for identifying these changes can be used.

Net capitation revenue as a percent of total medical revenue

Definition: Indicates the percentage of total revenue associated with capitation payments.

Goal: Depends on many practice factors; should be directly related to the proportion of average number of prepaid plan members to all charges

$$\frac{\text{Net capitation revenue}}{\text{Total net medical revenue}}$$

Net capitation revenue per-member per-month

Definition: Indicates the average revenue collected per-member per-month

Goal: Depends on many practice factors; should be directly related to the proportion of average number of prepaid plan members to all charges

$$\frac{\text{Net capitation revenue for 12 months}}{\text{Average number of prepaid plan members for 12 months}}$$

FFS equivalent charges (for capitation plan patients) per-member per-month

Definition: Indicates the average monthly FFS equivalent charges per-member per-month

Goal: Depends on many practice factors; should be directly related to the proportion of average number of prepaid plan members to all charges

$$\frac{\text{FFS equivalent charges (for capitation plan patients) for 12 months}}{\text{Average number of prepaid plan members for 12 months}}$$

Net capitation revenue as a percent of FFS equivalent charges

Definition: Indicates the ratio of capitation revenue over FFS equivalent charges

Goal: Depends on many practice factors; should be directly related to the proportion of average number of prepaid plan members to all charges

$$\frac{\text{Net capitation revenue}}{\text{FFS equivalent charges}}$$

REVENUE AND COST MEASURES

Medical revenue and costs are the bottom-line drivers of practice success and longevity since the difference between them is typically physician compensation. In general terms, profit is defined as revenue minus expenses. And provided revenue surpasses expenses, the practice will continue to operate. The greater the difference, the more profitable the practice will be and the higher the income of the physicians. Therefore, management and oversight of revenue and expenses should be a top priority for all practices.

Total medical revenue after operating cost (profitability)

Subtract the following:

$$\text{Total medical revenue } - \text{Total operating cost}$$

Total medical revenue

Take the following:

Net fee-for-service collections/revenue

+Net capitation revenue (gross capitation revenue –purchased services for capitation patients)

+Net other medical revenue (gross revenue from other medical activities –cost of sales and/or cost of other medical activities)

Total general operating cost

Take the following:

Cost of information technology (data processing, computer, telecommunication services, and telephone) +Cost of drug supply (chemotherapy/allergy drugs and vaccines) +Cost of medical and surgical supply (medical/surgical instruments and laundry) +Cost of building and occupancy (rental/lease, depreciation, interest on real estate loans, utilities, maintenance, and security) +Cost of furniture and equipment (exclude cost for furniture and equipment used in information technology, clinical laboratory, radiology and imaging, and other ancillary services) +Cost of administrative supplies and services (printing, postage, books, subscriptions, forms, stationary, purchased medical transcription services) +Cost of professional liability insurance premiums (malpractice and professional liability insurance for physicians and employees) +Cost of other insurance premiums (other policies such as fire, flood, theft, casualty, general liability, officers' and directors' liability, and reinsurance) +Cost of outside professional fees (infrequent services such as legal and accounting services and management, financial and actuarial consultants) +Cost of promotion and marketing (promotion, advertising and marketing activities, fliers, brochures, and yellow page listings) +Cost of clinical laboratory (CPT code 36415, 36416, and 80048 to 89356) +Cost of radiology and imaging (ultrasound, nuclear medicine, echocardiography) +Cost of other ancillary services (all ancillary services except clinical laboratory and radiology and imaging) +Cost of billing and collections purchased services (claims clearinghouse) +Cost of management fees paid to a MSO or PPMC +Cost of miscellaneous operating costs (recruiting, health, business and property taxes, other interest, charitable contributions, entertainment, and business transportation) +Cost allocated to medical practice from parent organization (indirect cost allocations or shared services)

Total operating cost

Add the following:

Total cost of support staff +Total general operating cost

Nonmedical revenue and cost

Nonmedical revenue and cost consist of nonmedical revenue (investment and rental revenue), extraordinary nonmedical revenue, financial support for operating costs (from parent organization), goodwill amortization, nonmedical cost (income taxes), extraordinary nonmedical cost, and net nonmedical revenue.

Net nonmedical revenue

Add the following:

Nonmedical revenue +Extraordinary nonmedical revenue +Financial support for operating costs

Goodwill amortization +Nonmedical cost (income taxes) +Extraordinary nonmedical cost

Net practice income or loss

Take the following:

(Total medical revenue after operation cost –Total providers cost) +Net nonmedical revenue

COST OF PROVIDERS AND PHYSICIANS

Non-physician providers are typically treated as employed staff in most practices; whereas, physicians function as owners. Therefore, the salaries and benefits of non-physician providers should be a component of the total cost of staff. However, since physicians are generally owners, their compensation generally consists of remaining revenue after operating costs. And in some cases, non-physician provider compensation is treated the same as physician-owner compensation so the importance of understanding how a benchmark is calculated and how the variables are defined is imperative for proper benchmarking.

Total providers cost

Add the following:

Total non-physician provider cost +Provider consultant cost +Total physicians cost

Total non-physician provider cost

Add the following:

Non-physician provider compensation +Non-physician provider benefit cost

Total physicians cost

Add the following:

Total physician compensation +Total physician benefit cost

Note: This is the amount received by all physician owners as compensation and benefits

COST OF STAFF

In many practices, the total cost of staff is the largest single expense category. Therefore, it is imperative these costs receive attention as part of the practice's cost management program. Related to this expense, a human resource policy that ensures performance reviews and associated raise maximums (explore local market maximums) is necessary to manage these costs. A practice can't provide every staff member with a 10% raise while reimbursement only increases 3%.

Total cost of business operations support staff

Cost of general administration staff (administrator, CFO, medical director, human resources, marketing) + Cost of patient accounting staff (billing, collection) + Cost of general accounting staff (controller, account manager, accounts payable, and budget) + Cost of managed care administration staff (contract administration and utilization review) + Cost of information technology staff (data processing, programming, telecommunications) + Cost of housekeeping, maintenance, and security staff

Total cost of front office support staff

Add the following:

Cost of medical receptionists +Cost of medical secretaries and transcribers +Cost of medical records staff +Cost of other administrative support staff

Total cost of clinical support staff

Add the following:

Cost of registered nurses +Cost of licensed practical nurses +Cost of Medical assistants and nurse's aides

Total cost of ancillary support staff

Add the following:

Cost of clinical laboratory staff +Cost of radiology and imaging staff +Cost of other ancillary medical support services staff

Total cost of employed support staff

Add the following:

Total cost of business operations support staff +Total cost of front office support staff +Total cost of clinical support staff +Total cost of ancillary support staff

RETURN ON INVESTMENT (ROI)[3]

Definition: A method of evaluating an investment's expected gains compared to its cost. In addition, this calculation has been used as a measure of profitability, efficiency, and as a financial control.

Goal: Higher the better

$$\frac{\text{Total revenue} - \text{Total costs}}{\text{Total costs}}$$

Note: There are many methods for calculating ROI and care should be taken when comparing ROIs.

COMPENSATION MEASURES

There are other measures that can be benchmarked against in a practice that don't require calculation. In general, these measures are either easily extracted from the practice's information system or hardcopy documents.

Physician compensation and benefits

Physician compensation is generally determined by subtracting practice overhead or total expenses from revenue. In most cases, the physicians, through their compensation method, share the remaining revenue after all expenses have been paid. And in many practices, physician benefits (e.g., health insurance, retirement plan, licenses) are treated as a practice expense.

Staff compensation and benefits

In many practices, the administrator or human resources department can produce staff compensation and benefit amounts.

OTHER FINANCIAL MEASURES

In addition to the previous formulas and ratios, there a several other financial measures that, if possible, should be collected, monitored, and communicated to physician leadership (see Exhibit 10.1).

EXHIBIT 10.1 OTHER FINANCIAL METRICS[4]

- GROSS CHARGES PER VISIT

- NET CHARGES PER VISIT

- STAFF PAYROLL AND BENEFITS OR TOTAL PERSONNEL COSTS TO NET CHARGES

- PROVIDER COMPENSATION AS A PERCENTAGE OF REVENUE AND NUMBER OF VISITS

Total assets

Definition: Includes current assets (short-term assets that can be liquefied quickly) and noncurrent and all other assets (long-term assets that cannot be liquefied quickly). Noncurrent and all other assets typically consist of investments and long-term receivables; property, furniture, fixtures and equipment; and intangibles and other assets.

Add the following:

Current assets +Noncurrent and all other assets

Total liabilities

Definition: Includes current liabilities (obligations from past transactions that must be paid within one year) and long-term liabilities (obligations from past transactions that don't have to be paid within one year). Current liabilities consist of accounts payable; claims payable; notes and loans payable; long-term debt (current portion); payroll withholdings; accrued payroll liabilities; accrued vacation, holiday, and sick pay; accrued liabilities (nonpayroll); patient deposits; and claims payable (incurred but not reported).[3] And long-term liabilities consist of long-term notes payable, mortgage payable, construction loans payable, capital lease obligation (long-term portion), and deferred income taxes (long-term portion).[4]

Add the following:

> Current liabilities +Noncurrent and all other liabilities

Total net worth

Subtract the following:

> Total assets −Total liabilities

---

[1] E.W. Woodcock, "Practice Benchmarking," in *Physician Practice Management: Essential Operations and Financial Knowledge* (Sudbury, MA: Jones and Bartlett Publishers, 2012)

[2] DecisionHealth, Part B News, A/R Benchmarks, October 16, 2006, v20, n40.

[3] Pavlock, E. J. *Financial Management for Medical Groups*, 2nd edition. Englewood: MGMA, 2000.

[4] The Coker Group. *Physician Ancillary Services: Evaluation, Implementation, and Management of New Practice Opportunities*. Boston: Jones and Bartlett Publishers, 2006.

CHAPTER 11

HOSPITAL AND INPATIENT METRICS

"Never compare your inside with somebody else's outside."
- *Hugh Macleod*

A s with other performance measurements, hospital and inpatient metrics should identify common goals, provide clear definitions, and focus on cause-and-effect relationships that impact an organization's strategies, goals, and mission. Metrics should allow for comparison against historical trends and industry standards, and ideally, they should help managers address issues proactively before they become serious problems.

Generally, metrics are categorized under broader areas of performance that are considered contributors to the organization's mission. These measures may include quality of care and patient satisfaction, as well as financial and productivity/efficiency measurements (see Exhibit 11.1). Standardizing metrics across departments and locations allows for meaningful comparison and analysis of common processes to identify best practices and areas for improvement. Because service-lines in hospitals are significantly different than private practices, standardizing into percentages or per FTE provider/ physician is necessary for service-line comparisons. Metrics should be used not just to monitor, but also to improve performance over time. However, sustained improvements often require changes in organization behavior, such as standardizing supplies to reduce costs or adopting clinical protocols to improve outcomes. Metrics are used to measure such aspects of the hospital environment as:

- Provider Profiling: Analyzing individual physician practice patterns by looking at clinical, quality, satisfaction, and economic indicators.
- Clinical Decision Support: Analyzing clinical performance to optimize resource utilization, cost effectiveness, and evidence-based decision making.
- Disease Management: Using metrics to identify high-risk patients in order to proactively manage conditions and optimize care.

- Benchmarking/Quality Measurement: Data analysis to support comparisons to internal and external benchmarks and to meet industry reporting requirements.
- Error Reduction/Safety: Analysis to track and trend clinical errors and safety incidents.

EXHIBIT 11.1 SOURCES FOR METRICS AND EXTERNAL BENCHMARKS

- NATIONAL COMMITTEE FOR QUALITY ASSURANCE (NCQA)
  WWW.NCQA.ORG

- AGENCY FOR HEALTHCARE RESEARCH & QUALITY (AHRQ)
  WWW.AHRQ.GOV

- JOINT COMMISSION FOR ACCREDITATION OF HEALTHCARE ORGANIZATIONS (JCAHO)
  WWW.JCAHO.ORG

- CENTERS FOR MEDICARE & MEDICAID SERVICES (CMS)
  WWW.CMS.HHS.GOV

- NATIONAL QUALITY FORUM
  WWW.QUALITYFORUM.ORG

- THE LEAPFROG GROUP
  WWW.LEAPFROGGROUP.ORG

Managers should be regularly identifying external benchmarks with which to evaluate internal metrics. Such comparison may help identify reasonable metric thresholds, as well as identify competitive opportunities and weaknesses among organizations. External benchmarks are available from numerous sources, including federal and state programs, industry organizations, and vendors. However, managers should be mindful of the limitations metrics present. Historical data represents the results of past decisions and do not predict future results particularly since context is difficult to apply to past data. Variations in operations and data quality among benchmarked facilities may diminish the value of comparisons.

The exhibits below list common metrics in the areas of quality of care, productivity and efficiency, financial performance, operations and maintenance, and patient demographics. The measures are not all inclusive and managers should identify metrics applicable to their organization per its goals, objectives, regulatory requirements, other pertinent factors, and questions being asked.

QUALITY

Quality of care is a measure of a patient's perceived and evaluated need as well as consumer satisfaction (see Exhibit 11.2). That is, the patient perceives a need for a level of care based on his/her health status, and the patient becomes a satisfied consumer when the care provided meets or exceeds his/her perceived need. From the patient's first impression of the building and reception area, to the greeting and check-in procedures by front-desk staff, to the time spent and friendliness of provider, to other environmental, process, and people factors, the practice is being measured by the patient for quality of care. Benchmarks for assessing patient perceived quality of care consist of surveys, mystery patient programs, patient longevity as a customer, and other factors.

More often, however, medical staff evaluate need and quality of care via professionally assigned triage categories, accepted protocols, evidence-based diagnosis, previous treatments and outcomes, other common metrics, and professional assessments.

EXHIBIT 11.2 COMMON QUALITY METRICS

METRICS	NOTES
AVERAGE LENGTH OF STAY (LOS)= TOTAL PATIENT DAYS / TOTAL DISCHARGES	UTILIZATION MEASURE THAT ESTIMATES THE AVERAGE LENGTH OF INPATIENT STAY. LOWER LOS IS GENERALLY PREFERRED
PATIENT SATISFACTION • OUTPATIENT • INPATIENT • EMERGENCY DEPT. • AMBULATORY SURGERY	REQUIRES SURVEY MECHANISM FOR PATIENTS MAY INCLUDE INDICATORS FOR : • COMMUNICATION WITH DOCTORS • COMMUNICATION WITH NURSES • RESPONSIVENESS OF HOSPITAL STAFF • CLEANLINESS AND QUIETNESS OF HOSPITAL • PAIN CONTROL • COMMUNICATION ABOUT MEDICINES • DISCHARGE INFORMATION • OVERALL RATING OF CARE • OVERALL RECOMMENDATION
PHYSICIAN SATISFACTION	REQUIRES SURVEY MECHANISM FOR PROVIDERS EXAMPLE: % REFERRING PHYSICIANS THAT "RECOMMEND TO OTHERS"
MEDICATION ERROR RATE = (TOTAL NUMBER OF MEDICATION ERRORS / TOTAL NUMBER OF DOSES ADMINISTERED) X 10,000	THE RATE OF TOTAL MEDICATION ERRORS THAT OCCURRED PER 10,000 DOSES ADMINISTERED.
PATIENT FALL RATE = (TOTAL NUMBER OF FALLS / TOTAL PATIENT DAYS) X 1,000	RATIO OF NUMBER OF PATIENT FALLS PER 1,000 PATIENT DAYS.

EXHIBIT 11.2 COMMON QUALITY METRICS (CONT'D)

METRICS	NOTES
MORTALITY RATES FOR MEDICAL CONDITIONS ACUTE MYOCARDIAL INFARCTION (AMI) (IQI 15) AMI, WITHOUT TRANSFER CASES (IQI 32) CONGESTIVE HEART FAILURE (IQI 16) STROKE (IQI 17) GASTROINTESTINAL HEMORRHAGE (IQI 18) HIP FRACTURE (IQI 19) PNEUMONIA (IQI 20)	INPATIENT QUALITY INDICATORS (IQI) DEFINED BY AGENCY FOR HEALTHCARE RESEARCH & QUALITY
MORTALITY RATES FOR SURGICAL PROCEDURES ESOPHAGEAL RESECTION (IQI 8) PANCREATIC RESECTION (IQI 9) ABDOMINAL AORTIC ANEURYSM REPAIR (IQI 11) CORONARY ARTERY BYPASS GRAFT (IQI 12) PERCUTANEOUS TRANSLUMINAL CORONARY ANGIOPLASTY (IQI 30) CAROTID ENDARTERECTOMY (IQI 31) CRANIOTOMY (IQI 13) HIP REPLACEMENT (IQI 14)	INPATIENT QUALITY INDICATORS (IQI) DEFINED BY AGENCY FOR HEALTHCARE RESEARCH & QUALITY

EXHIBIT 11.2 COMMON QUALITY METRICS (CONT'D)

METRICS	NOTES
HOSPITAL-LEVEL PROCEDURE UTILIZATION RATES CESAREAN SECTION DELIVERY (IQI 21) PRIMARY CESAREAN DELIVERY (IQI 33) VAGINAL BIRTH AFTER CESAREAN (VBAC), UNCOMPLICATED (IQI 22) VBAC, ALL (IQI 34) LAPAROSCOPIC CHOLECYSTECTOMY (IQI 23) INCIDENTAL APPENDECTOMY IN ELDERLY (IQI 24) BI-LATERAL CARDIAC CATHETERIZATION (IQI 25)	INPATIENT QUALITY INDICATORS (IQI) DEFINED BY AGENCY FOR HEALTHCARE RESEARCH & QUALITY
AREA-LEVEL UTILIZATION RATES CORONARY ARTERY BYPASS GRAFT (IQI 26) PERCUTANEOUS TRANSLUMINAL CORONARY ANGIOPLASTY (IQI 27) HYSTERECTOMY (IQI 28) LAMINECTOMY OR SPINAL FUSION (IQI 29)	INPATIENT QUALITY INDICATORS (IQI) DEFINED BY AGENCY FOR HEALTHCARE RESEARCH & QUALITY
VOLUME OF PROCEDURES ESOPHAGEAL RESECTION (IQI 1) PANCREATIC RESECTION (IQI 2) ABDOMINAL AORTIC ANEURYSM REPAIR (IQI 4) CORONARY ARTERY BYPASS GRAFT (IQI 5) PERCUTANEOUS TRANSLUMINAL CORONARY ANGIOPLASTY (IQI 6) CAROTID ENDARTERECTOMY (IQI 7)	INPATIENT QUALITY INDICATORS (IQI) DEFINED BY AGENCY FOR HEALTHCARE RESEARCH & QUALITY

PRODUCTIVITY AND EFFICIENCY

Beyond quality of care measures, healthcare managers also use metrics to help monitor and trend productivity and efficiency, as well as identify areas for improvement. Exhibit 11.3 identifies common management metrics used to identify and improve organizational performance and some recommended goals are identified.

EXHIBIT 11.3 PRODUCTIVITY AND EFFICIENCY METRICS

METRICS	NOTES
MAINTAINED BED OCCUPANCY RATE = OCCUPIED BED DAYS / MAX POSSIBLE OCCUPIED BED DAYS	HIGHER RATE INDICATES MORE EFFICIENT USE OF AVAILABLE RESOURCES
AVERAGE # FTEs PER OCCUPIED BED DAY (PER MONTH) = [# STAFF HOURS PER MONTH / 24 HOURS] / OCCUPIED BED DAYS PER MONTH	INDICATOR THAT ESTIMATES THE NUMBER OF EMPLOYEES ASSIGNABLE TO INPATIENT BEDS
CASE MIX INDEX (CMI) THE AVERAGE DIAGNOSTIC RELATED GROUP (DRG) WEIGHT FOR A HOSPITAL'S PATIENT VOLUME.	THOUGH NOT ITSELF AN ACTIONABLE METRIC, CMI INDICATES AN AVERAGE COMPLEXITY OF CARE AND IS USED TO COMPARE MEASUREMENTS (COSTS, BED DAYS, ETC.) ACROSS DISPARATE ORGANIZATIONS. EXAMPLE: A HOSPITAL REPORTS AN AVERAGE COST PER PATIENT OF $1000 IN A GIVEN YEAR AND ITS CMI IS .85. ITS CMI-ADJUSTED COST PER PATIENT = $1000/.85 = $1176
NUMBER OF CMI-WEIGHTED ADJUSTED DISCHARGES = TOTAL DISCHARGES / CMI	MEASURES INPATIENT WORKLOAD VOLUME
MONTHLY SURGICAL CASES	MEASURES WORKLOAD VOLUME SHOULD BE BROKEN OUT BY OUTPATIENT AND INPATIENT

EXHIBIT 11.3 PRODUCTIVITY AND EFFICIENCY METRICS (CONT'D)

METRICS	NOTES
SURGICAL CASES PERCENTAGE = TOTAL MEDICARE INPATIENT SURGICAL CASES / TOTAL MEDICARE INPATIENT CASES X 100	MEASURES PROPORTION OF INPATIENT CARE DRIVEN BY SURGICAL CASES
INPATIENT ADMISSIONS ERROR RATIO	MONITORS ADMITTING PROCESS PERFORMANCE GOAL: <3% ERROR
OUTPATIENT REGISTRATION ERROR RATIO	MONITORS REGISTRATION PROCESS PERFORMANCE GOAL: <3% ERROR

FINANCIAL PERFORMANCE

Financial Metrics analyze an organization's revenue cycle, operating expenses, profitability, profit & loss statements (income statement) and other financial statements to assess financial performance and uncover opportunities to improve overall fiscal health and profitability (see Exhibit 11.4). Key performance indicators should be monitored on a regular basis (for example, weekly, monthly, etc.) and trended over time. In addition, when using a trend, it is vital to know the context to ensure that appropriate conclusions are taken from the data. For instance, if an administrator were to trend a practice's current ratio (total current assets divided by total current liabilities) over time on a month-by-month basis for the past two years, there would be instances showing highs and lows. The highs and lows may indicate capital expenses like the purchase of a MRI unit or the receipt of funds from a loan. Without knowing the context of the practice's activities at the high and low points, it would be impossible to attribute the changes to anything specific—making this trend useless for evaluating the current state or predicting the future.

EXHIBIT 11.4 COMMON FINANCIAL METRICS

METRIC	NOTES
GROSS REVENUE PER PATIENT DAY = GROSS REVENUE / (DISCHARGES X AVERAGE LENGTH OF STAY)	MEASURED OVER A SPECIFIC TIME FRAME (QUARTER, FISCAL YEAR, ETC.). HIGHER RATE AND UPWARD TREND IS PREFERRED; LENGTH OF STAY (LOS).
NET INCOME PER PATIENT DAY = NET INCOME / (DISCHARGES X AVERAGE LOS)	MEASURED OVER A SPECIFIC TIME FRAME (QUARTER, FISCAL YEAR, ETC.). HIGHER RATE AND UPWARD TREND IS PREFERRED.
OPERATING EXPENSE PER INPATIENT DAY = OPERATING EXPENSE PER DAY = (TOTAL OPERATING EXPENSE X IP %) / TOTAL PATIENT DAYS	COST INDICATOR THAT ESTIMATES THE LEVEL OF RESOURCES USED TO TREAT A PATIENT DURING AN INPATIENT DAY. LOWER RATE AND DOWNWARD TREND IS PREFERRED.
EXPENSE PER CMI-WEIGHTED ADJUSTED DISCHARGE = EXPENSE / (CMI X TOTAL DISCHARGES)	USUALLY BROKEN OUT BY: • LABOR • OTHER DIRECT EXP. • MEDICAL SUPPLY • OTHER SUPPLY • TOTAL EXP.
OPERATING MARGIN (%) = (TOTAL OPERATING REVENUES − TOTAL OPERATING EXPENSES) / OPERATING REVENUE X 100	IDENTIFIES RELATIVE PROFITABILITY BASED ON HOSPITAL OPERATIONS
LONG-TERM DEBT-TO-CAPITALIZATION (%) = LONG-TERM DEBT / (LONG-TERM DEBT + FUND BALANCE) X 100	PERCENTAGE OF ASSETS FUNDED BY LONG-TERM DEBT. INDICATES THE ORGANIZATION'S CURRENT LEVERAGE AND ABILITY TO ASSUME ADDITIONAL.
DEBT-SERVICE COVERAGE (DSC) = (NET INCOME + INTEREST EXPENSE + DEPRECIATION) / (INTEREST EXPENSE + DEBT PRINCIPLE)	MEASURES ABILITY TO MEET DEBT SERVICE PAYMENTS FROM CASH FLOW. INDICATES THE ORGANIZATION'S ABILITY TO SAFELY ASSUME ADDITIONAL DEBT. A HIGHER RATIO AND UPWARD TREND IS PREFERRED.

Exhibit 11.4 Common Financial Metrics (cont'd)

Metric	Notes
Days Cash on Hand (Liquidity Ratio) = (Cash + Cash Equivalents + Limited-use Assets) / [(Total Operating Expenses – Depreciation - Amortization) / 365]	Higher ratio indicates a greater ability to meet liabilities.
Debt Financing Percentage = Total Assets-Net Assets / Total Assets x 100	Indicates what percentage of assets are financed by debt
Overall Charge Index = (Average Charge per Medicare Discharge (Case Mix Adjusted) / U.S. Median x Inpatient Revenue %) + (Average Charge per APC (Risk Weight Adjusted) / U.S. Median x Outpatient Revenue %)	Compares charges to U.S. median
Cost per Adjusted Patient Day	Efficiency measure; should be calculated separately for inpatient and outpatient services
Market Share Percentage = Net Patient Revenue / Sum of Net Patient Revenues in County x 100	Measures market penetration; can be broken out by product line for more granular view
Non-government Payers Percentage	% of Revenue from Sources Other Than Medicare or Medicaid
Net Operating Income (NOI) per FTE = NOI / Total FTEs	Measures how effectively staff time is utilized
Days in Accounts Receivable Days = Net Patient AR / (Net Annual Patient Revenue / 365)	Measures liquidity, as well as how efficient the organization manages its revenue cycle; lower value and downward trend is desirable
Current Ratio = Current Assets / Current Liabilities	Liquidity measure of an organization's ability to meet short-term debt obligations

Exhibit 11.4 Common Financial Metrics (cont'd)

Metric	Notes
Quick Ratio = Quick Assets / Current Liabilities	Liquidity measure of an organization's ability to use its "near cash" assets to immediately eliminate its current liabilities. Quick assets include current assets that can be quickly converted to cash at near book values (e.g. stocks).
Fixed Asset Turnover Ratio = Revenue / Value of Fixed Assets	Indicates how effectively an organization uses its fixed assets to generate revenue
Return on Assets (ROA) = Earnings Before Interest & Taxes (EBIT) / Total Assets	Measure how effectively assets are used to generate income
Charge Capture Quality	Measures charge accuracy; requires audit mechanism; typical benchmark: 98% compliance
Accounts Receivable[5]	Liquidity measure; % over 90 days (typical benchmark: <20%); % over 120 days (typical benchmark: <10%) % over 1 year (typical benchmark: <2%)
Clean Claims Submission[5]	Percentage of claims accepted on first submission; higher rate shortens revenue cycle; typical benchmark: 97%
Payer Turnaround Time[5]	Typical benchmark: 7-10 days (electronic), <45 days (paper)
Typical benchmark: 7-10 days (electronic), <45 days (paper) Denial Overturn Ratio[5]	Percentage of denied claims eventually accepted; typical benchmark: 95%
Underpayments Overturn Ratio[5]	Percentage of underpaid claims paid at full amount upon resubmission; typical benchmark: 95%

EXHIBIT 11.4 COMMON FINANCIAL METRICS (CONT'D)

METRIC	NOTES
BAD DEBT EXPENSE[5]	PERCENTAGE OF ACCOUNTS RECEIVABLE WRITTEN OFF AS UNCOLLECTIBLE; TYPICAL BENCHMARK: <4% OF GROSS REVENUE, <2% OF NET REVENUE

In addition to organizational financial measures, managers often monitor financial performance at the department level in order to pinpoint areas needing improvement. Below are common metrics used to measure the financial well-being of specific departments or cost centers (see Exhibit 11.5)

EXHIBIT 11.5 COMMON DEPARTMENTAL FINANCIAL METRICS[4]

DEPARTMENT	METRICS
MEDICAL/SURGICAL ICU	• AVERAGE LENGTH OF STAY (DAYS) • HOURS WORKED PER DISCHARGE • LABOR EXPENSE PER PATIENT DISCHARGE
EMERGENCY ROOM	• PERCENTAGE OF ER PATIENTS ADMITTED TO TOTAL ER VISITS • PERCENTAGE OF ER PATIENT ADMITTED TO TOTAL DISCHARGES • HOURS WORKED PER PATIENT VISIT • TOTAL EXPENSE PER PATIENT VISIT
FAMILY PRACTICE	• HOURS WORKED PER PATIENT VISIT • LABOR EXPENSE PER PATIENT VISIT
HOME HEALTH	• CLIENT VISITS • CLIENT VISITS PER DAY • HOURS WORKED PER CLIENT VISIT • LABOR EXPENSE PER CLIENT VISIT • TOTAL EXPENSE PER CLIENT VISIT

EXHIBIT 11.5 COMMON DEPARTMENTAL FINANCIAL METRICS[4] (CONT'D)

DEPARTMENT	METRICS
OPERATING ROOM (OR)	• INPATIENT OR CASES PER 100 GENERAL ACUTE DISCHARGES • PERCENTAGE OF AMBULATORY SURGERY CASES TO ALL OR CASES • OPERATING MINUTES PER OR CASE • OR CASES PER OR DAY • HOURS WORKED PER OR CASE • LABOR EXPENSE PER OR CASE • TOTAL EXPENSES PER OR CASE
LABORATORY SERVICES	• INPATIENT BILLED TESTS PER CMI-WEIGHTED DISCHARGE • PERCENTAGE OF OUTREACH BILLED TESTS TO TOTAL BILLED TESTS • TOTAL EXPENSE PER 100 BILLED TESTS
IMAGING SERVICES	• PROCEDURES PER ROOM PER DAY • PERCENTAGE OF INPATIENT PROCEDURES TO TOTAL PROCEDURES • PERCENTAGE OF PORTABLE PROCEDURES TO TOTAL PROCEDURES • INPATIENT PROCEDURES PER 100 CMI-WEIGHTED DISCHARGES • HOURS WORKED PER 100 PROCEDURES • TOTAL EXPENSE PER 100 PROCEDURES
HOME HEALTH	• CLIENT VISITS • CLIENT VISITS PER DAY • HOURS WORKED PER CLIENT VISIT • LABOR EXPENSE PER CLIENT VISIT • TOTAL EXPENSE PER CLIENT VISIT

EXHIBIT 11.5 COMMON DEPARTMENTAL FINANCIAL METRICS[4] (CONT'D)

DEPARTMENT	METRICS
PHARMACY SERVICES	• DOSES BILLED PER CMI-WEIGHTED DISCHARGE • DRUG EXPENSE PER 100 CMI-WEIGHTED DISCHARGES • TOTAL EXPENSE PER 100 CMI-WEIGHTED DISCHARGES
MATERIALS MANAGEMENT	• HOURS WORKED PER 100 ADJUSTED DISCHARGES • PERCENTAGE OF ALL DIVISION EXPENSES TO HOSPITAL EXPENSES

OPERATIONS AND MAINTENANCE

Another category of metrics evaluates cost and efficiency of operating and maintaining the healthcare facility (see Exhibit 11.6).

EXHIBIT 11.6 COMMON HEALTH FACILITIES METRICS

MANAGEMENT AREA	METRICS
FACILITIES OPERATIONS/ MAINTENANCE	• HOURS WORKED PER 100 ADJUSTED DISCHARGES • LABOR EXPENSE PER 100 ADJUSTED DISCHARGES • LABOR EXPENSE PER 1,000 GROSS SQ. FT. MAINTAINED • TOTAL EXPENSE PER 1,000 GROSS SQ. FT. MAINTAINED • PERCENTAGE OF DIVISION EXPENSES TO TOTAL HOSPITAL EXPENSES

MANAGEMENT AREA	METRICS
PLANT/GROUND MAINTENANCE	• HOURS WORKED PER 100 ADJUSTED DISCHARGES • LABOR EXPENSE PER 100 ADJUSTED DISCHARGES • LABOR EXPENSE PER 1,000 GROSS SQ. FT. MAINTAINED • TOTAL EXPENSE PER 1,000 GROSS SQ. FT. MAINTAINED
CLINICAL ENGINEERING	• HOURS WORKED PER BEDS SERVED • LABOR EXPENSE PER BEDS SERVED • HOURS WORKED PER 100 DEVICES SERVICED • LABOR EXPENSE PER 100 DEVICES SERVICED • HOURS WORKED PER 100 WORK REQUESTS • LABOR EXPENSE PER 100 WORK REQUESTS
HOUSEKEEPING / ENVIRONMENTAL SERVICES	• HOURS WORKED PER ADJUSTED DISCHARGE • LABOR EXPENSE PER ADJUSTED DISCHARGE • HOURS WORKED PER 1,000 NET SQ. FT. CLEANED • LABOR EXPENSE PER 1,000 NET SQ. FT. CLEANED • PERCENTAGE OF DIVISION EXPENSES TO TOTAL HOSPITAL EXPENSES
SECURITY	• HOURS WORKED PER ADJUSTED DISCHARGE • LABOR EXPENSE PER ADJUSTED DISCHARGE • HOURS WORKED PER 1,000 GROSS SQ. FT. PATROLLED • LABOR EXPENSE PER 1,000 GROSS SQ. FT. PATROLLED

EXHIBIT 11.6 COMMON HEALTH FACILITIES METRICS

MANAGEMENT AREA	METRICS
DIETARY/FOOD SERVICE	• HOURS WORKED PER ADJUSTED DISCHARGE • LABOR EXPENSE PER ADJUSTED DISCHARGE • HOURS WORKED PER 100 MEALS SERVED • LABOR EXPENSE PER 100 MEALS SERVED • PERCENTAGE OF DIVISION EXPENSES TO TOTAL HOSPITAL EXPENSES
MATERIALS MANAGEMENT	• HOURS WORKED PER 100 ADJUSTED DISCHARGES • LABOR EXPENSE PER 100 ADJUSTED DISCHARGES • STOCK INVENTORY TURNS • PERCENTAGE OF DIVISION EXPENSES TO TOTAL HOSPITAL EXPENSES

PATIENT DEMOGRAPHICS

A discussion of health care measures would be incomplete without considering how beneficiary populations are measured. Differences in demographics and patient complexity make "apples to apples" comparisons among different populations difficult. However, several proprietary models have been developed which classify patients according to risk-adjusted categories in order to normalize data (see Exhibit 11.7). By compensating for population differences, these data models allow for meaningful comparisons across populations and healthcare organizations. Risk-Adjustment models have two main functions:

1. To predict the costs of caring for different population groups. Such analysis is especially valuable for capitation-based systems, such as HMOs.

2. To facilitate efficiency comparisons (also known as economic profiling) across disparate organizations by normalizing patient data according to demographics and complexity.

EXHIBIT 11.7 RISK-ADJUSTMENT MODELS

MODEL	SOURCE	NOTES
ADJUSTED CLINICAL GROUPS (ACGs)	JOHNS HOPKINS UNIVERSITY	CLUSTERS BENEFICIARIES WITH SIMILAR COMORBIDITIES INTO GROUPS WITH SIMILAR CLINICAL CHARACTERISTICS RESOURCE INTENSITY
BURDEN OF ILLNESS SCORE (BOI)	MEDECISION, INC.	GROUPS CARE INTO EPISODES THAT SHARE SERVICES, MEDICATIONS, AND ACUITY
CLINICAL COMPLEXITY INDEX (CCI)	SOLUCIENT, INC.	CATEGORIZES PATIENTS ACCORDING TO AGE, ACUITY, COMORBIDITY, ADMISSIONS, AND DIAGNOSTIC CATEGORY
CHRONIC COMORBIDITY COUNT (CCC)	AGENCY FOR HEALTHCARE RESEARCH AND QUALITY (AHRQ)	THE TOTAL SUM OF SELECTED COMORBID CONDITIONS GROUPED INTO SIX CATEGORIES
DIAGNOSTIC COST GROUPS (DCGs)	DxCG, INC.	PROVIDES MULTIPLE LINEAR REGRESSION MODELS WHICH USE PATIENT DEMOGRAPHICS AND DIAGNOSES TO EXPLAIN HEALTH CARE EXPENDITURES
ELDER RISK ASSESSMENT (ERA)	HTTPS://WWW.NCBI.NLM.NIH.GOV/PMC/ARTICLES/PMC3914203/#R12/	FOR ADULTS OVER 60, ERA USES AGE, GENDER, MARITAL STATUS, NUMBER OF HOSPITAL DAYS OVER THE PRIOR TWO YEARS, AND SELECTED COMORBID MEDICAL ILLNESS TO ASSIGN AN INDEX SCORE TO EACH PATIENT
EPISODE RISK GROUPS (ERGs)	SYMMETRY HEALTH SYSTEMS	PROVIDES RISK SCORES FOR PATIENTS BASED ON AGE, GENDER, AND HISTORY OF CARE
GENERAL DIAGNOSTIC GROUPS (GDGs)	ALLEGIANCE, LLC	PREDICTS HEALTH CARE COSTS BASED ON DIAGNOSTIC CATEGORIES AND CLAIMS HISTORIES

EXHIBIT 11.7 RISK-ADJUSTMENT MODELS (CONT'D)

MODEL	SOURCE	NOTES
HIERARCHICAL CONDITION CATEGORIES (HCCs)	MEDICARE ADVANTAGE PROGRAM FOR CMS	HCC CONTAINS 70 CONDITION CATEGORIES SELECTED FROM ICD CODES AND INCLUDES EXPECTED HEALTH EXPENDITURES
MINNESOTA TIERING (MN)	HTTPS://WWW. HEALTHCATALYST.COM/ UNDERSTANDING- RISK-STRATIFICATION- COMORBIDITIES/	BASED ON MAJOR EXTENDED DIAGNOSTIC GROUPS (MEDCs), MN TIERING GROUPS PATIENTS INTO ONE OF FIVE TIERS
PATIENT AT RISK SCORE (PARS)	WORCESTERSHIRE ACUTE HOSPITALS NHS TRUST (CRITICAL CARE OUTREACH OPERATION POLICY, 2006)	IDENTIFIES "AT RISK" PATIENTS FOR A SPEEDY REFERRAL SO EARLY INTERVENTION CAN PREVENT DETERIORATION

OTHER KEY HOSPITAL RATIOS

There are many hospital metrics and ratios derived from internal reports and financial statements; however, in most hospitals, there is a short list of key ratios used to monitor the financial condition of the organization.

Excess margin

Definition: Profit margin related to overall revenues

Goal: Higher the better

Take the following:

$$\frac{\text{Total operating revenue} + \text{Non-operating revenues} - \text{Total operating expenses}}{\text{(Total operating revenues} + \text{Non-operating revenues)}} * 100$$

Cushion ratio

Definition: Available cash and total debt service relationship

Goal: Higher the better

Add the following:

$$\frac{\text{Cash +Short-term investments +Unrestricted long-term investments}}{\text{Principal +Interest payments}}$$

Average payment period in days

Definition: The length of time, in days, it takes to pay the bills

Goal: Lower the better

Subtract the following:

$$\frac{\text{Current liabilities}}{(\text{Total expenses} - \text{Depreciation}) / 365}$$

Average age of plant in years

Definition: Relative age of the facility and capital equipment

Goal: Lower the better

$$\frac{\text{Accumulated depreciation}}{\text{Depreciation expense}}$$

Debt-to-capitalization

Definition: Percentage of debt compared to net assets

Goal: Lower the better

Add the following:

$$\frac{\text{Long-term debt}}{(\text{Long-term debt} + \text{Net assets}) * 100}$$

Capital expense

Definition: Percentage of the purchase of fixed assets to total expenses

Goal: Downward trend is better; depends on many practice factors

$$\frac{\text{Interest expense} + \text{Depreciation expense}}{\text{Total expenses}} * 100$$

Personnel costs as a percentage of total operating revenues (labor compensation ratio)

$$\frac{\text{Total cost of salaries/wages} + \text{Total cost of benefits} + \text{Total cost of professional fees}}{\text{Total operating revenues}}$$

Bad debt expense as a percentage of total operating revenues

$$\frac{\text{Bad debt expense}}{\text{Total operating revenues}}$$

It is important to keep in mind that no two healthcare organizations are alike, and no two will need to monitor the same metrics in the same way. Likewise, many measures will only need to be monitored temporarily, until a process is fixed and performance improves. Monitoring a handful of key metrics at a time will yield better results than trying to measure every process at once. Given the extremely large number of metrics available, a pitfall for many managers is to try to measure too many metrics at once. This can easily overwhelm a manager, blur attempts to connect metrics and distill meaning, and with too many metrics, communicating to others, particularly physicians, can hinder more than help. Therefore, managers should strive to focus their efforts on those key performance indicators that truly impact their organization and have the greatest meaning and understanding to others.

[1] Centers for Medicare & Medicaid Services: Hospital CAHPS Survey

[2] John R. Griffith and Kenneth R. White, The Well-Managed Healthcare Organization, (Chicago: Health Administration Press, 2002).

[3] www.ahrq.gov

[4] Jennings, Marian C., editor, Health Care Strategy for Uncertain Times, San Francisco: Jossey-Bass, 2000, pp. 155-179.

[5] Healthcare Financial Management, Sep 2004

[6] Health Facilities Management, May 2003

[7] HSR: Health Services Research 39:4, Part I (August 2004) 987-988

[8] Crane SJ, Tung EE, Hanson GJ, Cha S, Chaudhry R, Takahashi PY. Use of an electronic administrative database to identify older community dwelling adults at high risk for hospitalization of emergency department visits: the Elder Risk Assessment Index. BMC Health Serv Res. 2010

CHAPTER 12

BENCHMARKING RESOURCES

"When you're finished changing, you're finished."
                                        - Benjamin Franklin

This chapter provides information on free resources for practice administrators to assist with the overall coding and chart documentation for the most-commonly utilized codes: office visits. It also discusses setting reasonable fees for office visits and the other services a practice provides. The free resources include: Medpar data, NCQA Medical Record Documentation standards, the Medicare regional E&M Chart Audit form, and the Medicare Physician Fee Schedule.

MEDPAR DATA

We often identify potential coding issues when looking at the frequency of Evaluation & Management (E&M) visits compared to a benchmark. In the absence of EHR benchmark data for a certain specialty, we use the Medicare MEDPAR claims' database, which has data from 2015.

E&M Distribution

While Medicare is for those 65 and over, and not necessarily comparable to all patients in a practice, the bell curve that Medicare's data illustrates for established and new patient visits is an industry-norm. The data is available at: https:// www.cms.gov/Research-Statistics-Data-and-Systems/Statistics-Trends-and-Reports/MedicareFeeforSvcPartsAB/Downloads/LEVEL1CHARG15. pdf?agree=yes&next=Accept.

Exhibit 12.1 and 12.2 are a visual representation of what could be over-coding (relative to 0% 99202s and 46% Level 3 and 53% Level 4 visits) and under-coding (relative to 1% Level 5):

EXHIBIT 12.1 SAMPLE PRATICE NEW PATIENT VISITS:

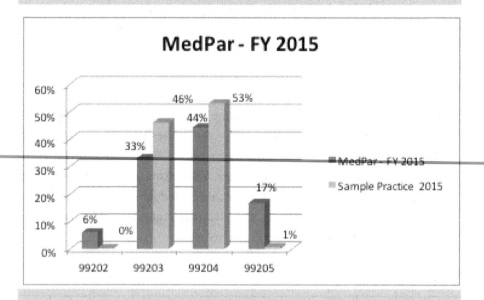

EXHIBIT 12.2 SAMPLE PRATICE ESTABLISHED PATIENT VISITS:
THE FOLLOWING IS AN EXAMPLE OF POTENTIAL UNDER-CODING OF
ESTABLISHED PATIENT VISITS (MOSTLY LEVEL 2S AND 3S):

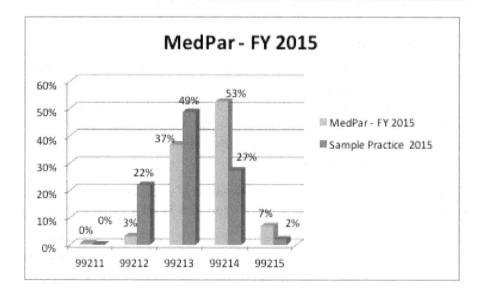

With findings like these, it is worth looking at chart documentation to be sure the correct code is appropriate based on the documentation. Otherwise, the documentation might need to be increased/more detailed to support the services performed.

NCQA MEDICAL RECORD DOCUMENTATION STANDARDS

A great tool to use to assess the 'acceptability' of the practice's documentation is the NCQA Chart Documentation Standards located at: http://www.ncqa. org/Portals/0/PolicyUpdates/Supplemental/Guidelines_Medical_Record_ Review.pdf?ver=2007-02-08-105600-000.

This is the industry-standard for consistent, current, and complete documentation in the medical record. There are 21 elements that reflect a set of commonly-accepted standards for medical record documentation. You'll see that the NCQA considers 6 of the 21 elements as core components, indicated by an asterisk (*). The entire list contains elements worth reviewing with your practice's documentation. This tool is an excellent resource for improving EHR templates (i.e., what is captured and displayed).

MEDICARE REGIONAL E&M CHART AUDIT

Once the general, overall medical record documentation looks acceptable, the next step is to review specific E&M coding. The CMS E&M Chart Audit tool is a scorecard for assessing E&M coding for a given visit. The scorecards are regional and the following is an example used by practices in Colorado (Novitas E/M Score Sheet):

http://www.novitas-solutions.com/webcenter/content/conn/ UCM_Repository/uuid/dDocName:00004968.

Using this template or similar ones from other regions, it is possible to identify areas for further assessment, provider education, EHR template adjustments, or changes to clinical workflows (all are good topics for discussion).

E&M Code Basics

There are three main components to an Evaluation and Management code:

1. history,
2. physical exam, and
3. medical decision making (MDM).

History is straightforward and consists of the patient's review of systems, their Past/Family/Social History and the history of the present illness.

The Physical Exam component of an E&M visit can vary based on whether the exam documentation is based on the 1995 or 1997 Medicare Exam Documentation Guidelines. From a consistency and standardization standpoint, it is recommended to establish a practice policy on which exam guidelines are used—if used 100% of the time—or when exceptions are made. Typically, comparing the documentation templates (prompts for the providers) to the guidelines reveals easy areas of extra documentation that can support documentation of additional organ systems or body areas being examined. An example of this for vision providers is a prompt in the EHR to document both "Exam of Lids" and "Exam of Conjunctiva" instead of a generic prompt, like "Eyes." Another example would be making sure one additional vital sign, like pulse, respiration, or height be added to the EHR template if only temperature and weight are included.

NOTE: It is in the exam documentation that we see the most cloning because of the EHR. Every chart looks identical, no matter the complexity. Be careful the visit isn't embellished beyond the need for the exam based on the reason for the visit.

In general, the first two components of an E&M visit (history and exam) are relatively easy to audit. The code selection primarily rests on the MDM, and this is typically where the documentation is lacking. This is the most subjective part of the audit and providers would be well-served to increase this documentation.

There are three components to MDM documentation, which can be followed on the Novitas (or another Medicare regional administrator) audit tool:

1. Number of Diagnoses or Treatment Options: It is often difficult to ascertain if the condition is new to the provider or established, worsening or improving, etc. These are all documentation cues that would be useful for providers to include, helping auditors score the first component of MDM.

2. Amount and/or Complexity of Data Reviewed: Was the history provided by the patient? Was a physician consulted on the case? Were records reviewed? Usually the record is silent on each of these possible areas of additional MDM points. Often, consultation, laboratory and imaging reports are filed in the chart, but not included in the documentation for the corresponding office visit. The status and timeliness of reviewing results should be verified and follow-up plans must be noted for abnormal results. If the order and results are kept outside of the E&M visit, and no mention is made, the provider gets no credit for reviewing/considering these additional sources of clinical information.

3. Risk of Complications and/or Morbidity or Mortality: In the absence of a specialty-specific table of risk, we make a lot of interpretations on where things fit (what is low? moderate? etc.). For example, do antibiotic injections at the time of the visit count as "Prescription Drug Management?" The practice's providers should agree on what is supported here for the types of patient conditions typically seen.

MEDICARE PHYSICIAN FEE SCHEDULE

When auditing the E&M code for a visit, it is important to also look at the appropriateness of the charges on the claim billed. With just a few data items, it is possible to generate an important deliverable for the practice: A Fee Schedule Analysis. What is needed is the practice's payor mix, CPT code utilization for a given time period, and an idea of what the best reimbursing payor agreement pays (typically as a percentage of the Medicare fee schedule).

It is common to see busy physician practices that haven't updated their fee schedules for several years. It is imperative a practice with charges too low, reset them. Payors take advantage of charges that are too low by adding language to the provider fee schedule stating the payor only has to pay the lesser of the billed charge or the fee schedule allowable.

You want to be mindful of the reasonableness of the charges. The majority of physician practices have charges in a normal range (200% - 400% of Medicare) for their market. In more competitive managed care markets, like Arizona, for example, charges might be closer to 150% of the Medicare allowable. In less competitive states, like Alaska, or super-specialized fields of medicine, the practice's charges should be closer to a higher multiple of Medicare, like 500%.

FEE SCHEDULE ANALYSIS

With a nominal amount of data and the publicly-available (and free) Medicare fee schedule database, a Fee Schedule Analysis can be accomplished with relative ease (a couple of hours for a typical practice, depending on the number of CPT codes). Ideally, at least one of the practice's commercial payor fee schedules is used as a baseline. So, if United Healthcare is paying 130% of Medicare, for example, and the charge master is set at only 115% of Medicare, then an increase to the charge master is clearly needed to ensure collections are maximized based on the maximum payor contracted allowable.

With a simple Excel spreadsheet, place the CPT codes on each row for your Fee Schedule Analysis with the following column headers:

Column 1:   CPT codes & HCPCS codes (by group, such as E&M, Procedures, Lab, etc. or in numerical order)

Column 2:   Frequency count (optional, but allows for weighting averages)

Column 3:   Most recent fee schedule charge per CPT/HCPCS code

Column 4:   Current-year Medicare with geographic adjustment for the practice's region and without, and with Non-Facility and Facility allowables, as applicable to the practice's settings

Column 5:   Payor allowable by codes from at least one commercial payor fee schedule (as described above)

Column 6:   Prior years of Medicare allowables, if available, for a base year of Medicare that a payor agreement is predicated upon

Exhibit 12.3 The spreadsheet will look like this (using a 1 as a placeholder for the frequency data):

PRACTICE CHARGE ANALYSIS & STATE FEE SCHEDULE COMPARISON

CPT Code	DESCRIPTION	2016 FREQ.	PHYSICIAN CHARGE	Current	Recommended New Charge	Scenario 1 Allowable is higher/lower than Current Charge	GPCI'd Medicare Non-facility (NF)	GPCI'd Medicare Facility (F)	Sample Payor Fee Schedule
				Charge as a % of 2016 NF (Column H)	300%		100%	100%	150%
					2016 NF	(Column D)	2016 NF	2016 F	2016 (As of 10/7/16)
Surgery									
10140	Drainage of hematoma/fluid	1	$378.00	227%	$500.00	$122.00	$166.66	$122.59	$222.83
11042	Deb subq tissue 20 sq cm/<	1	$400.00	335%	$359.00	($41.00)	$119.53	$64.36	$105.50
11055	Trim skin lesion	1	$62.00	128%	$146.00	$84.00	$48.52	$16.64	$71.07
11056	Trim skin lesions 2 to 4	1	$93.00	157%	$179.00	$86.00	$59.35	$23.52	$86.31
11057	Trim skin lesions over 4	1	$108.00	161%	$201.00	$93.00	$66.95	$30.77	$104.36
11420	Exc h-f-nk-sp b9+marg 0.5/<	1	$218.00	175%	$375.00	$157.00	$124.83	$83.98	$163.04
11421	Exc h-f-nk-sp b9+marg 0.6-1	1	$280.00	175%	$481.00	$201.00	$160.29	$114.43	$212.67
11720	Debride nail 1-5	1	$61.00	186%	$99.00	$38.00	$32.76	$15.20	$45.69
11721	Debride nail 6 or more	1	$110.00	240%	$138.00	$28.00	$45.82	$25.75	$64.31
11730	Removal of nail plate	1	$210.00	207%	$304.00	$94.00	$101.30	$52.94	$142.73
11750	Removal of nail bed	1	$440.00	240%	$551.00	$111.00	$183.66	$144.25	$309.71
11900	Inject skin lesions </w 7	1	$124.00	218%	$171.00	$47.00	$56.80	$32.79	$81.80
17110	Destruct b9 lesion 1-14	1	$170.00	150%	$340.00	$170.00	$113.21	$72.36	$159.09
17111	Destruct lesion 15 or more	1	$300.00	223%	$403.00	$103.00	$134.30	$89.16	$190.68
20550	Inj tendon sheath/ligament	1	$199.00	327%	$183.00	($16.00)	$60.90	$43.70	$82.37
20605	Drain/inj joint/bursa w/o us	1	$218.00	420%	$156.00	($62.00)	$51.86	$38.96	$84.05
20612	Aspirate/inj ganglion cyst	1	$211.00	337%	$189.00	($22.00)	$62.69	$44.06	$84.62
20670	Removal of support implant	1	$1,291.00	329%	$1,178.00	($113.00)	$392.36	$154.47	$478.95
28010	Incision of toe tendon	1	$458.00	191%	$719.00	$261.00	$239.34	$215.70	$340.17
28011	Incision of toe tendons	1	$624.00	187%	$1,002.00	$378.00	$333.83	$298.36	$482.34
29405	Apply short leg cast	1	$267.00	314%	$256.00	($11.00)	$85.14	$62.92	$122.42
29440	Addition of walker to cast	1	$89.00	197%	$136.00	$47.00	$45.10	$30.05	$72.21
29515	Application lower leg splint	1	$144.00	194%	$223.00	$79.00	$74.15	$51.94	$98.72
29540	Strapping of ankle and/or ft	1	$89.00	333%	$81.00	($8.00)	$26.75	$18.87	$62.06
29580	Application of paste boot	1	$111.00	204%	$163.00	$52.00	$54.29	$37.09	$74.46
64450	N block other peripheral	1	$200.00	243%	$247.00	$47.00	$82.24	$47.84	$149.49
64455	N block inj plantar digit	1	$200.00	407%	$148.00	($52.00)	$49.20	$36.30	$76.71
64640	Injection treatment of nerve	1	$150.00	110%	$411.00	$261.00	$136.93	$96.80	$306.89
Radiology									
73600	X-ray exam of ankle	1	$166.00	549%	$91.00	($75.00)	$30.25	$30.25	$29.30
73610	X-ray exam of ankle	1	$183.00	578%	$96.00	($87.00)	$31.69	$31.69	$32.39
73620	X-ray exam of foot	1	$60.00	228%	$79.00	$19.00	$26.31	$26.31	$28.79
73630	X-ray exam of foot	1	$180.00	609%	$89.00	($91.00)	$29.54	$29.54	$32.39
Medicine									
95851	Range of motion measurements	1	$396.00	2117%	$57.00	($339.00)	$18.71	$7.96	$23.69
97035	Ultrasound therapy	1	$50.00	396%	$38.00	($12.00)	$12.62	$12.62	$18.05
97597	Rmvl devital tis 20 cm/<	1	$185.00	243%	$229.00	$44.00	$76.11	$23.80	$97.02
Evaluation & Management									
99201	Office/outpatient visit new	1	$79.00	176%	$135.00	$56.00	$44.82	$27.62	$73.46
99202	Office/outpatient visit new	1	$135.00	177%	$229.00	$94.00	$76.22	$51.50	$124.91
99203	Office/outpatient visit new	1	$132.00	120%	$332.00	$200.00	$110.45	$78.92	$181.01
99212	Office/outpatient visit est	1	$85.00	192%	$134.00	$49.00	$44.38	$26.11	$72.72
99213	Office/outpatient visit est	1	$109.00	147%	$222.00	$113.00	$74.00	$52.14	$121.28
99214	Office/outpatient visit est	1	$158.00	145%	$327.00	$169.00	$108.98	$79.96	$178.59
99304	Nursing facility care init	1	$240.00	257%	$280.00	$40.00	$93.30	$93.30	$126.93
Supplies						300%			
A5500	Diab shoe for density insert	1	$75.00	107%	$211.00	$136.00	$70.29		$89.04
A5512	Multi den insert direct form	1	$27.50	96%	$87.00	$59.50	$28.67		$36.33
L1940	Afo molded to patient plasti	1	$810.00	184%	$1,323.00	$513.00	$440.84		$598.14
L1970	Afo plastic molded w/ankle j	1	$810.00	122%	$2,000.00	$1,190.00	$666.37		$860.63
L3030	Foot arch support remov prem	1	$50.00	68%	$221.00	$171.00	$73.53		$89.81
L3500	Ortho shoe add leather insol	1	$27.50	98%	$85.00	$57.50	$28.18		$34.41
L4386	Non-pneum walk boot pre cst	1	$243.00	159%	$459.00	$216.00	$152.80		$193.55
L4396	Static or dynami afo pre cst	1	$220.00	139%	$477.00	$257.00	$158.83		$201.18

In Exhibit 12.3, the practice had charges ranging from 68% of Medicare to 2,100%, with an average of 297% of Medicare. The one commercial payor fee schedule that was available was allowing 150% of Medicare. Ideally, their charges should be set at a consistent 300% of Medicare. This would show a clean 50% write-off (150% of Medicare is 50% of the charges, which are 300% of Medicare) for the payor's payments and would make policing the accuracy of the payor's reimbursement more easily done by a biller or anyone in the practice with a quick glance.

ADDRESSING SELF-PAY CONCERNS

Most physicians are reticent to increase charges because of the potential impact on self-pay patients. To address this concern, the practice can set a separate self-pay fee schedule that is above Medicare (because you don't want to disadvantage Medicare) and at the typical commercial payor fee schedule, like 120% of Medicare. This is fair for the patient who is not disadvantaged if they don't have health insurance because they are charged similarly if they did have insurance. Also, it is easier to explain by saying the self-pay discount is 40%, which would be the same as getting paid 120% of Medicare, if the practice's charges were 200% of Medicare (60% of 200 is 120; therefore, the discount from 200 down to 120 is 40% since 100% minus 60% is 40%).

CHAPTER 13

TALKING NUMBERS TO PHYSICIANS

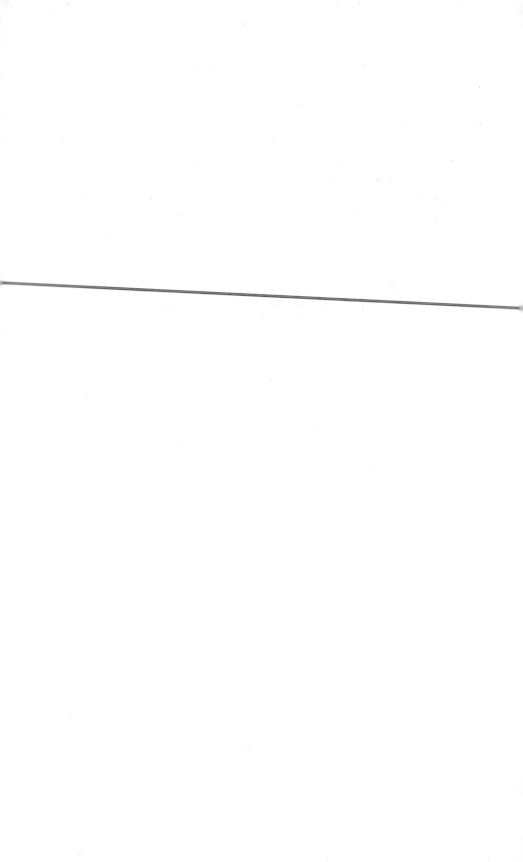

"The most important thing in communication is to hear what isn't being said."
- Peter Drucker

The value of memos, executive summaries, general correspondence, email, graphs, charts, exhibits, presentations, and dashboards cannot be overstated. Physician decisions, the physician-administrator relationship, and staff behavior determine practice success; therefore, it is imperative the administrator communicate efficiently and effectively to all members of the practice. Communication builds trust, improves decision-making, encourages an open and honest interaction, and develops buy-in. Also, there is a daily need to implement new processes and make decisions. In the ideal situation, staff and physician understand the details of any changes being suggested and there is buy-in. Unfortunately, the ideal is very rare so a strategy is needed to build it.

Organizing numbers is the cornerstone in the benchmarking process. An array or group of numbers only become valuable once they are arranged allowing for statistical methods and proper interpretation of the findings necessary to uncover the useful information behind the numbers. It is necessary to approach this systematically, through the use of averages (means), medians, standard deviations, percentiles, quartiles, and percent change (see Exhibit 4.1). These techniques can be used to measure and benchmark all practice attributes. In addition, these methods are easy to use, understand, and communicate as most people are familiar with at least some of the methods.

A framework to develop buy-in assumes that there are three ways to motivate people: the head, the heart, and WIIFM (what's in it for me). People motivated by "the head" respond to common-sense or logical arguments. Whereas, people driven by "the heart" will react if there is an emotional connection. And the "WIIFM" people are focused on their own self-interests. So if a business case analysis (BCA) is performed to implement a new service line, the strategy to develop buy-in should include supporting information for each of the three types of people. For "the head" person, a comprehensive BCA with a market analysis, all costs, estimated future revenues, ROI, and break-even analysis is needed to show the numbers look good. However, for "the heart" person, the emphasis should be on improved patient care, one-stop shop, increased goodwill, and better patient satisfaction/patient experience. And for the "WIIFM" people, if it is a staff member, job security, personal/professional growth, or another line for the resume would be a motivator. If it is a physician, the "WIIFM" might be projected future collections at the FTE physician-level.

Focus on the purpose, scope, and audience are necessary first steps. Ultimately, the purpose of presenting numbers to physicians is to efficiently relay important information. Physicians are most productive when treating patients; therefore, time reading lengthy explanations or deciphering busy graphs and charts is time wasted. Concise, brief, and clear communication should be your goal. The scope of your topic should be specific and related. Trying to present multiple, unrelated items on a single chart would only frustrate and potentially confuse a reader—thereby wasting the reader's time and teaching him or her to disregard future presentations. The information rich environment we live in makes us all susceptible to information overload (that is, too much information to process, associate, and commit to memory—information loses its value).

The educational and experiential background and your relationship with the audience must be considered when determining how and what to present. In addition, recognizing the differences in how people process information is necessary for effective communication. When preparing written documents, the follow characteristics will help ensure your message is delivered efficiently: (1) readability, (2) accuracy, (3) interest, and (4) polish, or professional look, feel, and style. Readability refers to the flow, organization, word choice, and sentence length; whereas, accuracy is the precision, attention to detail, and exactness of the content. Interesting writing will keep your audience's attention, increase the chances of your document being read from start to finish, and will entertain. And a professional look, feel, and style provide you and your report with credibility.[4]

Communication of data requires prioritization and emphasis (see Exhibit 13.1). Data should be ranked according to importance and the most important data should be emphasized. The Pareto Principle can be used as a guide to select data for emphasis—80% of practice variation is caused by 20% of practice activities. For example, if staff turnover is higher than the median found in the MGMA Performance and Practices of Successful Medical Groups, it may be possible to identify a list of potential causes. By comparing this list to the context/dynamics in the practice, it should be possible to narrow the list to a smaller set of most likely causes—this is the Pareto Principle at work. Typically, only a few causes affect the bulk of staff turnover. In addition, if the data is numeric, it is possible to graph in a Pareto chart (a bar chart with values ranked from highest to lowest). Often, however, the item to emphasize is not simply based on the numbers; rather, it is a judgment call based on the numbers, as well as the situation and the message the presenter wants to portray. Many methods are available to draw attention to specific data.

EXHIBIT 13.1 METHODS FOR EMPHASIZING DATA

- BOLD
- UNDERLINE
- ITALICS
- HUE (DARKER TEXT)
- COLOR INTENSITY (BRIGHT)

- LINE WIDTH (THICK)
- WORD ORIENTATION (SLANTING)
- SIZE (LARGE)
- BORDERS (LINES/SHAPES)

MEMOS AND EXECUTIVE SUMMARIES

Memos and executive summaries are one or two pages in length and include all the sections of a typical document in short-form. Memos tend to be less formal and loosely formatted; whereas, executive summaries should adhere to the structure of a formal report (see Exhibit 13.2).

EXHIBIT 13.2 EXAMPLE STRUCTURES OF MEMOS AND EXECUTIVE
SUMMARIES

EXAMPLE #1	EXAMPLE #2	EXAMPLE #3
FROM	INTRODUCTION	STATEMENT OF PURPOSE
TO	BACKGROUND	AND RATIONALE
SUBJECT	DEFINITIONS	THEORETICAL
BODY	PROBLEM STATEMENT	FRAMEWORK
SALUTATION	PROCEDURE	RESEARCH QUESTIONS
SIGNATURE	RESULTS	KEY TERMS AND
	EXAMPLES	VARIABLES
	DISCUSSION	DEFINITION OF
		POPULATION OF
		INTEREST
		DESCRIPTION OF
		RESEARCH DESIGN
		ASSUMPTIONS AND
		LIMITATIONS
		IMPLICATIONS OF
		FINDINGS
		DISSEMINATION OF
		FINDINGS

GENERAL CORRESPONDENCE AND EMAILS

These formats should follow the KISS principle—keep it short and simple (see Exhibit 13.3). For example, if there were multiple important issues that needed to be addressed by the physician staff, in keeping with the KISS principle, only one topic should be addressed in detail per email or correspondence. They should typically be no more than one page in length (less if email). General correspondence and emails should be used to relay a single thought, piece of information, or topic using the least number of words with few graphs/charts. In addition, the writing should be professional and adhere to accepted methods of grammar, punctuation, and spelling. Email writing style in particular incorporates a number of acronyms and symbols (for example, LOL = laugh out loud or emoticons [such as :)] created using a combination of keys) and the use of ALL CAPS for emphasis—almost universally regarded as shouting. Using acronyms, symbols, and all capitalized words should be used sparingly, if at all. The importance of maintaining professionalism in emails cannot be overstated—how you are perceived will be decided by your email style. A poor first impression can easily result from a poorly crafted email message. Furthermore, emails should be crafted with discretion and patient deliberation due to the ease and speed which they can be sent. Since most emails are short, sending a lengthy narrative with multiple attachments will quickly prompt a receiver to hit delete. And an email sent in haste or in the heat of the moment (sending an emotional, even invective-laced email to your boss, for example) can easily snowball into a serious problem.

EXHIBIT 13.3 GUIDELINES FOR CORRESPONDENCE AND EMAILS

- KEEP IT SHORT AND SIMPLE (KISS)
- PROFESSIONAL STYLE
- LIMIT ACRONYMS/SYMBOLS
- DISCRETION AND PATIENCE
- ONE PAGE, ONE TOPIC
- PROPER GRAMMAR, PUNCTUATION, AND SPELLING

GRAPHS, CHARTS, AND TABLES

Graphs, charts, and tables are excellent visual-aid type tools for supporting a message, but when used poorly can slow decision-making—they can help or hinder, clarify or confuse. Any visual aid should be used with a clear purpose in mind (see Exhibit 13.4). For instance, aids can be used to persuade, highlight, explain, or orient.[3] Visual aids are ideally suited to display benchmarking results such as percentage of total, ranking, changes over time, frequency distribution, and correlation.[2] Exhibit 13.4 recommends the percentage of time a particular type of chart should be used based on its practicality.[2]

EXHIBIT 13.4 CHART SELECTION[4]

CHART TYPE	% OF TIME	PRACTICALITY RATING
BAR CHART	25%	HIGH
COLUMN CHART (HISTOGRAM)	25%	HIGH
LINE CHART/GRAPH	25%	HIGH
DOT CHART (SCATTER PLOT)	10%	HIGH
PIE CHART	5%	LOW
COMBINATION CHART	10%	VARIES

Several key principles should be followed to effectively use visual aids (see Exhibit 13.5). First, understand the less is more model, since visual aids deliver information in such a concentrated form, using too many of them can be distracting.[2] Second, when revealing them, strongly consider the idea of "what the audience gets out of it" versus "what is put into it."[2] Third, "bigger is better"—ensure that the visual aid is easy to see and read. Fourth, consider the KISS principle again—keep it short and simple so the aid is easy for the audience to understand. Fifth, "make it memorable." And sixth, visuals should "stand on their own"—that is, the purpose, title, timeframe, and scope should be easy to find and understand.

EXHIBIT 13.5 KEY PRINCIPLES OF USING VISUAL AIDS

- FEWER IS BETTER[2]
- WHAT SHOULD THE AUDIENCE GET OUT OF THE IT?[2]
- BIGGER IS BETTER[3]
- KEEP IT SHORT AND SIMPLE[3]
- MAKE IT MEMORABLE[3]

Depending on what you want to show, certain visual aid formats are more appropriate (see Exhibit 13.6). For instance, graphs should be used when the message in the information is clearly represented by the shape of the data or to demonstrate relationships between multiple types of data.[2] Tables are best for presenting specific numbers, comparing numbers, or to show different types of numbers (for example, RVUs and RWPs by inpatient work center).[2]

EXHIBIT 13.6 RECOMMENDED METHODS FOR PRESENTING DATA

IF YOU WANT TO PRESENT:	USE A:
FREQUENCIES (DISCRETE DATA)	BAR CHART
FREQUENCIES (CONTINUOUS DATA)	HISTOGRAM
PERCENTAGES (RELATIVE	PIE CHART
FREQUENCIES)	LINE GRAPH
TRENDS (CONTINUOUS DATA)	SCATTER PLOT
RELATIONSHIPS (BETWEEN TWO	
VARIABLES)	

In addition, a visual aid that presents detailed information in an intuitive format is ideal for presenting meaningful information that can stand on its own. That is, the visual aid doesn't require significant explanation or a lengthy description and the chances of misinterpretation are minimal. Exhibit 13.7 is a template for illustrating a practice measure and associated benchmarks.

EXHIBIT 13.7 BENCHMARKING ILLUSTRATION

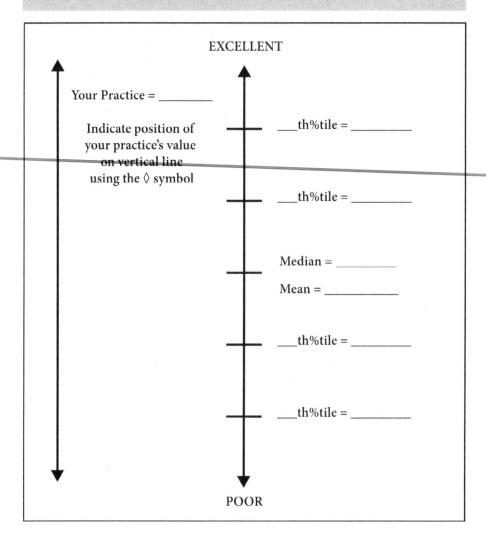

PRESENTATIONS

Nowadays, presentations are usually constructed using software applications such as Microsoft PowerPoint. When developing a presentation, care should be taken to consider the optimal or desired duration of the presentation, the audience, and the intended message. A presentation is an excellent tool for: introducing a new process, explaining the need for change or a decision, reinforcing an idea or position, highlighting a problem, presenting a sequence of events, or recommending a new course of action or process. Additionally, several considerations should be addressed to maximize the value, credibility, and overall readability of a presentation (see Exhibit 13.8).

EXHIBIT 13.8 PRESENTATION CONSIDERATIONS

- LIMIT TO LESS THAN ONE HOUR (PROVIDE AT LEAST 10 MINUTES TO ANSWER ANY QUESTIONS; IF YOU TELL YOUR AUDIENCE THE PRESENTATION WILL BE 50 MINUTES, STICK TO YOUR 50 MINUTES.)

- DESIGN AROUND PROSPECTIVE AUDIENCE (WHAT ARE YOUR AUDIENCE'S EXPECTATIONS, BACKGROUND, EDUCATION, ETC.?)

- DETERMINE PURPOSE OF PRESENTATION

- FONT OF TEXT

  □ CONSISTENT THROUGHOUT

  □ LARGE ENOUGH TO BE SEEN FROM A DISTANCE

  □ LIMIT NUMBER OF CHARACTERS PER SLIDE (TOO MUCH TEXT IS DISTRACTING AND DIFFICULT TO SEE)

- SPECIAL EFFECTS SHOULD BE USED SPARINGLY (ANIMATIONS, ACTION SETTINGS, AND SOUNDS CAN BE DISTRACTING)

- IMAGES SHOULD BE USED IN MODERATION BUT CAN BE USED TO CONSUME WHITE-SPACE (REAL-LIFE PICTURES ARE PREFERABLE TO CLIP-ART)

- LIMIT THE TOTAL NUMBER OF SLIDES BASED ON OTHER CONSIDERATIONS (HOW MUCH TIME DO YOU HAVE AND HOW LONG DOES IT TAKE TO PRESENT A SLIDE?)

- STRUCTURE PRESENTATION LOGICALLY (TITLE, OUTLINE/AGENDA, CONTENT, SUMMARY, Q&A)

- MAINTAIN PROFESSIONALISM (DON'T USE SLANG, TECHNICAL JARGON, PROPER APPEARANCE)

- MOVE AROUND (TRY NOT TO STAND IN ONE PLACE LIKE A STATUE)

- MAINTAIN A NATURAL DEMEANOR (DON'T APPEAR TO STIFF, ALLOW SOME ANIMATION IN YOUR HANDS, ETC.)

- ONCE PREPARED, TAKE A BREAK FROM THE PRESENTATION, THEN GO BACK TO RE-READ AND RE-PROOF

- ARRIVE EARLY TO THE PRESENTATION ROOM (WALK AROUND ROOM TO GET COMFORTABLE WITH IT AND CHECK TO MAKE SURE EQUIPMENT WORKS AND PRESENTATION CAN BE READ FROM THE BACK OF THE ROOM)

- DON'T READ FROM PRESENTATION, USE IT TO SUPPLEMENT, ILLUSTRATE, AND ORGANIZE

How many slides should be in a presentation? This is a common question and is dependent on many factors; however, a good rule of thumb at two to three minutes per slide is—around 20 slides for a 50-minute presentation. Other factors that can affect this formula are related to technique. For instance, talking too fast or reading from the slides.

Giving a good presentation that is memorable and valuable can be an elusive goal. Exhibit 13.9 identifies the top 10 presentation killers which should be avoided at all costs. To counter these pitfalls, practice, practice, practice. This doesn't mean practice a single presentation until it is memorized—this can be dangerous too if something unexpected happens during the presentation. Take every opportunity to give presentations of all kinds—the old adage, 'practice makes perfect' definitely applies.

EXHIBIT 13.9 PRESENTATION KILLERS

- MONOTONE VOICE

- READING DIRECTLY FROM THE SLIDE

- A BORING, UNINTERESTING MANNER

- THE "AND-UH" SYNDROME (UH, UM, YOU KNOW...)

- LACK OF PREPARATION: BEING UNORGANIZED, RAMBLING, BECOMING SIDETRACKED

- NERVOUS HABITS: FIDGETING, SWAYING, ANNOYING BODY LANGUAGE

- Speaking too long, going overtime

- Repeating, repeating, repeating

- Not making eye contact

- Not relating to the audience; no audience involvement, not tuned in to the audience's needs

101 WAYS TO CAPTIVATE A BUSINESS AUDIENCE by Sue Gaulke. Copyright 1997 by AMACOM Books. Reproduced with permission of AMACOM Books in the format Other book via Copyright Clearance Center.

Dashboards

Dashboards are typically visual representations of metrics, benchmarks, practice activities, and process status in a single (or few) display screens (see Exhibit 13.10). For example, an RVU dashboard might show Physician Work RVUs by physician in a line graph with an Exhibit populated by the specific number of RVUs below. In addition, the line graph might contain a line representing the practice average and a line depicting the MGMA average for the practice's specialty. The dashboard example below shows five metrics from the "Revenue by Payer" menu option that complies with the tenants of an effective report: accurate, brief, clear, and timely. In addition, this dashboard has multiple layers (see menu in lower left of figure) for displaying different practice metrics and when the cursor is placed over chart areas, additional information is automatically displayed.

FIGURE 13.10 EXAMPLE DASHBOARD

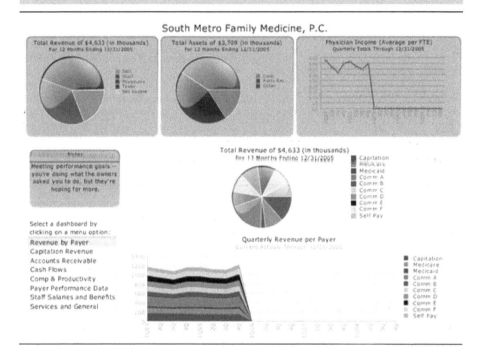

Ultimately, a dashboard functions as a "one-stop-shop" for quickly monitoring, comparing, and identifying current status and potential problems—a dashboard is an excellent early warning tool. Nowadays, many practices have automated dashboards that use web (Internet, Intranet, and Extranet) and database technologies. This enables users to access the dashboard from any PC with Internet connectivity. In addition, the benefits of web-enabling a dashboard permits custom calculations, flexibility, and real-time availability of practice measures. Dashboards improve management capabilities by automating data collection, display, and analysis. That is, they eliminate tedious hours of number crunching and analysis and speed decision response time driven by readily available, real-time practice information.

1 Balestracci, D. & Barlow, J. Quality Improvement, Practical Applications for Medical Group Practice, 2nd edition. Englewood: Center for Research in Ambulatory Health Care Administration; 1998.

2 Few, S. Show Me the Numbers, Designing Exhibits and Graphs to Enlighten. Oakland, CA: Analytics Press; 2004.

CHAPTER 14

USING LEAN SIX SIGMA TO IMPROVE OPERATIONS

"Perfection is not attainable, but if we chase perfection we can catch excellence."

> *- Vince Lombardi*

What do you do to improve and achieve best practices? The following is an introduction of how to move from benchmarking to applying work to improve every aspect of the patient care continuum. All medical practices can benefit from a structured, consistent, and standardized approach to addressing problems. Pick some key benchmarks or best practice ideas you have considered while reading this book and keep that in mind as you read on.

"Muda" is a Japanese word meaning futility, uselessness, or wastefulness. Therefore, muda should be identified, understood, and eliminated from today's medical practice. In general, there is muda throughout most every practice in virtually everything that is done. If we could eliminate muda, there would be maximum value to the customer. And the customer is not only the patient but also each employee, provider, visitor, or vendor that may be involved on a daily basis. In fact, it is documented there is at least a 25% waste factor with each employee's daily routine. What can be done to eliminate this waste?

A perfectly "lean" enterprise is one that is muda free and achieves the goal of meeting every customer's expectations. The application of lean principles from the manufacturing world can lead to the elimination of waste and to improved customer satisfaction.

LEAN AND SIX SIGMA

These are some key ways to apply lean principles to your practice.

- Create value—in the eyes of the customer, what they expect or what they are willing to pay for every time they come to the medical practice or are involved in the healthcare system

- Value stream—every step along the way adds value to the customer and does not include waste

- Flow—the cycle time of the patients visit, the processing of an insurance claim, the hiring of a new employee, all flow with no gaps

- Pull—the succeeding step signals that it is ready to receive; for example, triage or a treatment room is ready when the patient has completed check in

- Perfection—constantly strive for continuous process improvement

These principles were identified in 1996 with the publication of Lean Thinking by Womak and Jones and were mostly based upon manufacturing examples. Also, there are many examples in the service industry that can be adopted by healthcare.

A parallel concept is Six Sigma, which can also be applied to the medical practice. Sigma Six addresses defects or broken parts such as medication errors or wrong site surgery. It seeks near perfection through the elimination of errors down to 3.4 per million activities (99.99966% defect free).

The connection between the two concepts is Lean eliminates waste or gaps in the flow by being efficient and Six Sigma eliminates defects or broken parts by being effective. The concepts may be further understood when identifying how quality is generated in the medical practice. Avedis Donabedian, in 1966, identified three areas of focus in healthcare that are key to providing high quality: structure, process, and outcome (SPO).

STRUCTURE

Structure means there must be a framework or a foundation of evidence in order to proceed (also known as a deployment platform). In Lean terms the deployment platform is the "PDSA Cycle":

- Plan—define the problem, gather the data, and analyze

- Do—test the options

- Study—what worked and what didn't, develop the new best practice

- Act—implement across the practice

- In Six Sigma, this involves five steps referred to as "DMAIC":

- Define—identify the problem, keep focus, do not go too broad

- Measure—establish a baseline then identify at the conclusion if you have improved, first establishing a goal. This could be an internal benchmark or an external review of what or how others are meeting customer expectations

- Analyze—within the problem and appropriate metrics, what will lead to a successful change

- Improve—develop and test the solution to achieve the goal

- Control—implement and maintain the new way, seek to continuously improve the process

Process

This structure is supplemented through various tools which are key to process improvement. These tools include:

- Process maps—flow charts or graphics that show the steps in the process (for example, charting out a clinical workflow). Step one is to identify the current state or how things are done. Eventually, the process map should be the graphic of the new, better way of doing things. Figure 1 shows a paper exercise process map, high-tech tools are not necessary. The team through a brainstorming exercise developed this example. The key is to recognize the way things are done, which will identify where there is waste in that particular process.

FIGURE 1: PROCESS MAP

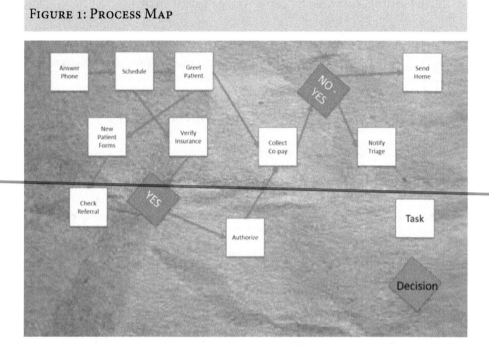

- Value Stream Map—this is a drill-down into the process map to identify the steps that are valuable and those that are wasteful. The goal is to eliminate any waste found in the process. Figure 2 reveals a 91-minute cycle time that includes 44 minutes of "value add" time, which is considered time that directly benefits the patient (direct contact with provider team) and the practice (check in and check out) and is not waste, and 47 minutes of "non-value" add time or muda!

FIGURE 2: VALUE STREAM MAP

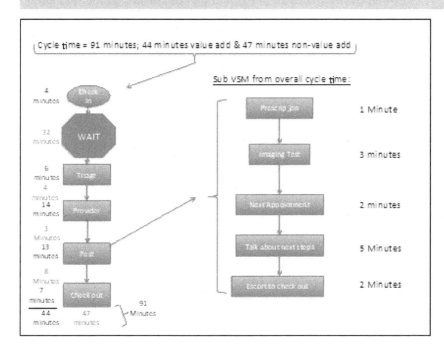

- Five whys—a simple technique is to ask an employee why they are doing the task or why they are doing it that way. Once the why is asked up to five times, it becomes clear there is no need, redundancy, and a need to change how the task is being accomplished. Involving the employee will very often lead to an improved process.

- Five or six "S" —sort, set in order, shine, standardize, and sustain with a sixth "S" sometimes added—safety. Keep the work area clean, remove clutter and insure consistency in action, things are always in their place

A key component of the process is the identification of a team. Achieving a best practice cannot be done alone. Team members should include the project manager or team leader, process owners (those who do the work in the process), subject matter experts (SMEs; inside or outside of the team who bring a level of expertise to the process), a "champion" who supports and represents the project improvement effort to others, and a recorder since it is necessary to track all the activity that occurs throughout the process. Documentation related to the process from the initial efforts of education through the final stages of each project is essential. This should be consolidated, maintained and become the basis for the practice's Lean Six Sigma efforts.

Outcome

The outcome of improved processes are dramatic improvements resulting in the customer's expectations being met. Examples of outcomes related to the application of the Lean Six Sigma approach include:

- Improved patient satisfaction scores

- Improved bottom line

- Reduced denial rate

- Increased number of patients treated per day

- Decreased costs per patient visit or ancillary service

- Reduced employee turnover through improved hiring practices and on-boarding programs

- Improved provider and employee satisfaction, reduced turnover and overtime

Model Case Study

What if patient satisfaction surveys for a primary care practice reveal an 85% overall satisfaction rate over the past quarter? Specifically, the results reveal wait time, attitude of the front desk, lack of time with the provider, and inefficiency at checkout as areas with low ratings.

The team leader decides the PDSA deployment platform will be used to assess the check-in/check-out cycle time. A week's worth of data is gathered which reveals a base line of 63 minutes for the average established patient visit. Checking with other benchmarks, there are many with a lower cycle time of 42 minutes.

A team of employees which included three process owners, one SME, and one patient is assembled to develop a current state process map (see figure 1 for example) with the goal of creating a value stream map to help detail the measures needed for improvement. This exercise reveals the big gaps occur at triage and immediately after the provider visit. In addition, there are clearly extra steps along the way; however, a disorganized nursing station where forms and devices are kept separate for each medical assistant is also identified and could benefit from the five "S" tool.

The team reviewed the value stream by asking why during the brainstorming session. One thing revealed is each exam room is set up differently, especially in one office that has three different doctors. And the scheduling template is inefficient since each doctor has his/her own approach to seeing patients.

At the conclusion of the "P," there are many causes and solutions. However, as part of brainstorming, all ideas are listed but not every solution will work. The Pareto principle (80% of the issues identified are caused by 20% of the occurrences in the cycle) indicated the big problems are the exam room setup and the duplication of tasks by both the doctor and the medical assistant. It is agreed these could be fixed and a pilot test (the "D") is designed and implemented.

After two weeks in the pilot, the team reconvenes to look at the data gathered ("S"). The new overall cycle time is now 58 minutes. These positive results show positive outcomes and a full practice-wide implementation plan should be developed. This was accomplished with new procedures defined, staff trained, and then full implementation ("A").

After two months, the team reconvenes again and finds one office has taken additional steps and reduced the cycle time by another three minutes. However, one office has shown only a two-minute reduction in its cycle time.

The bottom line: using Lean and Six Sigma tools can and will lead to successful outcomes but it takes time, coordination, and commitment on the part of all involved to achieve the desired outcome. The benchmarks generated and used from within and from other sources are key to follow-up activities and to evaluating improvement and success.

CHAPTER 15

PERFORMANCE AND PRACTICES OF SUCCESSFUL MEDICAL GROUPS

"The price is what you pay; the value is what you receive."
- Unknown

B etter performing practices are selected based on profitability and operating costs; productivity, capacity, and staffing; accounts receivable and collections, and managed care. Selection criteria to perform better in the profitability and operating costs category are (1) greater than the median for total medical revenue after operating costs per FTE physician and (2) less than the median for operating cost, not including non-physician providers, per medical procedure, inside the practice. Criteria for productivity, capacity, and staffing in nonsurgical specialties are (1) greater than the median for in-house medical procedures per square foot and (2) greater than the median for total gross charges per FTE physician. Criteria for productivity, capacity, and staffing in surgical specialties are (1) greater than the median for total medical procedures per FTE physician, (2) greater than the median for total gross charges per FTE physician, and (3) anesthesia practices, greater than the median for ASA units per FTE physician. And the criteria for accounts receivable and collections are (1) less than the median for percent of total A/R over 120 days, (2) greater than the median for adjusted fee-for-service collection percentage, and (3) less than the median for month's gross fee-for-services charges in A/R.Organizing numbers is the cornerstone in the benchmarking process. An array or group of numbers only become valuable once they are arranged allowing for statistical methods and proper interpretation of the findings necessary to uncover the useful information behind the numbers. It is necessary to approach this systematically, through the use of averages (means), medians, standard deviations, percentiles, quartiles, and percent change (see Exhibit 4.1). These techniques can be used to measure and benchmark all practice attributes. In addition, these methods are easy to use, understand, and communicate as most people are familiar with at least some of the methods.

TRAITS OF SUCCESSFUL MEDICAL GROUPS

Patient satisfaction and quality orientation are based on the premise that patients are the first reason why medical groups exist. Therefore, organizational systems must be designed to meet patient needs by treating the patient-practice relationship as most important while maintaining all other business relationships (see Exhibit 15.1). Ultimately, dedication to patients requires quality of care coupled with excellent service. Excellent service, however, is determined by the perception of the patient—not the practice, physicians, or staff.

EXHIBIT 15.1 PATIENT SATISFACTION AND QUALITY ORIENTATION OF SUCCESSFUL MEDICAL GROUPS

BEHAVIORS

- FORMAL PATIENT SATISFACTION SURVEY PROGRAM

- ESTABLISHED PROTOCOL FOR RESOLVING PATIENT COMPLAINTS

- INTERNAL PEER REVIEW PROGRAM/OBSERVANCE OF EVIDENCE-BASED CLINICAL METHODS

- REGULAR CODING AND DOCUMENTATION REVIEWS TO ENSURE COMPLIANCE

- PARTICIPATION IN DISEASE REGISTRIES

- CONTINUING EDUCATION REQUIREMENTS FOR PHYSICIANS AND STAFF

- ESSENTIAL PRACTICE INFORMATION IS MADE AVAILABLE TO PATIENTS IN PAPER AND WEB FORMATS

- EXTENDED HOURS FOR PATIENT CONVENIENCE

- IN-HOUSE DIAGNOSTIC SERVICES FOR PATIENT CONVENIENCE

- CUSTOMER SERVICE/COMMUNICATION TRAINING FOR PHYSICIANS AND STAFF

METRICS

- PATIENT SATISFACTION ASSESSMENT FOR PROVIDERS, STAFF, AND FACILITIES

- BOARD CERTIFICATION FOR PHYSICIANS

- CODING PROFILES FOR PHYSICIANS

- DOCUMENTATION STANDARDS

- CONFORMANCE WITH CLINICAL CARE GUIDELINES/PROTOCOLS

Operational and business discipline is based on sound financial management to ensure profitability. Continuous improvement should focus on operational methods that promote efficiency and cost effectiveness, eliminate water and reduce error, and involve physicians and staff in financial and cost management (see Exhibit 15.2).

EXHIBIT 15.2 OPERATIONAL AND BUSINESS DISCIPLINE OF SUCCESSFUL MEDICAL GROUPS

BEHAVIORS

- PERFORM ANNUAL BUDGET AND BUSINESS PLANNING

- INCORPORATE FINANCIAL GOALS INTO STRATEGIC PLAN

- MONITOR PERFORMANCE AGAINST BUDGET

- SET FINANCIAL OBJECTIVES TO EXCEED PEERS

- DOCUMENT ALL POLICIES AND PROCEDURES

- IMPLEMENT PERFORMANCE MANAGEMENT PLANS FOR EMPLOYEES

- REWARD EMPLOYEES FOR ORGANIZATIONAL CONTRIBUTIONS AND ELIMINATE POOR PERFORMERS

- MONITOR A/R AND CASH FLOW PERFORMANCE

- TREAT HEALTH PLANS AS BUSINESS PARTNERS, NOT ENEMIES

- NEGOTIATE ASSERTIVELY/HOLD HEALTH PLANS ACCOUNTABLE

- SCRUTINIZE ALL EXPENSES, REGULARLY BID VENDOR CONTRACTS, AND PARTICIPATE IN GROUP PURCHASING ORGANIZATIONS

- REWARD PHYSICIANS AND STAFF FOR COST SAVINGS

- MAXIMIZE USE OF INFORMATION SYSTEMS AND OFFICE AUTOMATION TECHNOLOGIES

- Develop formal marketing programs

Metrics

- Revenue and collections
- Total operating expense, support staff expenses, and general operating expenses
- Expenses as a percent of revenue
- Revenue after operating expenses
- Physician/provider compensation
- Staff per FTE physician
- Staff turnover rates
- A/R aging
- Adjusted collection percent
- Denial rates
- Payer mix
- Revenue and expense per RVU

The purpose of focusing on provider productivity is to ensure provider activities drive revenue (see Exhibit 15.3). This also includes creating system to leverage physician effort while monitoring productivity.

Exhibit 15.3 Focus on Provider Productivity of Successful Medical Groups

Behaviors

- Utilize productivity-based compensation programs for providers and staff
- Set productivity expectations for providers and staff
- Use non-physician providers to leverage physician skills
- Maintain optimal staffing level to maximize efficiency

- DEVELOP MENTORING PROGRAM FOR NEW PHYSICIANS

- ENSURE NEW PHYSICIANS ARE CREDENTIALED BEFORE BEGINNING BILLABLE WORK

- DEVELOP PRACTICE CULTURAL VALUES THAT PROMOTE WORK ETHIC

- IMPLEMENT A HIRING PROCESS THAT ENSURES NEW PHYSICIANS WILL EMBRACE PRODUCTIVITY EXPECTATIONS

- DESIGN OPERATIONAL SYSTEM AND FACILITIES SUCH AS SCHEDULING METHODS, OFFICE AUTOMATION, AND EXTENDED HOURS TO FACILITATE PRODUCTIVITY

- EVALUATE PHYSICIANS FOR OPTIMAL CODING PATTERNS TO MINIMIZE LOST REVENUE DUE TO INAPPROPRIATE UNDER CODING

METRICS

- RVUS PER PHYSICIAN

- ENCOUNTERS OR PROCEDURES PER PHYSICIAN

- REVENUE PER PHYSICIAN

- STAFF PER PHYSICIAN

- BILLABLE DAYS PER MONTH PER PHYSICIAN

- NO-SHOW RATES

- REFERRAL PATTERNS AND TRENDS

The purpose of innovation and improvement is to identify more advanced methods of doing business. This also includes evaluating operational activities for efficiency and quality, assessing organizational and provider performance to uncover improvement opportunities, promote provider and staff buy-in, and reduce resistance to change (see Exhibit 15.4).

EXHIBIT 15.4 INNOVATION AND IMPROVEMENT IN SUCCESSFUL MEDICAL GROUPS

BEHAVIORS

- BENCHMARK INTERNALLY AGAINST PAST PERFORMANCE AND EXTERNALLY

AGAINST PEERS

- DEVELOP FORMAL BUSINESS AND PROJECT PLANS TO ENSURE EFFICIENT MANAGEMENT AND IMPLEMENTATION OF CHANGE INITIATIVES

- INVEST IN TECHNOLOGY AND OFFICE AUTOMATION PRUDENTLY

- SEE MUTUALLY BENEFICIAL COLLABORATIONS WHEN INDEPENDENT ACTION IS NOT POSSIBLE

- TEST OPERATIONAL CHANGES BEFORE FULL IMPLEMENTATION

METRICS

- ADVANCES IN PROCESS EFFICIENCY

- STATUS OF TECHNOLOGY ADOPTION COMPARED TO PEERS SUCH AS USE AND INTEGRATION OF ELECTRONIC HEALTH RECORDS

- STATUS OF FACILITY UPDATES SUCH AS THE TIME SINCE THE LAST REMODEL OR EXPANSION

The purpose of entrepreneurialism and growth perspective is to strive to expand the revenue base. This also includes being competitive and leading the market by taking risks as a group (see Exhibit 15.5).

EXHIBIT 15.5 ENTREPRENEURIALISM AND GROWTH PERSPECTIVE OF SUCCESSFUL MEDICAL GROUPS

BEHAVIORS

- MAINTAIN AND EXPAND RELATIONSHIPS WITH REFERRAL SOURCES

- ANTICIPATE COMMUNITY NEEDS SUCH AS DEVELOPING NEW FACILITIES IN POPULATION GROWTH AREAS

- EXPLOIT ADVANTAGES OFFERED BY NEW TECHNOLOGIES

- MAXIMIZE PROFITABILITY OF ANCILLARY SERVICES

- NURTURE RELATIONSHIPS WITH POTENTIAL BUSINESS PARTNERS INCLUDING HOSPITALS, OTHER GROUPS, PROFESSIONAL SERVICE PROVIDERS, AND BANKERS

- PERFORM THOROUGH AND COMPLETE BUSINESS PLANNING REGARDING NEW

BUSINESS ENDEAVORS

- PARTICIPATE IN COMMUNITY HEALTH PROGRAMS AND CHARITABLE EVENTS ALONG WITH PROFESSIONAL ASSOCIATIONS

- MAINTAIN A MANAGED MARKETING PROGRAM

- ADAPT SUCCESSFUL BEHAVIORS OF OTHER MEDICAL GROUPS

METRICS

- REVENUE INCREASE PER YEAR

- NEW PATIENTS PER MONTH

- ADDITIONS TO NEW SERVICE OFFERINGS AND ADDITION OF NEW PHYSICIANS

- REVENUE AND EXPENSE PER ANCILLARY SERVICE LINE

- RETURN ON INVESTMENT PER MARKETING PROGRAM

- REFERRAL PHYSICIAN SATISFACTION

The purpose of aligned incentives is to create individual and collective incentives to promote achievement of organizational goals. This also includes ensuring key operating systems support organizational objectives while seeking goal alignment among physicians and staff (see Exhibit 15.6).

EXHIBIT 15.6 ALIGNED INCENTIVES OF SUCCESSFUL MEDICAL GROUPS

BEHAVIORS

- PROVIDE MARKET-BASED COMPENSATION FOR STAFF WITH INCENTIVES FOR ACHIEVEMENT OF INDIVIDUAL AND ORGANIZATIONAL GOALS

- DEVELOP STAFF BONUS PROGRAMS THAT REWARD AT THE TIME GOALS ARE ACHIEVED RATHER THAN JUST AT THE END OF THE YEAR

- DISCLOSE ORGANIZATIONAL PERFORMANCE INFORMATION TO STAFF SUCH AS FINANCIAL STATEMENTS AND PATIENT SATISFACTION SURVEY RESULTS

- INVOLVE STAFF IN OPERATIONAL PLANNING TO ENLIST THEIR SUPPORT IN ACHIEVING GOALS AND IMPROVING PERFORMANCE

- ACKNOWLEDGE (SHOW VISIBLE APPRECIATION) INDIVIDUAL STAFF

CONTRIBUTIONS TO ORGANIZATIONAL SUCCESS

- INVOLVE PHYSICIANS IN OPERATIONAL AND BUSINESS IMPROVEMENT INITIATIVES
- DESIGN POLICIES AND PROCEDURES TO ENSURE CONSISTENCY WITH ORGANIZATIONAL GOALS AND VALUES

METRICS

- SUPPORT STAFF COSTS PER PHYSICIAN
- PHYSICIAN COMPENSATION TO PRODUCTION RATIOS SUCH AS COMPENSATION PER RVU
- PHYSICIAN SATISFACTION
- EMPLOYEE/STAFF SATISFACTION
- OPERATING EFFICIENCIES SUCH AS CLAIMS PROCESSED PER BILLING STAFF

The purpose of having a clear vision and cohesive culture is to define the direction of the organization. This also includes instilling a common value system among physicians and staff, working as a team to achieve organizational objectives, and confronting issues that cause dissatisfaction (see Exhibit 15.7).

EXHIBIT 15.7 CLEAR VISION AND COHESIVE CULTURE OF SUCCESSFUL MEDICAL GROUPS

BEHAVIORS

- CONDUCT COMPREHENSIVE, FORMAL STRATEGIC PLANNING EXERCISES REGULARLY AND ESTABLISH EXPLICIT GROUP VALUES AND ARTICULATE THE VISION
- REMIND PHYSICIANS AND STAFF OF GOALS AND VISION
- CONDUCT REGULAR STAKEHOLDER NEEDS ASSESSMENTS OF PATIENTS, PHYSICIANS, AND STAFF
- ASSESS ALIGNMENT OF EXPECTATIONS AMONG PHYSICIANS AND STAFF
- ENSURE PRACTICE LEADERSHIP CONNECTS WITH AND ESTABLISHES AND

NURTURES RELATIONSHIPS WITH STAFF

- CONDUCT FORMAL TEAMBUILDING EXERCISES
- CREATE OPPORTUNITIES FOR PHYSICIANS AND STAFF TO INTERACT SOCIALLY
- IDENTIFY A CULTURAL PROFILE
- RECRUIT PHYSICIANS AND STAFF OR CULTURAL FIT

METRICS

- CULTURAL PROFILE
- STRATEGIC PLANNING UPDATES
- PHYSICIAN AND STAFF SATISFACTION
- PHYSICIAN AND STAFF VOLUNTARY TURNOVER RATES

The environment most practices must contend with are, in general, very similar: declining reimbursement, rising costs, lack of qualified staff, and complicated and ever changing regulatory and payer issues. However, better performing practices typically have more satisfied patients, more fulfilling work environments for physicians and staff, and better economic outcomes. Among better performing practices, Operational and Business Discipline was identified as most the important overall factor in determining practice success, and in particular, superior management was considered the most influential.

PROFITABILITY AND OPERATING COSTS

Many practices identified as better performers have provided tips for maximizing revenue and accurately allocating, analyzing, understanding, and controlling costs. In general, there are several steps that are associated with better performing practices (see Exhibit 15.8).

EXHIBIT 15.8 SEVEN STEPS TO BETTER PROFITABILITY AND OPERATING COSTS PERFORMANCE

- DETAILED COST ACCOUNTING
- TRANSACTION COSTING
- ZERO-BASED BUDGETING
- PHYSICIAN INCENTIVES

- EFFECTIVE MANAGED CARE CONTRACTING
- EFFECTIVE CODING
- IMPROVED SERVICE DELIVERY

Practices selected by MGMA as better performing in the profitability and operating costs category provided several of their keys to success (see Exhibit 15.9). These keys were used by real practices and resulted in success through best practices. The use of these keys does not guarantee success but they will increase a practice's potential.

EXHIBIT 15.9 KEYS TO PROFITABILITY AND OPERATING COSTS SUCCESS

- PHYSICIANS WHO SEE THEIR PATIENTS IN THE HOSPITAL
- GROWING COMMUNITY
- UNIQUE APPROACHES TO BILLING AND STAFF RETENTION
- LONG-TIME EMPLOYEES
- ENTREPRENEURIAL CULTURE
- STAFFING MIX THAT ALLOWS FOR GREATER PRODUCTIVITY
- PHYSICIANS WHO ARE INVOLVED IN PRACTICE OPERATIONS
- STRONG POSITIVE PRESENCE IN THE COMMUNITY
- BILLING STAFF RESPONSIBLE FOR A PHYSICIAN SITE

- VISIONARY LEADER
- TEAM APPROACH TO PRACTICE OPERATIONS
- STRONG EMPHASIS PLACED ON EFFICIENCIES
- WORKING SMARTER NOT HARDER
- WORLD-WIDE FELLOWSHIP PROGRAM
- SHIFT IN CULTURE
- ESTABLISHED PHYSICIANS MENTORING OTHERS
- CHANGE IN STAFF RECRUITMENT PROCEDURES

$$\frac{\text{Total gross charges}}{\text{Total FTE physicians}}$$

Gross Charges per Medical Procedure Inside the Practice

Goal: Higher the better

$$\frac{\text{Total gross charges (generated from inside the practice)}}{\text{Total number of medical procedures (provided from inside the practice)}}$$

Total Employed Support Staff Cost per FTE Physician

Goal: Depends on the practice; however, according to the research, a balance between practice productivity and number of support staff is necessary

$$\frac{\text{Total employed support staff cost}}{\text{Total FTE physicians}}$$

Total General Operating Cost per FTE Physician

Goal: Lower the better

$$\frac{\text{Total general operating cost}}{\text{Total FTE physicians}}$$

Total Operating Cost per FTE Physician

Goal: Lower the better

$$\frac{\text{Total operating cost}}{\text{Total FTE physicians}}$$

Total Medical Revenue After Operation Cost per FTE Physician

Goal: Higher the better

$$\frac{\text{Total medical revenue} - \text{operating cost}}{\text{Total FTE physicians}}$$

Total Operating Cost as a Percentage of Total Medical Revenue

Goal: Lower the better

$$\frac{\text{Total operating cost} * 100}{\text{Total medical revenue}}$$

EXHIBIT 15.10 OTHER PROFITABILITY AND OPERATING COSTS MEASURES[5]

- MEDICAL PROCEDURES INSIDE THE PRACTICE TO TOTAL GROSS CHARGES

- SURGICAL PROCEDURES INSIDE THE PRACTICE TO TOTAL GROSS CHARGES

- LABORATORY PROCEDURES TO TOTAL GROSS CHARGES

- RADIOLOGY PROCEDURES TO TOTAL GROSS CHARGES

- TOTAL GROSS CHARGES PER TOTAL PROCEDURES

- TOTAL GROSS CHARGES PER SURGICAL/ANESTHESIA PROCEDURE INSIDE THE PRACTICE

- TOTAL GROSS CHARGES PER CLINICAL LAB AND PATHOLOGY PROCEDURE INSIDE THE PRACTICE

- TOTAL GROSS CHARGES PER DIAGNOSTIC RADIOLOGY/IMAGING PROCEDURE INSIDE THE PRACTICE

- NET FEE-FOR-SERVICE REVENUE PER FTE PHYSICIAN

- NET CAPITATION REVENUE PER FTE PHYSICIAN

- OTHER MEDICAL REVENUE PER FTE PHYSICIAN

- NONMEDICAL REVENUE PER FTE PHYSICIAN

- TOTAL MEDICAL REVENUE AFTER OPERATING COST AS A PERCENT OF TOTAL MEDICAL REVENUE

- TOTAL NON-PHYSICIAN PROVIDER COST PER FTE PHYSICIAN

- TOTAL SUPPORT STAFF COST AS A PERCENTAGE OF TOTAL MEDICAL REVENUE

- TOTAL NON-PHYSICIAN PROVIDER COST AS A PERCENTAGE OF TOTAL MEDICAL REVENUE

- TOTAL PROVIDER COST PER MEDICAL PROCEDURE INSIDE THE PRACTICE

- TOTAL PROVIDER COST PER SURGICAL/ANESTHESIA PROCEDURE INSIDE THE PRACTICE

- TOTAL PROVIDER COST PER CLINICAL LABORATORY AND PATHOLOGY PROCEDURE INSIDE THE PRACTICE

- TOTAL PROVIDER COST PER DIAGNOSTIC RADIOLOGY/IMAGING PROCEDURE INSIDE THE PRACTICE

- NOTE: THERE ARE SEVERAL OTHER MEASURES INVOLVING PROCEDURES CONDUCTED "OUTSIDE" THE PRACTICE THAT SHOULD ALSO BE CONSIDERED, PARTICULARLY WHEN ANALYZING REVENUE GENERATING CENTERS/ACTIVITIES

PRODUCTIVITY, CAPACITY, AND STAFFING

Many practices identified as better performers have provided tips for maximizing physician productivity, optimizing capacity, and investing time and energy into their support staff. Physician productivity is the primary revenue generating activity of a practice that consists of patient visits/encounters and procedures. Better performing practices focus on capacity by inventing in the proper resources and optimizing the efficient use of those resources. The common characteristics of better performing practices are related to infrastructure, policies and procedures, staffing numbers and mix, hiring, training, physician compensation methods, information systems, and patient satisfaction. In general, there are several steps that are associated with better performing practices (see Exhibit 15.11).

EXHIBIT 15.11 FIVE STEPS TO BETTER PRODUCTIVITY, CAPACITY, AND
STAFFING PERFORMANCE

- BUILD CAPACITY
- COMPENSATION FORMULA
- APPROPRIATE STAFFING
- PATIENT SATISFACTION
- SCHEDULING SYSTEM

Practices selected by MGMA as better performing in the productivity, capacity, and staffing category provided several of their keys to success (see Exhibit 15.12). These keys were used by real practices and resulted in success through best practices. The use of these keys does not guarantee success but they will increase a practice's potential.

EXHIBIT 15.12 KEYS TO PRODUCTIVITY, CAPACITY, AND STAFFING
SUCCESS

- STAFF EDUCATION ON PROCEDURES AND TREATMENTS
- ONSITE PHARMACIST AND TECHNICIANS
- WELL-TRAINED NURSES
- DEDICATED, HARDWORKING, AND INVOLVED PHYSICIANS
- INVOLVE STAFF IN DECISION-MAKING
- STAFF INCENTIVE PLANS
- AS A GROUP, FOCUS ON IMPROVING OPERATIONAL EFFICIENCIES
- RELAXED AND COMFORTABLE ATMOSPHERE FOR PATIENTS
- GOOD WORKING RELATIONSHIP WITH LOCAL HOSPITAL(S)
- EXPERIENCED STAFF
- PROVIDE STATE-OF-THE-ART CARE
- HIRE THE RIGHT TEAM
- BENCHMARK FOR CONTINUED IMPROVEMENT
- IMPLEMENT TECHNOLOGY TO IMPROVE SERVICE AND PRODUCTIVITY
- USE OF INFORMATION TECHNOLOGY

Total Gross Charges per FTE Physician

Goal: Higher the better

$$\frac{\text{Total gross charges}}{\text{Total FTE physicians}}$$

Total Medical Revenue per FTE Physician

Goal: Higher the better

$$\frac{\text{Total medical revenue}}{\text{Total FTE physicians}}$$

Physician Work RVUs per FTE Physician

Goal: Higher the better

$$\frac{\text{Total physician Work RVUs}}{\text{Total FTE physicians}}$$

Patient Encounters per FTE Physician

Goal: Depends on the practice, specialty, and patient mix; typically, the higher the better

$$\frac{\text{Total number of patient encounters}}{\text{Total FTE physicians}}$$

In-house Professional Procedures per Square Foot

Goal: Higher the better

$$\frac{\text{Total number of professional (physician/provider) procedures}}{\text{Total square footage of entire practice}}$$

Total Procedures per Square Foot

Goal: Higher the better

$$\frac{\text{Total number of all types of procedures}}{\text{Total square footage of entire practice}}$$

Total Procedures per FTE Physician

Goal: Higher the better

$$\frac{\text{Total number of all types of procedures}}{\text{Total FTE physicians}}$$

Total Procedures per Patient

Goal: Higher the better

$$\frac{\text{Total number of all types of procedures}}{\text{Total number of unique patients}}$$

Total Employed Support Staff per FTE Physician

Goal: Depends on the practice; however, according to the research, a balance between practice productivity and number of support staff is necessary

$$\frac{\text{Total number of employed support staff}}{\text{Total FTE physicians}}$$

Total Employed Support Staff Cost per FTE Physician

Goal: Depends on the practice; however, according to the research, a balance between practice productivity and number of support staff is necessary

$$\frac{\text{Total employed support staff cost}}{\text{Total FTE physicians}}$$

Total Employed Support Staff Cost as a Percentage of Total Medical Revenue

Goal: Depends on the practice; however, according to the research, a balance between practice productivity and number of support staff is necessary

$$\frac{\text{Total employed support staff cost} * 100}{\text{Total medical revenue}}$$

EXHIBIT 15.13 OTHER PRODUCTIVITY, CAPACITY, AND STAFFING MEASURES [5]

- TOTAL RVUS PER FTE PHYSICIAN

- PATIENT PER FTE PHYSICIAN

- TOTAL NON-PHYSICIAN PROVIDERS PER FTE PHYSICIAN

- GENERAL ADMINISTRATIVE STAFF PER FTE PHYSICIAN

- MANAGED CARE ADMINISTRATIVE STAFF PER FTE PHYSICIAN

- MEDICAL RECORDS STAFF PER FTE PHYSICIAN

- CLINICAL SUPPORT STAFF PER FTE PHYSICIAN

- CLINICAL LABORATORY STAFF PER FTE PHYSICIAN

- RADIOLOGY AND IMAGING STAFF PER FTE PHYSICIAN

- INSIDE MEDICAL/SURGICAL PROCEDURES PER FTE CLINICAL SUPPORT STAFF

- MEDICAL PROCEDURES INSIDE THE PRACTICE PER FTE PHYSICIAN

- SURGICAL PROCEDURES INSIDE THE PRACTICE PER FTE PHYSICIAN

- ALL LABORATORY PROCEDURES PER FTE PHYSICIAN

- ALL RADIOLOGY/IMAGING PROCEDURES PER FTE PHYSICIAN

- TOTAL SQUARE FEET PER FTE PHYSICIAN

ACCOUNTS RECEIVABLE AND COLLECTIONS

Since accounts receivable (A/R) is usually the single largest balance sheet item, most practices identified as better performers generally invest significant time and energy managing this asset. In particular, better performing practices treat A/R and collections as a practice-wide endeavor, that is, every department, staff member, and physician are involved in the process. Therefore, better performing practices have provided the following tips for actively managing A/R and collections to increase cash flow and improve working capital position (see Exhibit 15.14).

EXHIBIT 15.14 FIVE STEPS TO BETTER A/R AND COLLECTIONS
PERFORMANCE

- CONSIDER BILLING TO BE
  EVERYONE'S RESPONSIBILITY
- PUSH BILLING "TO THE FRONT" OF
  THE CYCLE
- ENTER CHARGES INTO THE
  SYSTEM IMMEDIATELY AND WITH
  ACCURACY

- ENSURE BILLING FOR ALL SERVICES
- ANALYZE A/R BY VARIOUS
  COMPONENTS

Practices selected by MGMA as better performing in the A/R and collections category provided several of their keys to success (see Exhibit 15.15). These keys were used by real practices and resulted in success through best practices. The use of these keys does not guarantee success but they will increase a practice's potential.

5.15 KEYS TO A/R AND COLLECTIONS SUCCESS

- USE OF INFORMATION
  TECHNOLOGY
- INVOLVED PHYSICIANS
- CLOSE WATCH ON TRENDS IN THE
  HEALTHCARE MARKET
- OUTSOURCED BILLING FUNCTIONS
- LOOKING AT DATA FROM
  DIFFERENT ANGLES
- USE OF AN ELECTRONIC HEALTH
  RECORD SYSTEM
- IN-HOUSE BILLING AND
  COLLECTIONS PROCEDURES
- VOLUNTEER EFFORTS IN THE
  COMMUNITY

- AGGRESSIVE INCENTIVE PLAN FOR
  EMPLOYEES
- CODING AUDITS
- PHYSICIANS ENGAGED IN BILLING
  PROCESSES
- PHYSICIANS DEDICATED TO THEIR
  PATIENTS
- AN INTERNAL REPORT CARD FOR
  BENCHMARKING
- DEDICATED STAFF WORKING AS A
  TEAM
- STAFF WITH A VESTED INTEREST IN
  MAKING THE PRACTICE SUCCESSFUL

Total A/R per FTE Physician

Goal: Higher the better

$$\frac{\text{Total A/R}}{\text{Total FTE physicians}}$$

Gross Fee-For-Service (FFS) Collection Percentage

Goal: Higher the better

$$\frac{\text{Gross FFS charges}}{\text{Gross FFS collections}}$$

Gross FFS Charges per FTE Physician

Goal: Higher the better

$$\frac{\text{Gross FFS charges}}{\text{Total FTE physicians}}$$

Adjustments to FFS Charges per FTE Physician

Goal: Lower the better

$$\frac{\text{Gross FFS charges} - \text{adjusted FFS charges}}{\text{Total FTE physicians}}$$

Number of Business Office Support Staff per FTE Physician

Goal: Depends on the practice; however, according to the research, a balance between practice productivity and number of support staff is necessary

$$\frac{\text{Total number of business office support staff}}{\text{Total FTE physicians}}$$

Business Office Support Staff Cost per FTE Physician

Goal: Depends on the practice; however, according to the research, a balance between practice productivity and number of support staff is necessary

$$\frac{\text{Total cost of business office support staff}}{\text{Total FTE physicians}}$$

Bad Debt as a % of Charges (or per FTE physician or provider)6

Goal: Lower the better

$$\frac{\text{Total A/R written off to bad debt (e.g., three-month time period)}}{\text{Total gross charges (same time period as above)}}$$

EXHIBIT 15.16 OTHER METHODS/MEASURES FOR IMPROVING A/R AND COLLECTIONS[5]

- A/R AS A PERCENT OF GROSS CHARGES6

- ADJUSTED COLLECTIONS PERCENT

- ADJUSTMENTS TO FSS CHARGES

- AGED ACCOUNTS BY PAYER

- BAD DEBTS DUE TO FFS ACTIVITY PER FTE PHYSICIAN

- CLAIM TURNAROUND

- COLLECTIONS PER TOTAL RVU (OR PER TOTAL WORK RVU)6

- (AGING REPORTS)

- DAYS AND MONTHS GROSS FFS CHARGES IN A/R

- EOB REVIEW (USED TO DETERMINE DENIAL RATES, AUDIT PAYERS, AND ASSESS FEE SCHEDULE)

- GENERAL ACCOUNTING SUPPORT STAFF COST PER FTE PHYSICIAN

- PATIENT ACCOUNTING SUPPORT STAFF COST PER FTE PHYSICIAN

- PAYER MIX AS A PERCENT OF CHARGES

- PAYER MIX AS A PERCENT OF COLLECTIONS

- PERCENT OF TOTAL A/R 0 – 30 DAYS, 31 – 60 DAYS, 61 – 90 DAYS, 91 – 120 DAYS, AND 120+ DAYS

- TIME TO GENERATE A CLAIM (INCLUDING AMBULATORY AND HOSPITAL ENCOUNTERS)

- TOTAL A/R

- TOTAL NUMBER OF GENERAL ACCOUNTING SUPPORT STAFF PER FTE PHYSICIAN

- TOTAL NUMBER OF PATIENT ACCOUNTING SUPPORT STAFF PER FTE PHYSICIAN

PATIENT SATISFACTION

The healthcare environment has increasingly become more competitive and consumer-driven; therefore, most practices have recognized the key role patient satisfaction plays as patient loyalty and word-of-mouth advertising determine practice success and longevity. Many practices identified as better performers have provided tips for maximizing patient satisfaction and reducing the costs associated with poor patient satisfaction (see Exhibit 15.17).

EXHIBIT 15.17 FIVE STEPS TO BETTER PATIENT SATISFACTION AND THE COSTS OF POOR PATIENT SATISFACTION[4]

FIVE STEPS TO BETTER PATIENT SATISFACTION	COSTS OF POOR PATIENT SATISFACTION
• ENSURE PHYSICIANS AND STAFF UNDERSTAND THE PRACTICE'S PHILOSOPHIES IN DELIVERING CARE	• COSTS OF HANDLING IRATE CUSTOMERS OFTEN TAKE MULTIPLE LEVELS OF PERSONNEL
• DEFINE THE FEEDBACK PROCESS	• COST OF NEGATIVE PUBLICITY
• LINK SERVICE DELIVERY WITH PERFORMANCE PLAN	• LOST REVENUE FROM THE INABILITY TO ACCEPT NEW PATIENTS IN A TIMELY MANNER
• COMMUNICATE PRACTICE VALUES REGULARLY	• LOST REVENUE DUE TO STAFF WHO DO NOT FOCUS ON PATIENT SATISFACTION
• DEFINE AND EXPLAIN HOW PHYSICIANS AND STAFF WILL BE MEASURED	• COST OF DAMAGED MARKETING EFFORTS
	• LOSS OF REFERRAL RELATIONSHIPS

Practices selected by MGMA as better performing in the patient satisfaction category provided several of their keys to success (see Exhibit 15.18). These keys were used by real practices and resulted in success through best practices. The use of these keys does not guarantee success but they will increase a practice's potential.

EXHIBIT 15.18 KEYS TO PATIENT SATISFACTION SUCCESS

- KEEP A SMALL-PRACTICE PERSPECTIVE
- SURVEYING PATIENTS ON MANY SATISFACTION MEASURES
- RETAINING EMPLOYEES
- FOCUSING ON ONE PATIENT FOR ONE PHYSICIAN FOR LIFE
- HIGH PATIENT SATISFACTION FEEDBACK FROM SURVEYS
- STAFF FOCUS AND DEDICATION TO QUALITY CARE AND VALUED SERVICES
- BENCHMARKING WITH KEY INDICATOR REPORTS
- ADDING OPEN-ACCESS SCHEDULING

- LOW MANAGEMENT OVERHEAD
- STRONG, DECISIVE PHYSICIAN OWNERS
- COMMITMENT TO AN ESTABLISHED VISION AND CORE VALUES
- RESPECT FOR ALL PATIENTS AND STAFF
- PHILOSOPHY THAT ENCOURAGES STAFF INVOLVEMENT IN DECISION-MAKING
- CONTINUAL PROCESS IMPROVEMENT AND STREAMLINING PATIENT CARE
- PHYSICIANS WHO CREATE A GOOD WORKING ENVIRONMENT

Better performing practices have identified the following key patient satisfaction measures: access, staff performance, practice and patient communication, physician performance, overall patient satisfaction, willingness to refer other patients to the practice, and facilities (see Exhibit 15.19).5 In addition, many practices seeking improved patient satisfaction measured their progress using metrics related to ease of making an appointment, facility access, waiting time, staff courtesy, physician treatment of patients, and quality of medical care.[4]

EXHIBIT 15.19 OTHER METHODS FOR IMPROVING PATIENT SATISFACTION[5]

- USE OF...

- PATIENT SATISFACTION SURVEYS

- PHYSICIAN SATISFACTION SURVEYS

- EMPLOYEE/STAFF SATISFACTION SURVEYS

- REFERRAL PHYSICIAN SATISFACTION SURVEYS

- EXISTENCE OF A PATIENT SAFETY PROGRAM

- PHYSICIANS FORMALLY MEET TO DISCUSS CLINICAL ISSUES

- PRACTICE HAS A WEB SITE

- PRACTICE CONSIDERS THE FOLLOWING IMPORTANT AREAS FOR EXTRA ATTENTION:

- A/R

- INFORMATION TECHNOLOGY

- HUMAN RESOURCE MANAGEMENT

- GOVERNANCE

- PHYSICIAN-ADMINISTRATOR TEAM

- PHYSICIAN COMPENSATION PROGRAM

- PATIENT SATISFACTION

- PRACTICE RELATIONSHIPS WITH HOSPITALS AND PAYERS

- PRACTICE RESPONSE TO ENVIRONMENTAL CHANGES

- DEVELOPMENT OF NEW REVENUE SOURCES

- BALANCING PHYSICIAN AUTONOMY

- CONTAINING COSTS

MANAGED CARE OPERATIONS

Practices identified as better performers seek to optimize their managed care operations, to include, negotiating contracts, managing charges and collections, utilization reviews, and credentialing.5 Ultimately, improved managed care operations result in increased quality of care and profits and decreased costs.5 Better performing practices have provided the following behaviors for improving managed care operations performance (see Exhibit 15.20).

EXHIBIT 15.20 BEHAVIORS FOR IMPROVING MANAGED CARE OPERATIONS PERFORMANCE[5]

- SUPPORT MANAGED CARE OBJECTIVES BY PROVIDING PREVENTATIVE AND QUALITATIVE PATIENT CARE

- IMPROVE PATIENT OUTCOMES THROUGH A VARIETY OF CHRONIC DISEASE MANAGEMENT PROGRAMS

- REVIEW AND MANAGE CONTRACTS

- ADDRESS OPERATIONAL PROBLEMS THAT DELAY TIMELY ACCESS TO CARE

- ESTABLISH AND MONITOR PERFORMANCE GOALS

Practices selected by MGMA as better performing in the managed care operations category provided several of their keys to success (see Exhibit 15.21). These keys were used by real practices and resulted in success through best practices. The use of these keys does not guarantee success but they will increase a practice's potential.

EXHIBIT 15.21 KEYS TO MANAGED CARE SUCCESS[4, 5]

- PROVIDE PHYSICIANS WITH MOBILE TECHNOLOGY TO INCREASE EFFICIENCY

- COORDINATE EHR, LABORATORY, AND COMPUTER SYSTEMS TO COMMUNICATE WITH ONE ANOTHER

- STAY INFORMED OF ADVANCES IN TECHNOLOGY AND CHANGES IN YOUR COMMUNITY

- USE STATE LAWS TO LOOK FOR INNOVATING WAYS TO STRUCTURE OPERATIONS

- OFFER EXTENSIVE PROVIDER NETWORKS TO KEEP REFERRALS IN-HOUSE

- BE CREATIVE IN THE REFERRAL AUTHORIZATION PROCESS

- HAVE SPECIALIST IN-SERVICE PROGRAMS FOR PRIMARY CARE PHYSICIANS

- MULTIPLE SITE LOCATIONS CLOSE TO WORK AND HOME FOR PATIENTS

- ALTERNATE WORK SCHEDULE FOR STAFF WITH EXTENDED PRACTICE HOURS

- TREAT PHYSICIANS WHO ARE EMPLOYEES AS OWNERS

- INSTITUTE A SINGLE FORMULARY THAT INCORPORATES ALL INSURANCE PLAN FORMULARIES

- INVEST IN NEW TECHNOLOGY THAT PROVIDES PATIENTS WITH SUBSTANTIAL RESULTS

- INCORPORATE NEW POSITIONS INTO THE PRACTICE THAT INCREASE CARE AND COST CONTAINMENT

- PARTNER WITH LOCAL AREA HOSPITALS TO EXPAND PRODUCTS AND SERVICES

- CREATE PROGRAMS THAT HELP THE PHYSICIAN BE MORE EFFICIENT

- USE TECHNOLOGY TO FOSTER CROSS-COMMUNICATION BETWEEN PRIMARY AND SPECIALTY CARE PHYSICIANS

- COLLABORATION AND INNOVATION

- BILINGUAL STAFF

- MIX OF ON-SITE AND ANCILLARY SERVICES

Net Capitation Revenue as a Percent of Gross Capitation Charges

Goal: Higher the better

$$\frac{\text{Net capitation revenue} * 100}{\text{Gross capitation charges}}$$

Number of Visits by per Member per Month (PMPM)

Goal: Depends on the proportion of total revenue derived from capitation payments; if capitation payments account for the majority share of total revenue, then higher the better (direct relationship)

$$\frac{\text{Total number of visits by capitation patients}}{\text{Total number of unique capitation patients seen}}$$

Number of Referrals per 1000 Members

Goal: Depends on many practice factors; should be balanced between physician and practice productivity expectations and needs of the patients

Step 1:

$$\frac{\text{Total number of unique patients seen}}{1000}$$

Step 2:

$$\frac{\text{Number of referrals}}{\text{Result from Step 1}}$$

Number of Bed Days per 1000 Members

Goal: Depends on many practice factors; should be balanced between physician and practice productivity expectations and needs of the patients

Step 1:

$$\frac{\text{Total number of unique patients seen}}{1000}$$

Step 2:

$$\frac{\text{Number of bed days}}{\text{Result from Step 1}}$$

Total Physician Work Relative Value Units (RVUs) per Physician

Goal: Depends on many practice factors; should be balanced between physician and practice productivity expectations and needs of the patients

Total physician work RVUs per physician

Total Relative Value Units (RVUs) per Physician

Goal: Depends on many practice factors; should be balanced between physician and practice productivity expectations and needs of the patients

Total RVUs per physician

Cost per Visit per Case

Goal: Depends on many practice factors; should be balanced between physician and practice productivity expectations and needs of the patients

$$\frac{\text{Total cost}}{\text{Total number of capitation patient encounters/visits}}$$

Cost per Visit per Covered Life

Goal: Depends on many practice factors; should be balanced between physician and practice productivity expectations and needs of the patients

$$\frac{\text{Total cost}}{\text{Total number of unique capitation patients seen}}$$

Patient Panel Size per Physician

Goal: Depends on many practice factors; should be balanced between physician and practice productivity expectations

Total number of unique capitation patients seen per physician

Charges by Payer Type

Goal: Depends on many practice factors; should be directly related to the type of coverage by patient seen

Sum of charges organized by payer type

Revenue by Payer Type

Goal: Depends on many practice factors; should be directly related to the type of coverage by patient seen and contracted rates

Revenue organized by payer type

EXHIBIT 15.22 OTHER MANAGED CARE OPERATIONS MEASURES

- NET CAPITATION REVENUE AS A PERCENT OF TOTAL REVENUE
- TOTAL MEDICAL REVENUE PER FTE PHYSICIAN
- MEDICAL REVENUE AFTER OPERATING COST PER FTE PHYSICIAN
- NET CAPITATION REVENUE PER FTE PHYSICIAN
- CAPITATION REVENUE PER FTE PHYSICIAN
- GROSS CAPITATION CHARGES PER FTE PHYSICIAN
- TOTAL GROSS CHARGES PER FTE PHYSICIAN
- PATIENTS PER FTE PHYSICIAN
- TOTAL PROCEDURES PER FTE PHYSICIAN
- SQUARE FEET PER FTE PHYSICIAN
- PURCHASED SERVICES FOR CAPITATION PATIENTS PER FTE PHYSICIAN
- TOTAL NON-PHYSICIAN PROVIDERS PER FTE PHYSICIAN
- TOTAL EMPLOYED SUPPORT STAFF PER FTE PHYSICIAN

OTHER FORMULAS

The following formulas were also used to evaluate practices in the categories presented earlier (e.g., profitability and cost management, etc.). In addition to formulas presented earlier in this chapter, the following calculations can be used to gain additional insight into the operational and business discipline activities of a practice.

Adjusted Fee-For-Service Charges

Goal: Higher the better

$$\text{Gross FFS Charges - Adjustments to FFS Charges}$$

Adjusted Fee-For-Service Collection Percentage

Goal: Higher the better

$$\frac{\text{Net FFS Revenue} * 100}{\text{Adjusted FFS Charges}}$$

Days of Gross Fee-For-Service Charges in A/R

Goal: Lower the better

$$\frac{\text{Total A/R}}{\text{Gross FFS charges}}$$

Months of Gross Fee-For-Service Charges in A/R

Goal: Lower the better

$$\frac{\text{Total A/R}}{\text{Gross FFS charges}}$$

Gross Fee-For-Service Collection Percentage

Goal: Higher the better

$$\frac{(\text{Net FFS revenue} * 100)}{\text{Gross FFS charges}}$$

Net Capitation Revenue to Gross Capitation Charges Ratio

Goal: Higher the better

$$\frac{\text{Net capitation revenue} * 100}{\text{Gross capitation charges}}$$

[1] The Traits of Successful Medical Groups. *Performance and Practices of Successful Medical Groups*, 2005 Report Based on 2004 Data. Englewood: Medical Group Management Association; 2005.

[2] MGMA. *Performance and Practices of Successful Medical Groups*, 1998 Report Based on 1997 Data. Englewood: Medical Group Management Association.

[3] MGMA. (2005). *Performance and Practices of Successful Medical Groups*, 2005 Report Based on 2004 Data. Englewood: Medical Group Management Association.

[4] MGMA. (2004). *Performance and Practices of Successful Medical Groups*, 2004 Report Based on 2003 Data. Englewood: Medical Group Management Association.

[5] MGMA. (2003). *Performance and Practices of Successful Medical Groups*, 2003 Report Based on 2002 Data. Englewood: Medical Group Management Association.

[6] *The Physician Billing Process*, 3rd edition (2016). Englewood: Medical Group Management Association.

CONCLUSION AND FUTURE IMPLICATIONS

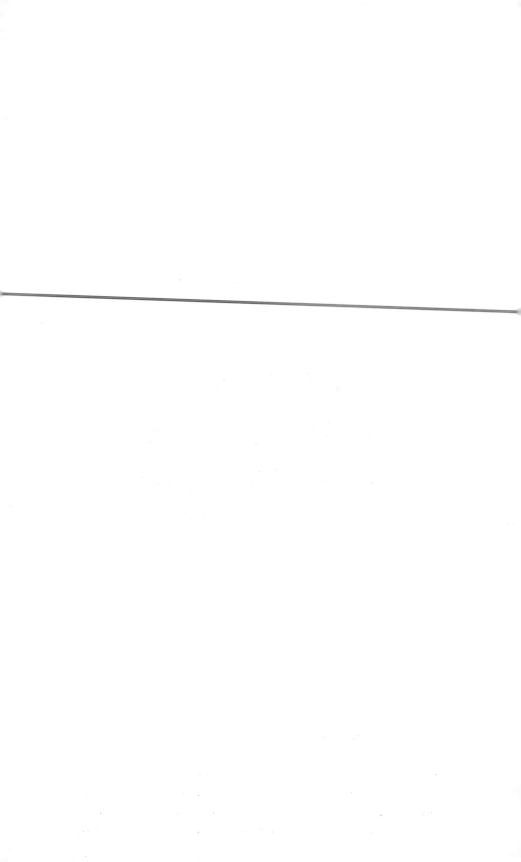

"If you only have a hammer, you tend to see every problem as a nail."
- Abraham Maslow

B enchmarking will continue to be an invaluable tool for comparison and practice improvement as challenges and changes in the practice continue to emerge. Legislation, costs, compensation plans, value-based care, health savings accounts, advances in technology, and an emphasis on outcomes and patient satisfaction, to name a few, all contribute to the need for measurement, benchmarking, and practice improvement. More than likely, the methods, formulas, and ratios presented in this book will not change significantly. However, the focus on particular benchmarks may change depending on the particular needs of a given practice, changes in the regulatory environment, or due to changes in payment/reimbursement methods or physician compensation (e.g., pay-for-performance or value-based) programs.

There are several frameworks that can be used to design and focus benchmarking activities. For instance, the Institute of Healthcare Improvement Triple Aim Initiative[1]: (1) improving the patient experience of care, (2) improving the health of populations, and (3) reducing the per capita cost of healthcare. Also, other frameworks for designing and focusing benchmarking activities can be used such as (1) cost, quality, and access and (2) people, environment, and process, or (3) the 3-Ps of success (profitability, productivity, and performance).

Historically, benchmarking and operational improvement have been focused on the financial performance area, and although this area remains very important to the success and longevity of a practice, greater emphasis is being placed on patient satisfaction and clinical quality/outcomes. With this shift to add greater attention to non-financial measures, the development and wide-spread use of new patient satisfaction and clinical metrics will start to appear. In particular, high patient satisfaction results in high perceived quality of care, fewer no-shows and cancellations, and greater patient loyalty. And clinical metrics are being used to establish reimbursement, physician pay-for-performance (P4P) programs, monitor population health initiatives, and satisfy value-based payment contracts (or risk-based contracts).

"The healthcare industry is the only service industry that doesn't act like one." This was a profound statement made at a MGMA Conference during a session that presented a case study of a practice using techniques proven to be successful by non-healthcare companies (e.g., customer service methods used by Disney, supply chain management by Wal-Mart). Best practices and lessons learned can be found and adapted from any industry and the methods, measures, and data used to benchmark will continue to evolve. In addition, the ability of the healthcare industry to adapt and remain flexible will ensure its long-term success and value.

Therefore, the techniques presented in this book will serve as a foundation and guide to benchmarking, but their limitations should not be overlooked. Don't use a hammer to put in a screw—use the right tool for the right job. When benchmarks and benchmarking are used properly, they can uncover hidden treasures, open people's eyes, create buy-in, improve financial performance, and increase patient and staff satisfaction and clinical quality/outcomes.

---

[1] www.ihi.org/Engage/Initiatives/TripleAim/Pages/default.aspx (2017).

APPENDIX I: EXAMPLE PRACTICE

As stated in the Introduction, the items in this Appendix are meant to help organize the benchmarking tools presented in this book. Most variables for the formulas and ratios are associated with the following example accounts receivable aging report, operational report, balance sheet, and income statement.

Description:

Single-specialty family practice without OB services

12 FTE physicians (no non-physician providers)

Physician compensation based partly on collections for professional charges (incentive/bonus based on service quality)

Accounting method: Income Tax basis; Internal Revenue Code Section 446(a) requires that taxable income be computed on the same basis of accounting the taxpayer uses in keeping its books.

Legal organization: Professional Corporation (physicians as sole owners)

Centralized administrative department

Local area: Metropolitan (population of 250,001 to 1,000,000)

Balance Sheet and Income Statement adapted from Physician Practice Management: Essential Operational and Financial Knowledge, Edited by Lawrence F. Wolper (2005)

PATIENT AGED TRIAL BALANCE (AGED A/R)		
0 - 30 days	$ 399,338	58%
31 - 60 days	$ 96,392	14%
61 - 90 days	$ 55,081	8%
91 - 120 days	$ 27,541	4%
> 120 days	$ 110,162	16%
Total	$ 688,514	100%

OPERATIONS REPORT (FOR THE YEAR ENDING DECEMBER 31)

Total FTE physicians	12	
Total FTE business operations support staff	12.36	22%
Total FTE front-office support staff	18.84	34%
Total FTE clinical support staff	18.48	34%
Total FTE ancillary support staff	5.28	10%
Total FTE support staff	54.96	100%
Payers:		
Medicare: fee-for-service		14.0%
Medicare: managed care FFS		2.0%
Medicare: capitated		0.4%
Medicaid: FFS		4.0%
Medicaid: managed care FFS		0.7%
Medicaid: capitated		0.3%
Commercial: FFS		43.0%
Commerical payer #1		40.0%
Commercial payer #2		31.0%
Commercial payer #3		17.0%
Commercial payer #4		12.0%
Commerical: managed care FFS		24.0%
Commerical: capitated		2.5%
Workers' compensation		1.1%
Charity care and professional courtesy		1.6%
Self-pay		6.0%
Other government payers		0.1%
Total gross charges		100%
Total square footage	22,800	
Total Physician Work RVUs	61,476	
Total RVUs	123,576	
Total unique patient seen	29,352	
New patients	3,229	11%
Established patients	26,123	89%
Total procedures	121,452	
Total encounters	70,692	
Clinical services hours worked per week	Average = 36.74	Median = 36
Weeks worked per year	Average = 46.99	Median = 47

BALANCE SHEET (FOR THE YEAR ENDING DECEMBER 31)

		2017
Assets		
Current assets:		
Cash	$	25,000
Marketable securities	$	25,000
Accounts receivable - other	$	1,300
Total current assets	$	51,300
Investments:		
Investment in securities	$	-
Property held for future use	$	50,000
Total investments	$	50,000
Long-Term Receivables:		
Notes receivable - physicians	$	10,000
Property and Equipment, at Cost:		
Leasehold improvements	$	68,200
Equipment	$	688,100
	$	756,300
Less Accumulated Depreciation:	$	429,400
Property and equipment, net	$	326,900
Other Assets:		
Goodwill, net of accumulated amortization of $200,000	$	40,000
Total assets	$	478,200
Liabilities and stockholders' equity		
Current liabilities:		
Notes and loans payable	$	23,500
Current maturities of long-term debt	$	102,000
Accrued benefits and payroll taxes	$	45,000
Total current liabilities	$	170,500
Long-term notes payable		
Long-term debt, less current maturities	$	285,000
Total liabilities	$	455,500
Stockholders' Equity:		
Common stock, $1 par, authorized 200,000 shares; issued and outstanding 100,000 shares	$	10,000
Capital contributed in excess of par	$	140,000
Retained earnings (deficit)	$	(127,300)
Total stockholders' equity	$	22,700
Total liabilities and stockholders' equity	$	478,200

Source: adapted from Physician Practice Management: Essential Operational and Financial Knowledge, edited by Lawrence F. Wolper (2005), Jones and Bartlett Publishers.

Income Statement (for the year ending December 31)

		2017
Revenues:		
Net FFS revenue	$	4,180,700
Capitation revenue	$	551,100
Other revenue	$	133,500
Net revenue	$	4,865,300
Operating expenses:		
Salary and fringe benefits:		
Business operations support staff salaries	$	405,280
Front office support staff salaries	$	357,600
Clinical support staff salaries	$	429,120
Ancillary support staff salaries	$	178,100
Payroll taxes	$	108,400
Employee benefits	$	129,100
Total salaries and benefits	$	1,607,600
Service and general expenses:		
Professional liability insurance (malpractice insurance)	$	85,900
Medical supplies and drugs (clinical and other)	$	201,300
Depreciation	$	190,200
Amortization	$	4,000
Rent	$	186,000
Other general and administrative	$	474,600
Total services and general expenses	$	1,142,000
Purchased services:		
Purchased outside professional services	$	294,000
Purchased data processing services	$	-
Total purchased services	$	294,000
Provider-Related Expenses:		
Physician salaries and benefits	$	1,828,800
Total operating expenses	$	4,872,400
Income (Loss) from operations	$	(7,100)
Other Income (Expenses):		
Interest expense (net)	$	(34,100)
Income from long-term investments	$	3,500
Other income (expense), net	$	(30,600)
Income before provision for income taxes	$	(37,700)
Provision for income taxes		
Net income (loss)	$	(37,700)
Retained earnings (deficit), beginning of year	$	(89,600)
Retained earnings (deficit), end of year	$	(127,300)

Source: adapted from Physician Practice Management: Essential Operational and Financial Knowledge, edited by Lawrence F. Wolper (2005), Jones and Bartlett Publishers.

GLOSSARY

A

accounting methods:

cash: An accounting system in which revenues are recorded when cash is received and costs are recorded when cash is paid out. Receivables, payables, accruals, and deferrals arising from operations are ignored. On a pure cash basis, long-lived (fixed) assets are expensed when acquired, leaving cash and investments as the only assets and borrowings and payroll withholds as the only liabilities.

accrual: An accounting system in which revenues are recorded as earned when services are performed rather than when cash is received. Cost is recorded in the period during which it is incurred; that is, when the asset or service is used, regardless of when cash is paid. Costs for goods and services that will be used to produce revenues in the future are reported as assets and recorded as costs in future periods. The accrual system balance sheet includes not only the assets and liabilities from the cash basis balance sheet but also the receivables from patients, prepayments and deferrals of costs, accruals of costs and revenues, and payables to suppliers.

income tax: A system used to file an income tax return and based on federal tax laws.

modified cash: An accounting system that is primarily a cash basis system but allows the cost of long-lived (fixed) assets to be expensed through depreciation. The modified cash system recognizes inventories of goods intended for resale as assets. Under a modified cash system, purchases of buildings and equipment, leasehold improvements, and payments of insurance premiums applicable to more than one accounting period are normally recorded as assets. Costs for these assets are allocated to accounting periods in a systematic manner over the length of time the practice benefits from the assets.

accounts receivable current to 30 days: Amounts owed to the practice by patients, third-party payers, employer groups, and unions for fee-for-service activities before adjustments for anticipated payment reductions or allowances for adjustments or bad debts. Amounts assigned to accounts receivable (A/R) are due to "gross fee for service charges." Assignment of a charge into A/R is initiated at the time an invoice is submitted to a payer or patient for payment. For example, if an obstetrics practice establishes an open account for accumulation of charges when a patient is accepted into a prenatal program and the account will not be invoiced until after delivery, then A/R will not reflect these charges until an invoice is created. Deletion of charges from A/R is done when the account is paid, turned over to a collection agency, or written off as bad debt. "Accounts payable to patients and payers" are subtracted from A/R before reporting A/R. This is the net amount owed after patient refunds. Do not include capitation payments owed to the practice by HMOs.

adjusted RVU values for modifier usage: Modifiers that cause adjustments to RVU values include ones for additional complexity or multiple procedures such as -21, -22, -51, -80 and modifiers for technical and professional component billing such as -26, -TC (technical component).

administrative supplies and services cost: This consists of cost of printing, postage, books, subscriptions, administrative and medical forms, stationery, bank processing fees, and other administrative supplies and services. This should also include purchased medical transcription services.

ambulatory surgery center: Freestanding entity that is specifically licensed to provide surgery services performed on a same-day outpatient basis.

ASA units: American Society of Anesthesiology relative units.

average: Measure of central tendency and the arithmetic mean of a data set (or mathematical center; also known as the mean).

adjusted charges: See adjustments to fee-for-service charges.

adjustments to fee-for-service charges: Difference between "gross fee-for-service charges" and the amount expected to be paid by patients or third-party payers. This represents the value of services performed for which payment is not expected. This should also include (1) Medicare and Medicaid charge restrictions (the difference between the practice's full, undiscounted charge and the Medicare limiting charge); (2) third-party payer contractual adjustments (commercial insurance and/or managed care organization);

(3) charitable, professional courtesy, or employee adjustments; and (4) the difference between a gross charge and the Federally Qualified Health Center payment.

B

bad debts due to fee-for-service activity: Difference between adjusted fee-for-service charges and the amount actually collected. This should also include (1) losses on settlements for less than the billed amount; (2) accounts written off as not collectible; (3) accounts assigned to collection agencies; and (4) the provision for bad debts, in the case of accrual accounting.

bell-shaped curve: See normal distribution.

benchmarking: Continual process of measuring and comparing key work process indicators with those of best performers. The overall objective is to facilitate organizational improvement by identifying best processes and practices through accurate and relevant measurement. In other words, successful benchmarking demonstrates to organizations how to improve their performance and profitability through evidence-based management.

best practices: Proven services, functions, or processes that have been shown to produce superior outcomes or results in benchmarks that meet or set a new standard. However, there is no single best practice or "silver bullet." Instead, "best" refers to what is optimal for a particular organization, given its patients, mission, community, culture, and external environment.

billing and collections purchased services: When a medical practice decides to purchase billing and collections services from an outside organization as opposed to hiring and developing its own employed staff to conduct billing and collections activities, the cost for such purchased services should be considered "billing and collections purchased services." This should also include claims clearinghouse cost.

branch or satellite clinic: Smaller clinical facility for which the practice incurs occupancy costs, such as lease, depreciation, and utilities. A branch is in a separate location from the practice's principal facility. Merely having physicians practice in another location does not qualify that location as a branch or satellite clinic. For example, if a physician sees patients in a hospital, this would not normally be counted as a branch or satellite clinic unless the practice pays rent for the space.

building and occupancy cost: Cost of general operation of buildings and grounds. Include (1) rental, operating lease, and leasehold improvements for buildings and grounds; (2) depreciation cost for buildings and grounds; (3) interest paid on loans for real estate used in practice operations; (4) cost of utilities such as water, electric power, and space heating fuels; (5) cost of supplies and materials used in housekeeping and maintenance; and (6) other costs such as building repairs and security systems. Do not include (1) interest paid on short-term loans, which is included in "miscellaneous operating cost"; (2) interest paid on loans for real estate not used in practice operations such as non-medical office space in practice-owned properties; such interest is included in nonmedical costs; or (3) cost of producing revenue from sources such as parking lots or leased office space from practice-owned properties.

business corporation: For-profit organization recognized by law as a business entity separate and distinct from its shareholders. Shareholders need not be licensed in the profession practiced by the corporation.

C

capacity: see *throughput*

capitation: Process when a provider organization receives a fixed, previously negotiated periodic payment per member covered by the health plan in exchange for delivering specified health care services to the members for a specified length of time regardless of how many or how few services are actually required or rendered. Per member per month is the commonplace calculation unit for such capitation payments.

capitation contract: Contract in which the practice agrees to provide medical services to a defined population for a fixed price per beneficiary per month, regardless of actual services provided. Capitation contracts always contain an element of risk.

centralized administrative department: Provides leadership and has the authority and responsibility for the operations of the various physician practices within the entity. This department provides oversight and encompasses many or all of the following types of activities: establishing policies, negotiating managed care agreements, strategic planning, physician contracting, approving expenditures, and affording any other resources required to manage the physician practices.

central tendency: Center of the distribution of data, which consists of the mean, median, and mode.

charity care and professional courtesy: Charity patients are those not covered by either commercial insurance or federal, state, or local governmental health care programs and who do not have the resources to pay for services. Charity patients must be identified at the time that service is provided so that a bill for service is not prepared. Professional courtesy charges are included in this category. Fee-for-service gross charges, at the practice's undiscounted rates, for all services provided to charity patients.

clinical laboratory and pathology procedures: This consists of (1) 36415 and 36416, venous and capillary blood collection; (2) 80048-89356, a panel of tests represented by a single current procedural terminology (CPT) code and considered to be one procedure; (3) HCPCS P codes; (4) all clinical laboratory and pathology procedures conducted by laboratories outside of the practice's facilities as long as the practice pays the outside laboratory directly for the procedures and the procedures are only for the practice's fee-for-service patients. The cost for these purchased laboratory services should be reported as a subset of "clinical laboratory"; and (5) all procedures done either at the practice (where the practice bills at a global rate for both the technical and professional components) or procedures done at an outside facility (where the practice bills at a professional rate only). This should not include purchased laboratory services from external providers and facilities on behalf of the practice's capitation patients for which costs are reported as "purchased services for capitation patients."

clinical laboratory cost: This consists of cost of clinical laboratory and pathology procedures defined by CPT codes 80048-89356, 36415, and 36416. This should also include (1) rental and/or depreciation cost of major furniture and equipment subject to capitalization; (2) repair and maintenance contract cost; (3) cost of supplies and minor equipment not subject to capitalization; (4) other costs unique to the clinical laboratory; and (5) cost of purchased laboratory technical services for fee-for-service patients. This should not include: cost of purchased laboratory technical services for capitation patients. Such cost should be reported as purchased services for capitation patients.

clinical laboratory FTE: This consists of procedures for clinical laboratory and pathology CPT codes 80048-89356, 36415, and 36416. This should also include (1) FTE and cost of support staff such as nurses, secretaries, and technicians and (2) FTE and cost of department director or manager.

clinical science department: A unit of organization in a medical school with an independent chair and a single budget. The department's mission is to conduct teaching, research and/or clinical activities related to the entire spectrum of health care delivery to humans, from prevention through treatment.

clinical support staff: Registered nurses, licensed practical nurses, medical assistants, and nurse's aides.

commercial—capitation: Fee-for-service (FSS) equivalent gross charges, at the practice's undiscounted rates, for all services provided to patients under a commercial capitated contract. This should not include: (1) charges for FSS patients; or (2) charges for patients covered under discounted FSS contract arrangements.

commercial—fee-for-service: Fee-for-service gross charges, at the practice's undiscounted rates, for all services provided to fee-for-service patients who were covered by commercial contracts that do not include a withhold but may or may not include a performance-based incentive. A commercial contract is any contract that is not Medicare, Medicaid, or workers' compensation. This should not include charges for: (1) Medicare patients; (2) Medicaid patients; (3) capitation patients; (4) patients covered by a managed care plan; (5) workers' compensation patients; (6) charity or professional courtesy patients; or (7) self-pay patients.

commercial—managed care fee-for service: Fee-for-service gross charges, at the practice's undiscounted rates, for all services provided to patients who were covered by managed care contracts that include a withhold and may or may not include a performance- based incentive. A commercial contract is any contract that is not Medicare, Medicaid, or workers' compensation. This should also include charges for patients covered under discounted fee-for-service contract arrangements. This should not include charges for (1) Medicare patients; (2) Medicaid patients; (3) capitation patients; (4) workers' compensation patients; (5) charity or professional courtesy patients; or (6) self-pay patients.

continuous data: Data that can be divided and subdivided into equal-sized subunits (e.g., a meter can be subdivided into centimeters, which can be subdivided into millimeters, and so on; for the opposite of continuous data, see discrete data).

cost: Amount of resources used to acquire an asset.

cost allocated to medical practice from parent organization: When a medical practice is owned by a hospital, integrated delivery system, or other entity, the parent organization often allocates indirect costs to the medical practice. These indirect costs may have different names depending on the situation, for example, "shared services costs" or "uncontrollable costs." These costs may be arbitrarily assigned to the medical practice, may be the result of negotiations between the practice and the parent organization, or the result of some sort of cost accounting system. Often, these indirect costs include a portion of the salaries of the senior management team of the parent organization, a portion of corporate human resources costs, or a portion of corporate marketing costs. Depending on the type of cost, the cost may be allocated to the medical practice as a function of the ratio of medical practice FTE to total system FTE, the ratio of medical practice square footage to total system square footage, or the ratio of medical practice gross charges to total system gross charges. Depending on the culture of the integrated system, these indirect costs may or may not show up on the financial statements of the medical practice. This should not include cash loans made to subsidiaries.

cost of sales and/or cost of other medical activities: Cost of activities that generate revenue included in "revenue from the sale of medical goods and services," as long as this cost is not also included in total operating cost or nonmedical cost. This should also include cost of pharmaceuticals, medical supplies, and equipment sold to patients primarily for use outside the practice. Examples include prescription drugs, hearing aids, optical goods, and orthopedic supplies. This should not include (1) cost of drugs used in providing services, including vaccinations, allergy injections, immunizations, chemotherapy, and anti-nausea drugs (such cost is included in "drug supply") or (2) cost of supplies and instruments used in providing medical and surgical services (such cost is included in "medical and surgical supply").

current assets: Cash and other assets expected to be converted to cash, sold, or consumed in the normal course of operations within one year.

current liabilities: This consists of (1) payables such as liabilities that mature and require payment from current assets or through the creation of other liabilities within one year; (2) payroll liabilities such as amounts withheld from employees or otherwise accrued; and (3) other current liabilities such as accrued nonpayroll liabilities, advances from settlements due to third-party agencies, patient deposits, estimated contract claims payable (incurred but not reported claims), deferred revenue, and deferred income taxes.

D

diagnostic radiology and imaging procedures: This consists of (1) 70010–76499, diagnostic radiology; (2) 76506–76999, diagnostic ultrasound; (3) 78000—78999, diagnostic nuclear medicine; (4) all diagnostic radiology and imaging procedures conducted by laboratories outside of the practice's facilities as long as the practice pays the outside laboratory directly for the procedures and the procedures are only for the practice's fee-for-service patients; and (5) all procedures done either at the practice (where the practice bills at a global rate for both the technical and professional components) or procedures done at an outside facility (where the practice bills at a professional rate only). This should not include (1) 77261–77799, radiation oncology; (2) 79000–79999, therapeutic nuclear medicine (radiation oncology and therapeutic nuclear medicine activity is included in "medical procedures" on line 111 or 112, depending on location code); or (3) purchased radiology services from external providers and facilities on behalf of the practice's capitation patients for which costs are reported as "purchased services for capitation patients."

discrete data: Unlike continuous data, discrete data cannot be divided or subdivided into equal-sized subunits (e.g., people are nondivisible entities and cannot be subdivided; if there is a group of 10 people, subdividing the group in half and then in half again would result in 2.5 people, and it is not possible to have 0.5 of a person).

drug supply cost: Cost of drugs purchased for general practice use. This should also include cost of chemotherapy drugs, allergy drugs, and vaccines used in providing medical and surgical services. This should not include (1) cost of specialized supplies dedicated for exclusive use in the departments of clinical laboratory, radiology, and imaging or other ancillary services departments or (2) cost of pharmaceuticals sold to patients primarily for use outside the practice and not used in providing medical and surgical services; for example, prescription drugs (such cost is included in "cost of sales and/or cost of other medical activities").

E

encounter: see patient encounters.

expense: Resources consumed by the practice when generating revenue.

extraordinary nonmedical cost: Cost unusual in nature and infrequent in occurrence. This should also include (1) legal settlement cost and (2) environmental disaster recovery cost.

extraordinary nonmedical revenue: Revenue unusual in nature and infrequent in occurrence. This should also include (1) legal settlement receipts and (2) environmental disaster recovery funds.

F

faculty practice plan: Formal framework that structures the clinical practice activities of the medical school faculty. The plan performs a range of services, including billing, collections, contract negotiations, and the distribution of income. Plans may form a separate legal organization or may be affiliated with the medical school through a clinical science department or teaching hospital. Faculty associated with the plan must provide patient care as part of a teaching or research program.

financial support for operating costs: Operational support received from a parent organization such as a hospital, integrated delivery system, or other entity. This should also include operating subsidies received from a hospital, health system, physician practice management company, or management services organization.

freestanding ambulatory surgery center: See **ambulatory surgery center**; a freestanding ambulatory surgery center does not employ physicians.

full-time equivalent (FTE) physicians: Primary care physicians, nonsurgical specialty physicians, and surgical specialty physicians. A full-time physician works whatever number of hours the practice considers to be the minimum for a normal work week, which could be 37.5, 40, 50 hours, or some other standard. To compute the FTE of a part-time physician, divide the total hours worked by the number of hours that your practice considers to be a normal work week. A physician working 30 hours compared to a normal work week of 40 hours would be 0.75 FTE (30 hours divided by 40 hours). A physician working full-time for three months during a year would be 0.25 FTE (3 months divided by 12 months). A medical director devoting 50 percent effort to clinical activity would be 0.5 FTE. A physician cannot be counted as more than 1.0 FTE regardless of the number of hours worked. This should also include (1) practice physicians such as shareholders and partners, salaried associates, employed and contracted physicians and locum tenens; (2) residents and fellows working at the practice; and (3) only physicians involved in clinical care. This should not include full-time physician administrators or the time that a physician devotes to medical director activities. The FTE and cost for such activities should be included as "general administrative."

furniture and equipment cost: Cost of furniture and equipment in general use in the practice. This should also include (1) rental and/or depreciation cost of furniture and equipment used in reception areas, patient treatment and exam rooms, physician offices, and administrative areas and (2) other costs related to clinic furniture and equipment such as maintenance cost. This should not include cost of specialized furniture and equipment dedicated for exclusive use in the information technology, clinical laboratory, radiology and imaging, or other ancillary services departments.

G

general accounting: FTE and cost of general accounting office staff, such as department supervisor, controller, and financial accounting manager; and accounts payable, payroll, bookkeeping, and financial accounting input staff.

general administrative FTE and cost: FTE and cost of general administrative and practice management staff, supporting secretaries, and administrative assistants. This should include FTE and cost of executive staff such as administrator, assistant administrator, chief financial officer, medical director, and site and branch office managers; and human resources, marketing, credentialing and purchasing department staff. This should not include FTE and cost of directors of departments, such as information technology director, medical records director, laboratory director, and radiology director. Credentialing staff as they pertain to managed care departments, such FTE and cost, should be accounted for as "managed care administrative."

general operating cost: This should not include costs (1) for sales and/or other medical activities; (2) for support staff; (3) for nonphysician provider; (4) included in "Purchased services for capitation patients;" and (5) for nonmedical.

goodwill amortization: When an integrated delivery system, hospital, or physician practice management company purchases a medical practice, the purchase price can be thought of as having two components: (1) the value of the tangible assets; and (2) the value of the goodwill. Goodwill is the premium paid in excess of the value of the tangible assets and may be amortized over a period of time. The tangible assets are depreciated over a period of time. This should not include depreciation of tangible assets, such as the building or equipment. These depreciation costs are reported as a component of costs for information technology, building and occupancy, furniture and equipment, clinical laboratory, radiology and imaging, and other ancillary services.

government-owned practice: Ownership by a governmental organization at the federal, state, or local level. Government funding is not a sufficient criterion for ownership. An example would be a medical clinic at a federal, state, or county correctional facility.

gross capitation revenue: Revenue received in a fixed per member payment, usually on a prospective and monthly basis, to pay for all covered goods and services due to capitation patients. This should include (1) per member per month capitation payments including those received from an HMO, Medicare AAPCC (average annual per capita cost), the state for Medicaid beneficiaries, and other medical groups; (2) portions of the capitation withholds returned to a practice as part of a risk-sharing arrangement; (3) bonuses and incentive payments paid to a practice for good capitation contract performance; (4) patient copayments or other direct payments made by capitation patients; (5) payments received due to a coordination of benefits and/or reinsurance recovery situation for capitation patients; and (6) payments made by other payers for care provided to capitation patients. This should not include payments paid to a practice by an HMO under the terms of a discounted fee-for-service managed care contract. Such payments should be included in "net fee-for-service collections/revenue."

gross charges for patients covered by capitation contracts: Full value, at a practice's undiscounted rates, of all covered services provided to patients covered by all capitation contracts, regardless of payer (also known as fee-for-service equivalent gross charges). Include: fee-for-service equivalent gross charges for all services covered under the terms of the practice's capitation contracts, such as: (1) professional services provided by physicians, nonphysician providers, and other physician extenders such as nurses and medical assistants; (2) both the professional and technical components of laboratory, radiology, medical diagnostic, and surgical procedures; (3) drug charges, including vaccinations, allergy injections, immunizations, chemotherapy, and anti-nausea drugs; (4) charges for supplies consumed during a patient encounter inside the practice's facilities; (charges for supplies sold to patients for consumption outside the practice's facilities are reported as a subset of "revenue from the sale of medical goods and services"); and (5) facility fees, including for the operation of an ambulatory surgery unit or of a medical practice owned by a hospital where split billing for professional and facility services is utilized.

This should not include (1) pharmaceuticals, medical supplies, and equipment sold to patients primarily for use outside the practice, including prescription drugs, hearing aids, optical goods, and orthopedic supplies (if such goods are not covered under the capitation contract, the revenue from these charges is included in "revenue from the sale of medical goods and services"); (2) the value of purchased services from external providers and facilities on behalf of the practice's capitation patients (cost of these purchased services is included in "purchased services for capitation patients"); (3) charges for fee-for-service activity allowed under the terms of capitation contracts (such charges are reported as "gross fee-for-service charges"); or (4) capitation revenue (if capitation charges are not tracked, leave space blank).

gross fee-for-service charges: Full value, at the practice's undiscounted rates, of all services provided to fee-for-service (FSS), discounted FSS, and noncapitated patients for all payers. This should include (1) professional services provided by physicians, nonphysician providers, and other physician extenders such as nurses and medical assistants; (2) both the professional and technical components of laboratory, radiology, medical diagnostic, and surgical procedures; (3) contractual adjustments such as Medicare charge restrictions, third-party payer contractual adjustments, charitable adjustments, and professional courtesy adjustments; (4) drug charges, including vaccinations, allergy injections, immunizations, chemotherapy, and anti-nausea drugs; (5) charges for supplies consumed during a patient encounter inside the practice's facilities and charges for supplies sold to patients for consumption outside the practice's facilities, reported as a subset of "revenue from the sale of medical goods and services"; (6) facility fees, including for the operation of an ambulatory surgery unit or of a medical practice owned by a hospital where split billing for professional and facility services is utilized; (7) charges for FFS allowed under the terms of capitation contracts; (8) charges for professional services provided on a case-rate reimbursement basis; and (9) charges for purchased services for FFS patients, defined as services that are purchased by the practice from external providers and facilities on behalf of the practice's FFS patients. For purchased services, note the following: (1) the revenue for such services should be included in "net fee-for-service collections revenue"; (2) the cost for such services should be included, as appropriate, in "clinical laboratory," "radiology and imaging," "other ancillary services" and/

or "provider consultant cost"; and (3) the count of the number of purchased procedures for FFS patients should be included in "number of procedures." This should not include (1) charges for services provided to capitation patients, which are included in "gross charges for patients covered by capitation contracts"; (2) charges for pharmaceuticals, medical supplies, and equipment sold to patients primarily for use outside the practice, including prescription drugs, hearing aids, optical goods, and orthopedic supplies (revenue generated by such charges is included in "revenue from the sale of medical goods and services"); or (3) charges for any other activities that generate the revenue reported in "revenue from the sale of medical goods and services."

gross revenue from other medical activities: In general, this consists of revenue generated from ancillary services and indirect patient care activities. This should not include (1) interest income, which is reported as "nonmedical revenue"; (2) income from practice nonmedical property such as parking areas or commercial real estate, which is reported as "nonmedical revenue"; (3) income from business ventures such as a billing service or parking lot, which is reported as "nonmedical revenue"; (4) onetime gains from the sale of equipment or property, which is reported as "nonmedical revenue"; and (5) cash received from loans.

gross square footage: Total number of finished and occupied square feet within outside walls for all the facilities (both administrative and clinical) that comprise the practice, including hallways, closets, elevators, and stairways. For anesthesia practices, any leased or rented administrative office space, regardless of whether inside or outside a hospital setting, should be included.

H

histogram:

health maintenance organization (HMO): Insurance company that accepts responsibility for providing and delivering a predetermined set of comprehensive health maintenance and treatment services to a voluntarily enrolled population for a negotiated and fixed periodic premium.

hospital: Inpatient facility that admits patients for overnight stays, incurs nursing care costs, and generates bed-day revenues.

housekeeping, maintenance, security: This consists of FTE and cost of housekeeping, maintenance, and security staff. This should not include: FTE and cost of parking attendants if parking generates revenue, which is reported as "nonmedical revenue." The cost of parking attendants should be included as "nonmedical cost."

I

incurred but not reported liability accounts (IBNR): Special liability accounts used by medical practices with capitation contracts to keep track of amounts owed to providers outside the practice for services provided to the practice's capitated patients.

independent practice association (IPA): Association or network of licensed providers and/or medical practices. An IPA is usually a unique legal entity, most often operating on a for-profit basis. Typically, the primary purpose of the IPA is to secure and maintain contractual relationships between providers and health plans.

individual patient: Person who received at least one service from the practice during the 12-month reporting period, regardless of the number of encounters or procedures received by that person. If a person was a patient two years ago but did not receive any services at all last year, that person would not be counted as a patient for last year. A patient is not the same as a covered life. The number of capitated patients, for example, could be less than the number of capitated covered lives if a subset of the covered lives did not utilize any services during the 12-month reporting period.

information technology cost: Cost of practice-wide data processing, computer, telephone, and telecommunications services. This should include (1) cost of local and long-distance telephone, radio paging, and answering services; (2) rental and/or depreciation cost of major data processing, computer, and telecommunications furniture, equipment, hardware, and software subject to capitalization; (3) hardware and software repair and maintenance contract cost; (4) cost of data-processing services purchased from an outside service bureau; and (5) cost of data-processing supplies and minor software and equipment not subject to capitalization. This should not include cost of specialized information services equipment dedicated for exclusive use in the departments of clinical laboratory, radiology and imaging, or other ancillary services departments.

information technology FTE: FTE staff such as data processing, computer programming, telecommunications, and department director or manager.

in-house professional procedures: Medical, surgery, and anesthesia procedures conducted inside the practice's facilities.

in-house professional gross charges: Medical, surgery, and anesthesia gross charges conducted inside the practice's facilities.

intangibles and other assets: Organization costs (legal, accounting, and fees), goodwill, and deposits.

integrated delivery system (IDS): Network of organizations that provide or coordinate and arrange for the provision of a continuum of health care services to consumers and are willing to be held clinically and fiscally responsible for the outcomes and the health status of the populations served. Generally consists of hospitals, physician groups, health plans, home health agencies, hospices, skilled nursing facilities, or other provider entities, these networks may be built through "virtual" integration processes encompassing contractual arrangements and strategic alliances as well as through direct ownership.

insurance company: Organization that indemnifies an insured party against a specified loss in return for premiums paid, as stipulated by a contract.

investments and long-term receivables: Investments meant for purposes that do not include supporting current operations (e.g., long-term receivables, long-term investments, investments in affiliates, and property held for future use).

K

kurtosis: Measures the "peakedness" of a data distribution. If the kurtosis is clearly different than zero, then the distribution is either flatter or more peaked than normal; the kurtosis of a normal distribution is zero. Kurtosis values above zero (positive) indicate a distribution that is too peaked, with short, thick tails; whereas values less than zero (negative) indicate a distribution that is too flat, with too many data points in the tails.

L

levels of measurement: Categories of numerical values related to the aspects of the objects, items, or events they represent (also known as scales of measurement); the levels of measurement are nominal, ordinal (categorical), interval, and ratio.

licensed practical nurses (LPN): This consists of FTE and cost of licensed practical nurses functioning in clinical/direct patient care capacities. This should not include: FTE and cost of licensed practical nurses who worked exclusively in the departments of clinical laboratory, radiology, and imaging or other ancillary departments.

limited liability company (LLC): Legal entity that is a hybrid between a corporation and a partnership, because it provides limited liability to owners such as a corporation while passing profits and losses through to owners such as a partnership.

locum tenens: These are temporary employees and typically consist of temporary providers and physicians hired specifically as employees for a specific period of time (e.g., gap fill).

M

managed care: System in which the provider of care is given incentives to establish mechanisms to contain costs, control utilization, and deliver services in the most appropriate settings. There are three key factors: (1) controlling the utilization of medical services; (2) shifting financial risk to the provider; and (3) reducing the use of resources in rendering treatments to patients.

managed care administrative: FTE and cost of managed care administrative staff, such as supporting secretaries and administrative assistants. This should include health maintenance organization and preferred provider organization contract administrators; case management staff; actuaries; managed care medical directors; and managed care marketing, quality assurance, referral coordinators, utilization review, and credentialing staff.

management fees paid to a management services organization (MSO) or physician practice management company (PPMC): Fees paid for management or other services from an MSO, PPMC, hospital, or other parent organization. The fee could be a contracted fixed amount, a percentage of collections, or any other mutually agreed upon arrangement. This should include (1) fees paid to an MSO/PPMC, hospital, or parent organization for management services, including management, administrative, and/or related support services; and (2) the cost of support staff employed by the MSO or PPMC. If FTE data for the MSO or PPMC support staff is accurate and easily obtainable, it is preferable to report the MSO/PPMC support staff FTE and cost. If the FTE counts are not known, it is suggested that the support staff cost be treated as a purchased service and be reported. This should not include the cost of support staff employed by the MSO or PPMC.

management services organization (MSO): Entity organized to provide various forms of practice management and administrative support services to health care providers. These services may include centralized billing and collections services, management information services, and other components of the managed care infrastructure. MSOs, which do not actually deliver health care services, may be jointly or solely owned and sponsored by physicians, hospitals, or other parties. Some MSOs also purchase assets of affiliated physicians and enter into long-term management service arrangements with a provider network. Some expand their ownership base by involving outside investors to help capitalize the development of such practice infrastructure.

mean: See average.

median: Data point in the true center of the dataset.

Medicaid—capitation: Fee-for-service equivalent gross charges, at the practice's undiscounted rates, for all services provided to Medicaid or similar state health care program patients under a capitated contract. This should not include (1) charges for fee-for-service patients; or (2) charges for patients covered under discounted fee-for-service contract arrangements.

Medicaid—fee-for-service: Fee-for-service (FFS) gross charges, at the practice's established undiscounted rates, for all services provided to Medicaid or similar state health care program patients on a FFS basis. This should not include (1) FFS equivalent gross charges for services provided to Medicaid or other state health care program patients under capitated, prepaid, or other "at-risk" arrangements; (2) charges for patients covered under discounted FFS contract arrangements.

Medicaid—managed care fee-for-service: Fee-for-service (FFS) gross charges, at the practice's established undiscounted rates, for all services provided to Medicaid or similar state health care program patients under a managed care plan. If patients are covered by both Medicare and Medicaid or a similar state health care plan on a FFS basis, all charges for such patients should be included as Medicare FFS charges. This should also include charges for patients covered under discounted FFS contract arrangements. This should not include (1) charges for FFS patients; or (2) FFS equivalent gross charges for services provided to patients under capitated, prepaid arrangements.

medical assistants and nurse's aides: FTE and cost of medical assistants and nurse's aides. This should not include FTE and cost of medical assistants and nurse's aides who worked exclusively in the departments of clinical laboratory, radiology and imaging, or other ancillary departments.

medical procedures conducted inside the practice's facilities: This consists of evaluation and management (E&M) services and Current Procedural Terminology® (CPT) (given an appropriate location code) (1) 99201–99215, office or other outpatient services; (2) 99241–99245, office or other outpatient consultations; (3) 99271–99275, confirmatory consultations; (4) 99354–99360, prolonged and standby services; (5) 99361–99373, case management services; (6) 99374–99380, care plan oversight services; (7) 99381–99429, preventive medicine services; (8) 99431–99432, newborn care; (9) 99450–99375, special evaluation and management services, radiology services (given an appropriate location code); (10) 77261–77799, radiation oncology; (11) 79000–79999, therapeutic nuclear medicine, medicine services (given an appropriate location code); and (12) 90281–99090; and (13) 99170–99199. This should not include: (1) 10021–69990, surgery procedures, which are reported as "surgery and anesthesia procedures"; (2) 70010–76499, diagnostic radiology, which are reported as "diagnostic radiology and imaging procedures"; (3) 76506–76999, diagnostic ultrasound; (4) 78000–78999, diagnostic nuclear medicine; and (5) 80048–89399, clinical laboratory and pathology, which are reported as "clinical laboratory and pathology procedures."

medical procedures conducted outside the practice's facilities: This consists of (1) 99217–99220, hospital observation services; (2) 99221–99239, hospital inpatient services; (3) 99251–99255, initial inpatient consultations; (4) 99261–99263, follow-up inpatient consultations; (5) 99281–99290, emergency services; (6) 99291–99292, critical care services; (7) 99293–99294, pediatric critical care services; (8) 99295–99299, neonatal intensive care services; (9) 99301–99316, nursing facility services; (10) 99321–99333, custodial care services; (11) 99354–99360, prolonged services; (12) 99341–99350, home services; (13) 99431–99440, newborn care; and (14) 99500–99602, home health services.

medical receptionists: FTE and cost of medical receptionist staff such as switchboard operators, schedulers, and appointment staff. This should not include FTE and cost of medical receptionists who worked exclusively in the departments of clinical laboratory, radiology and imaging, or other ancillary departments.

medical records: FTE and cost of medical records staff such as medical records clerks and department director or manager. This should not include FTE and cost of medical records and coding staff who worked exclusively in the departments of clinical laboratory, radiology and imaging, or other ancillary departments.

medical school: Institution that trains physicians and awards medical and osteopathic degrees.

medical secretaries and transcribers: This consists of FTE and cost of medical secretaries and transcribers. This should not include: FTE and cost of medical secretaries and transcribers who worked exclusively in the departments of clinical laboratory, radiology and imaging, or other ancillary departments.

medical and surgical supply cost: Cost of supplies purchased for general practice use. This should include (1) cost of medical and surgical supplies and instruments used in providing medical and surgical services; and (2) cost of laundry and linens. This should not include: (1) cost of specialized supplies dedicated for exclusive use in the departments of clinical laboratory, radiology and imaging, or other ancillary services departments; (2) cost of pharmaceuticals, medical supplies, and equipment sold to patients primarily for use outside the practice and not used in providing medical or surgical services; for example, prescription drugs, hearing aids, optical goods, and orthopedic supplies (such cost is included in "cost of sales and/or cost of other medical activities)" or (3) the cost of any equipment subject to depreciation.

Medicare—capitation: Fee-for-service (FFS) equivalent gross charges, at the practice's undiscounted rates, for all services provided to patients under a Medicare/TEFRA (Tax Equity and Fiscal Responsibility Act), received from a capitated contract. This should not include (1) charges for FFS patients; or (2) charges for patients covered under discounted FFS contract arrangements.

Medicare—fee-for-service: Fee-for-service (FFS) gross charges, at the practice's established undiscounted rates, for all services provided to Medicare patients on a FFS basis. If patients are covered by both Medicare and Medicaid or a similar state health care plan, all charges for such patients should be included as Medicare FFS charges. This should not include (1) FFS equivalent gross charges for services provided to Medicare/TEFRA (Tax Equity and Fiscal Responsibility Act) patients under capitated, prepaid, or other "at-risk" arrangements; or (2) charges for patients covered under discounted FFS contract arrangements.

Medicare—managed care fee-for-service: Fee-for-service (FFS) gross charges, at the practice's established undiscounted rates, for all services provided to Medicare patients through a managed care plan. If patients are covered by both Medicare and Medicaid or a similar state health care plan on a FFS basis, all charges for such patients should be included as Medicare FFS charges. This should include charges for patients covered under discounted FFS contract arrangements. This should not include FFS equivalent gross charges for services provided to Medicare/TEFRA (Tax Equity and Fiscal Responsibility Act) patients under capitated, prepaid arrangements.

Military Health System (MHS): Health care system of the U.S. Department of Defense consisting of medical services from the Army, Navy, and Air Force. The system consists of a multi-billion-dollar budget, millions of beneficiaries, outpatient and inpatient services covering the entire continuum of health care services, and large number of medical centers, hospitals, and clinics. The Coast Guard is not part of the MHS since it is part of the Department of Homeland Defense.

miscellaneous operating cost: Operating cost not stated in other operating cost categories such as charitable contributions; employee relations dinners and picnics; entertainment; uniforms; business transportation; interest on loans; health, business, and property taxes; recruiting cost; job position classified advertising; moving cost; and payouts to retired physicians from accounts receivable. This should not include (1) federal or state income taxes, which are included in "nonmedical cost"; or (2) principal paid on loans.

mode: Value that occurs most frequently in the data set.

multispecialty with primary and specialty care: Medical practice that consists of physicians practicing in different specialties, including at least one of the following primary care specialties: family practice—general with or without obstetrics, sports medicine, urgent care, geriatrics, internal medicine—general and urgent care, and pediatrics—adolescent medicine, general, and sports medicine.

multispecialty with primary care only: Medical practice that consists of physicians practicing in more than one of the primary care specialties listed in multispecialty with primary and specialty care or the surgical specialties of obstetrics/gynecology, gynecology (only), or obstetrics (only).

multispecialty with specialty care only: Medical practice that consists of physicians practicing in different specialties, none of which are the following primary care specialties: family practice—general, sports medicine, urgent care, and with or without obstetrics; geriatrics; internal medicine—general and urgent care; and pediatrics— adolescent medicine, general, or sports medicine.

N

net collections: Revenue received from all payers.

net fee-for-service charges: See gross fee-for-service charges.

net fee-for-service collections and revenue: Revenue collected from patients and third-party payers for services provided to fee-for-service (FFS), discounted FFS, and non-capitated Medicare and Medicaid patients. This is the revenue remaining after patient refunds and checks returned to patients. If the practice used accrual basis accounting, "net fee-for-service collections and revenue" should equal "gross fee-for-service charges" minus "adjustments to fee-for-service charges" minus "bad debts due to fee-for-service activity." This should also include (1) portions of the withholds returned to a practice as part of a risk-sharing arrangement; (2) bonuses and incentive payments paid to a practice for good performance; (3) patient copayments; (4) payments received due to a coordination of benefits and/or reinsurance recovery situation; and (5) revenue due to purchased services (i.e., purchased by the practice from external providers and facilities on behalf of the practice's patients) for FFS patients.

net practice income or loss:

noncurrent and all other assets: This should include (1) investments and long-term receivables such as long-term investments in securities, restricted cash, property not used for operations, and receivables due beyond one year (assets recorded in these accounts are not used to finance operations); (2) noncurrent tangible assets such as long-lived tangible assets used in practice operations (assets recorded in these accounts generally have a useful life in excess of one year); and (3) intangible and other assets such as cost of property rights without physical substance that benefits future operations (such assets are purchased from external sources, provide future benefit, and are relatively long lived). Other assets include long-term prepayments, deferred charges, and assets not included in other categories.

noncurrent and all other liabilities: Long-term liabilities that mature and require payment at some time beyond one year.

nonmedical cost: This should include (1) income taxes based on net profit that is paid to federal, state, or local government; (For cash basis accounting, income taxes equal the cash payment or refund for the tax year paid or received in following tax year plus periodic withholding paid. For accrual accounting, the income tax equals the total tax liability regardless of when the tax was paid or refunds were received.) (2) all costs required to maintain the productivity of income- producing rental property and parking lots; (3) losses on the sale of real estate or equipment and from the sale of marketable securities; (4) other nonmedical cost; (5) all direct costs related to business ventures such as rental property, parking lots, or billing services, for which gross revenue is reported as "nonmedical revenue," as long as these costs are not also included in "total operating cost;" and (6) state taxes on medical revenue.

nonmedical revenue: This should include (1) interest and investment revenue such as interest, dividends, and/or capital gains earned on savings accounts, certificates of deposit, securities, stocks, bonds, and other short-term or long-term investments; (2) gross rental revenue such as rent or lease income earned from practice-owned property not used in practice operations; (3) capital gains on the sale of practice real estate or equipment; (4) interest paid by insurance companies for failure to pay claims on time; (5) bounced check charges paid by patients; and (6) gross revenue from business ventures such as a billing service or parking lot (the direct costs of such ventures should be reported as "nonmedical cost"). This should not include: cash received from loans.

nonphysician provider benefit cost: This should include (1) employer's share of FICA, payroll, and unemployment insurance taxes; (2) employer's share of health, disability, life, and workers' compensation insurance; (3) employer payments to defined benefit and contribution, 401(k), 403(b), and nonqualified retirement plans; (4) deferred compensation paid or expensed during the year; (5) dues and memberships in professional organizations and state and local license fees; (6) allowances for education, professional meetings, travel, and automobile; and (7) entertainment, country and athletic club membership, and travel for spouse. This should not include: (1) voluntary employee salary deductions used as contributions to 401(k) and 403(b) plans; and (2) expense reimbursements.

nonphysician provider compensation: Nonphysician providers are specially trained and licensed providers who can provide medical care and billable services. Examples of nonphysician providers include audiologists, certified registered nurse anesthetists, dieticians and nutritionists, midwives, nurse practitioners, occupational therapists, optometrists, physical therapists, physician assistants, psychologists, social workers, speech therapists, and surgeon's assistants. This should include the total compensation paid to nonphysician providers who comprise the count of "Total nonphysician provider," cost column. This should also include (1) compensation for both employed and contracted nonphysician providers; (2) compensation for full-time and part-time nonphysician providers; (3) salaries, bonuses, incentive payments, research contract revenue, honoraria, and profit distributions; and (4) voluntary employee salary deductions used as contributions to 401(k), 403(b), or Section 125 plans. Do not include: (1) amounts included in "nonphysician provider benefit cost"; or (2) expense reimbursements.

nonprocedural gross charges: This should include (1) facility fee charges for the operation of an ambulatory surgery unit; (2) facility fee charges in a hospital-affiliated practice that utilizes a split billing system where both facility fees and professional charges are billed; (3) charges for drugs and medications administered inside the practice's facilities, such as chemotherapy drugs; and (4) charges for HCPCS A, J, R, and V codes. This should not include charges for the sale of medical goods and services.

normal distribution: Also known as a Poisson distribution, a normal curve, or a bell-shaped curve.

not-for-profit corporation or foundation: Organization that has obtained special exemption under Section 501(c) of the Internal Revenue Service code that qualifies the organization to be exempt from federal income taxes. To qualify as a tax-exempt organization, a practice or faculty practice plan would have to provide evidence of a charitable, educational, or research purpose.

O

objective: Measurement not affected by the person taking the measurement. No emotional or personal interpretations affect the result; in general, the more objective a measurement, the more reliable.

operating expenses: Expense generated by the practice when engaged in medical revenue-producing activities.

other administrative support: FTE and cost of other administrative staff such as shipping and receiving, cafeteria, mailroom, and laundry staff.

other ancillary services: Operating costs for all ancillary services departments except clinical laboratory and radiology and imaging. This should include (1) operating costs for departments such as physical therapy, optical, ambulatory surgery, radiation oncology, and therapeutic nuclear medicine; (2) rental and/or depreciation cost of major furniture and equipment subject to capitalization; (3) repair and maintenance cost; (4) cost of supplies and minor equipment not subject to capitalization; (5) other costs unique to the ancillary services departments; and (6) cost of purchased "other ancillary" technical services for fee-for-service patients. This should not include (1) cost of purchased "other ancillary" technical services for capitation patients, which should be reported as "purchased services for capitation patients"; (2) cost of physical therapy and orthopedic items such as crutches and braces sold to patients, which should be included in "cost of sales and/or cost of other medical activities"; or (3) cost of optical items such as eyeglasses and contact lenses sold to patients, which is included in "cost of sales and/or cost of other medical activities."

other federal government payers: Fee-for-service gross charges, at the practice's undiscounted rates, for all services provided to patients who are covered by other federal government payers other than Medicare. This should include charges for TRICARE patients. This should not include charges for Medicare and Medicaid patients.

other insurance premiums: Cost of other policies such as fire, flood, theft, casualty, general liability, officers' and directors' liability, and reinsurance.

other medical revenue: Grants, honoraria, research contract revenues, government support payments, and educational subsidies. This should include (1) federal, state, or local government or private foundation grants to provide indigent patient care or for case management of the frail and elderly; (2) honoraria income for practice participation in educational programs; (3) research contract revenues for activities such as pharmaceutical studies; and (4) educational subsidies used to train residents. This should not include (1) charges for the delivery of services made possible by subsidies or grants (such charges are included in "gross fee-for-service charges" and/or "gross charges for patients covered by capitation contracts") or (2) the value of operating subsidies from parent organizations such as hospitals or integrated systems (such subsidies should be included in "financial support for operating costs").

other medical support services: FTE and cost of support staff in any ancillary services department other than clinical laboratory and radiology and imaging. This should include (1) FTE and cost of support staff who provide assistance to patients such as patient relations staff or lay counselors; (2) FTE and cost of support staff such as nurses, secretaries, technicians, physical therapy aides, and assistants in ancillary services departments such as physical therapy, optical, ambulatory surgery, radiation oncology, therapeutic nuclear medicine, clinical research, pharmacists, and pharmacy support staff; and (3) FTE and cost of the department directors and managers in these ancillary services departments. This should not include nonphysician providers such as nurse practitioners, physician's assistants, and physical therapists.

output measures: When calculating procedure counts and gross charges for practice activities, it is necessary to identify whether the activity occurred inside or outside the practice's facilities. This inside/outside distinction enables the proper assignment of operating costs to develop cost per unit output statistics. The Centers for Medicare and Medicaid Services' "place of service" codes are used to make this inside/outside distinction. While one place of service code, the "office" code (11), indicates activity inside the practice's facilities, all other place of service codes (12–81) are for activities occurring outside the practice's facilities. Examples of "outside" locations are the patient's home, inpatient or outpatient hospital, psychiatric or rehabilitation facility, emergency room, freestanding ambulatory surgery center, birthing center, skilled nursing or custodial care facility, hospice, ambulance, independent laboratory, radiology and imaging center, and ambulatory emergency center. This should include (1) procedures performed by all practice physicians, nonphysician providers, and other health care professionals such as nurses, medical assistants, and technicians; and (2) purchased procedures from external providers and facilities on behalf of the practice's fee-for-service patients for which revenue is reported as a subset of "net fee-for-service collections/ revenue" and for which costs are reported as a subset of "clinical laboratory," "radiology and imaging," "other ancillary services" and/or "provider consultant cost." This should not include purchased procedures from external providers and facilities on behalf of the practice's capitation patients, for which costs are reported as "Purchased services for capitation patients."

outside professional fees: Fees for professional services performed on a one-time or sporadic basis. This should include (1) fees for legal and accounting services; and (2) fees for management, financial, and actuarial consultants. This should not include (1) information services, architectural, and public relations consultant fees (such costs are included in "information technology," "building and occupancy," and "promotion and marketing") and (2) cost for contracted support staff, which is reported as "total contracted support staff."

P

partnership: An unincorporated organization where two or more individuals have agreed to share profits, losses, assets, and liabilities although not necessarily on an equal basis. The partnership agreement may or may not be formalized in writing.

patient accounting: FTE and cost of patient accounting (billing and collections) staff such as department supervisor, billing/accounts receivable manager, coding, charge entry, insurance, billing, collections, payment posting, refund, adjustment, and cashiering staff.

patient encounters: Documented, face-to-face contact between a patient and a provider who exercises independent judgment in the provision of services to the individual. If a patient with the same diagnosis sees two different providers on the same day, it is one encounter. If a patient sees two different providers on the same day for two different diagnoses, then it is considered two encounters. The total number of patient encounters should include only procedures from the evaluation and management chapter (CPT codes 99201–99375) or the medicine chapter (CPT codes 90800--99199) of the Physicians' Current Procedural Terminology (4th edition, copyrighted by the American Medical Association). This should include (1) pre- and post-operative visits and other visits associated with a global charge; (2) for diagnostic radiologists, the total number of procedures or reads; (3) for obstetric care, if a single CPT-4 code is used for a global service, each ambulatory contact, such as a prenatal and postnatal visit, is a separate ambulatory encounter, whereas the delivery is a single surgical case; (4) administration of chemotherapy drugs; (5) administration of immunizations; (6) ambulatory encounters attributed to nonphysician providers; and (7) visits where there is no identifiable contact between a patient and a physician or nonphysician provider (for example, a patient comes into the practice solely for an injection, vein puncture, EKGs, EEGs, etc., administered by an RN or technician). This should not include (1) encounters for the physician specialties of pathology or diagnostic radiology (see No. 2 under "Include"); (2) encounters that include procedures from surgery (CPT codes 10040–69979) or anesthesia (CPT codes 00100–01999); or (3) number of procedures, because a single encounter can generate multiple procedures.

percentile: Provides indication of the relative position with respect to other data points and is simply a value indicating the percent of values less than or equal to the percentile.

physician: Any doctor of medicine (MD) or doctor of osteopathy (DO) who is duly licensed and qualified under the law of jurisdiction in which treatment is received.

physician practice management company (PPMC): Usually publicly held or entrepreneurial directed enterprise that acquires total or partial ownership interests in physician organizations. PPMC is a type of management services organization (MSO), although the motivations, goals, strategies, and structures arising from its unequivocal ownership character—development of growth and profits for its investors rather than for the participating providers—differentiate it from other MSO models.

physician work relative value units (RVUs): This should include (1) RVUs for the "physician work RVUs" only; (2) physician work RVUs for all professional medical and surgical services performed by physicians, nonphysician providers, and other physician extenders, such as nurses and medical assistants; (3) physician work RVUs for the professional component of laboratory, radiology, medical diagnostic, and surgical procedures; (4) physician work RVUs for all procedures performed by the medical practice (for procedures with either no listed CPT code or with an RVU value of zero, RVUs can be estimated by dividing the total gross charges for the unlisted or unvalued procedures by the practice's known average charge per RVU for all procedures that are listed and valued); (5) physician work RVUs for procedures for both fee-for-service and capitation patients; (6) physician work RVUs for all payers, not just Medicare; and (7) physician work RVUs for purchased procedures from external providers on behalf of the practice's fee-for-service patients. This should not include (1) RVUs for "malpractice RVUs" or "nonfacility practice expense RVUs"; (2) RVUs for the technical components of laboratory, radiology, medical diagnostic, and surgical procedures; (3) RVUs for other scales, such as McGraw-Hill and California; (4) RVUs for purchased procedures from external providers on behalf of the practice's capitation patients; (5) RVUs that have been weighted by a conversion factor (do not weigh the RVUs by a conversion factor); and (6) RVUs where the geographic practice cost index (GPCI) equals any value other than 1 (GPCI must be set to 1.000 [neutral]).

population designation:

> *Non-metropolitan (less than 50,000):* The community in which the practice is located is generally referred to as "rural". It is located outside of a "metropolitan statistical area" (MSA), as defined by the United States Office of Management and Budget, and has a population less than 50,000.

> *Metropolitan (50,000 to 250,000):* The community in which the practice is located is an MSA or Census Bureau defined urbanized area with a population of 50,000 to 250,000.

> *Metropolitan (250,001 to 1,000,000):* The community in which the practice is located is an MSA or Census Bureau defined urbanized area with a population of 250,001 to 1,000,000.

Metropolitan (more than 1,000,000): The community in which the practice is located is a "primary metropolitan statistical area" (PMSA) with a population more than 1,000,000.

practice affiliated with a medical school: This consists of clinicians from the medical group practice who hold non-tenured appointments as medical school faculty and/or are part of a health system that is associated with a medical school that grants a doctor of medicine degree, or practices that have a legal standing with a medical school, faculty practice plan, or clinical science department. Practices that provide residency rotations but do not meet these criteria should not be considered affiliated with a medical school.

primary clinic location: This consists of clinic with the most FTE physicians of all the practice branches.

professional corporation or association: This consists of for-profit organization recognized by law as a business entity separate and distinct from its shareholders. Shareholders must be licensed in the profession practiced by the organization.

professional gross charges: This consists of medical, surgery, and anesthesia gross charges conducted inside the practice's facilities and medical, surgery, and anesthesia gross charges conducted outside the practice's facilities

professional liability insurance premiums: This consists of premiums paid or self-insurance cost for malpractice and professional liability insurance for practice physicians, nonphysician providers, and employees.

professional procedures: This consists of medical, surgery, and anesthesia procedures conducted inside the practice's facilities and medical, surgery, and anesthesia procedures conducted outside the practice's facilities.

promotion and marketing: This consists of cost of promotion, advertising, and marketing activities, including patient newsletters, information booklets, fliers, brochures, Yellow Page listings, and public relations consultants.

property, furniture, fixtures, and equipment: This consists of tangible, long-lived assets used in practice operations (e.g., land, land improvements, buildings, furniture, fixtures, equipment, and capital leases).

provider consultant cost: This consists of fee-for-service fees paid to consulting pathologists, radiologists, and other consulting physicians and/or nonphysician providers who are not included in the count of "total physician" or the count of "total nonphysician provider." This should not include: costs for purchased physician and/or nonphysician provider consultation services for capitation patients. Such cost is included in "purchased services for capitation patients."

purchased services for capitation patients: Fees paid to health care providers and organizations external to the practice for services provided to capitation patients under the terms of capitation contracts. This should include (1) payments to providers outside the practice for physician professional, nonphysician professional, clinical laboratory, radiology and imaging, hospital inpatient and emergency, ambulance, out-of-area emergency and pharmacy services and (2) accrued expenses for "incurred but not reported" claims for purchased services for capitation patients for which invoices have not been received.

Q

quartile: Provides indication of the relative position with respect to the other data points (similar to percentile) and is simply the 25th (25 percent), 50th (50 percent or median), or 75th (75 percent) percentiles.

R

radiology and imaging cost: Cost of diagnostic radiology and imaging procedures defined by diagnostic radiology CPT codes 70010–76499, diagnostic ultrasound CPT codes 76506–76999, diagnostic nuclear medicine CPT codes 78000–78999, echocardiography CPT codes 93303–93350, non-invasive vascular diagnostic studies CPT codes 93825–93990, and electrocardiograph CPT codes 93300–93350. This should also include (1) rental and/or depreciation cost of major furniture and equipment subject to capitalization; (2) repair and maintenance contract cost; (3) cost of radiological diagnostics (isotopes); (4) cost of supplies and minor equipment not subject to capitalization (this amount is the net after subtracting the revenue from silver recovery from X-ray film and processing fixer); (5) other costs unique to the radiology and imaging department; and (6) cost of purchased radiology technical services for fee-for-service patients. This should not include (1) cost of purchased radiology technical services for capitation patients, which should be reported as "purchased services for capitation patients" or (2) cost of procedures for radiation oncology CPT codes 77261–77799 or therapeutic nuclear medicine CPT codes 79000–79999, which are included in "other ancillary services."

radiology and imaging FTE: Film library staff and the diagnostic radiology and imaging department that conduct procedures for diagnostic radiology CPT codes 70010–76499, diagnostic ultrasound CPT codes 76506–76999, diagnostic nuclear medicine CPT codes 78000–78999, echocardiography CPT codes 93303–93350, noninvasive vascular diagnostic studies CPT codes 93875–93990, and electrocardiograph CPT codes 93000–93350. This should also include (1) FTE and cost of support staff such as nurses, secretaries, and technicians; and (2) FTE and cost of department director or manager. This should not include FTE and staff cost for radiation oncology CPT codes 77261–77799 or therapeutic nuclear medicine CPT codes 79000–79999, which are included as "other medical support services."

registered nurses: This consists of FTE and cost of registered nurse staff and registered nurses working as frontline managers or lead nurses. This should not include (1) FTE and cost of nonphysician providers such as nurse practitioners, certified registered nurse anesthetists, or nurse midwives or (2) FTE and cost of registered nurses who worked exclusively in the departments of clinical laboratory, radiology and imaging, or other ancillary departments.

relative value unit (RVU): Non-monetary standard unit of measure that indicates the value of services provided by physicians, nonphysician providers, and other health care professionals. RVUs are associated with procedural codes performed by medical providers and are used for reimbursement purposes. RVU tables (procedural codes and their associated RVU weight) are published by the Centers for Medicare and Medicaid on a calendar year basis. RVUs consist of three components: (1) physician work (includes physician time, mental effort, technical skill, judgment, stress, and amortization of the physician's education); (2) practice expense (direct expenses such as supplies, nonphysician labor, equipment expenses, and indirect expenses); and (3) malpractice expense. RVUs do not include a component for clinical outcomes, quality, or severity.

relative weighted product (RWP): Similar to relative value unit and used by the Military Health System for inpatient services.

reliability: Consistency across repeated measures.

resource based relative value scale (RBRVS): This consists of total and physician work relative value units (RVUs) and/or American Society of Anesthesiologists (ASA) units. Report the relative value units, as measured by the RBRVS, not weighted by a conversion factor, attributed to all professional services. The RVU system is explained in detail in the November 7, 2003 Federal Register, pages 63,261 to 63,386. Total RVUs for a given procedure consist of three components: (1) physician work RVUs; (2) practice expense (PE) RVUs; and (3) malpractice RVUs. Thus, total RVUs = physician work RVUs + practice expense RVUs + malpractice RVUs. There are two different types of practice expense RVUs: (1) fully implemented nonfacility practice expense RVUs; and (2) fully implemented facility practice expense RVUs. "Nonfacility" refers to RVUs associated with a medical practice that is not affiliated with a hospital and does not utilize a split billing system that itemizes facility (hospital) charges and professional charges. "Nonfacility" also applies to services performed in settings other than a hospital, skilled nursing facility or ambulatory surgery center. "Facility" refers to RVUs associated with a hospital affiliated medical practice that utilizes a split billing fee schedule where facility (hospital) charges and professional charges are billed separately. "Facility" also refers to services performed in a hospital, skilled nursing facility or ambulatory surgery center. This should not include total RVUs that are a function of "facility" practice expense RVUs. To summarize, there are two different types of total RVUs: (1) fully implemented nonfacility total RVUs and (2) fully implemented facility total RVUs. If you are a hospital affiliated medical practice that utilizes a split billing fee schedule, total RVUs should be calculated as if you were a medical practice not affiliated with a hospital.

revenue: Income generated from the delivery of products and services.

revenue from the sale of medical goods and services: This consists of (1) revenue from pharmaceuticals, medical supplies, and equipment sold to patients primarily for use outside the practice, including prescription drugs, hearing aids, optical goods, and orthopedic supplies (this amount should be net of write-offs and discounts); (2) compensation paid by a hospital to a practice physician for services as a medical director; (3) hourly wages of physicians working in a hospital emergency room; (4) contract revenue from a hospital for physician services in staffing a hospital indigent care clinic or emergency room; (5) contract revenue from a school district for physician services in conducting physical exams for high school athletes; (6) revenue from the preparation of court depositions, expert testimony, postmortem reports, and other special reports; and (7) fees received from patients for the photocopying of patient medical records. This should not include capitation revenue used to pay for covered goods and services for capitation patients (such revenue is included in "gross capitation revenue").

S

self-pay: Fee-for-service gross charges, at the practice's undiscounted rates, for all services provided to patients who pay the medical practice directly. Note that these patients may or may not have insurance. This should include (1) charges for patients who have no insurance but have the resources to pay for their own care and do so and (2) charges for patients who have insurance but choose to pay for their own care and submit claims to their insurance company directly. Because the practice may or may not be aware of this situation, all charges paid directly by the patient should be considered as self-pay.

single specialty: Medical practice that focuses its clinical work in one specialty. The determining factor for classifying the type of specialty is the focus of clinical work and not necessarily the specialties of the physicians in the practice. For example, a single specialty neurosurgery practice may include a neurologist and a radiologist. Practices that include only the subspecialties of internal medicine should be classified as a single specialty internal medicine practice. Internal medicine subspecialties include: allergy and immunology, cardiology, endocrinology/metabolism, gastroenterology, hematology/oncology, infectious disease, nephrology, pulmonary disease, and rheumatology.

skew: Skewness measures the deviation of the distribution from symmetry. If the skewness is clearly different from zero, then that distribution is asymmetrical, while normal distributions are perfectly symmetrical. If skewness is greater than zero (positive), then a large number of data points are to the right and the left tail is too long. If skewness is less than zero (negative), then a large number of data points are to the left and the right tail is too long.

sole proprietorship: Organization with a single owner who is responsible for all profit, losses, assets, and liabilities.

standard deviation: Measure of variation or dispersion, which represents the spread of the data around the mean.

subjective: Measurement affected by the person taking the measurement. Emotional or personal interpretations affects the result; in general, the more subjective a measurement, the less reliable.

support staffing: This consists of (1) FTE for all support staff employed by all the legal entities working in support of the medical practice and (2) FTE for both full-time and part-time support staff. To compute FTE, add the number of fulltime (1.0 FTE) support staff to the FTE count for the part-time support staff. A full-time support staff employee works whatever number of hours the practice considers to be the minimum for a normal work week, which could be 37.5, 40, 50 hours, or some other standard. To compute the FTE of a part-time support staff employee, divide the total hours worked in an average week by the number of hours that your practice considered to be a normal work week. An employee working 30 hours compared to a normal work week of 40 hours would be 0.75 FTE (30 divided by 40 hours). An employee working full-time for three months during a year would be 0.25 FTE (3 divided by 12 months). A support staff employee cannot be counted as more than 1.0 FTE regardless of the number of hours worked; and (3) the allocated FTE where the practice consists of multiple legal entities. For example, a management services organization managing two medical practices and employing one billing clerk who devotes an equal amount of time to each practice would add 0.5 FTE to the total FTE count in "patient accounting," for each managed practice. This should not include the FTE of contracted support staff, which should be reported as "total contracted support staff."

support staff cost: This consists of (1) salaries, bonuses, incentive payments, honoraria, and profit distributions; (2) voluntary employee salary deductions used as contributions to 401(k), 403(b), or Section 125 plans; (3) compensation paid to the total FTE count; (4) compensation for all support staff employed by all of the legal entities working in support of the medical practice; (5) the allocated support staff cost where the practice consists of multiple legal entities (for example, a management services organization managing two medical practices and employing one billing clerk who devotes an equal amount of time to each practice would add 50 percent of the one billing clerk's compensation to the total cost of "patient accounting, for each managed practice); and (6) compensation for both full-time and part-time employed support staff. This should not include (1) nonphysician provider cost; (2) any benefits for employed support staff, which should be reported as "total employed support staff benefit cost"; (3) expense reimbursements; and (4) any benefits or the cost of contracted support staff who do not work for any of the legal entities that comprise the medical practice (these costs should be reported as "total contracted support staff").

surgery and anesthesia procedures conducted inside the practice's facilities: This consists of (1) 00100–01999, anesthesia procedures; (2) 10021–36410, 36420–69990, surgery procedures; (3) 99100–99142, anesthesia procedures; and (4) surgery and anesthesia procedures performed in the practice's own ambulatory surgery unit. This should not include 36415 and 36416, venous and capillary blood collection.

surgery and anesthesia procedures conducted outside the practice's facilities: This consists of surgery and anesthesia procedures performed in an inpatient hospital or a freestanding ambulatory surgery center. This should not include 36415 and 36416, venous and capillary blood collection.

T

throughput: Often synonymous with "capacity," throughput is typically an amount of something per unit time that processes into and out of a system. In the case of a typical medical practice, throughput is referring to the practice's (system) ability to handle/treat patients (process) from the time a patient enters until he/she leaves the facility.

total contracted support staff (temporary): Represents all the staff hired on a contract basis that are not employed by any of the legal entities that comprise the medical practice. The utilization of contracted support staff occurs when the medical practice (including all the associated legal entities that comprise the medical practice) contracts to have full-time and/or ongoing support staff activities conducted by contracted staff. A defining characteristic of contracted support staff is that the hours worked (hence the FTE) by the contracted support staff are easily identified and reported. If the hours worked are not easily identified and reported, then the FTE count cannot be accurately reported. One example of this type of cost would be purchased services for billing and collections activities. When a practice decides to hire a billing company to conduct billing activities, it is often not possible to track the hours that the billing company devotes to the given practice. Such cost should be reported as "Billing and collections purchased services." Include: (1) temporary staff working for temporary agencies. Do not include: (1) the FTE and cost of support staff employed directly by the practice or any of the legal entities comprising the medical practice; or (2) the FTE and cost for legal, accounting, management, and/or other consultants for services performed on a one-time or sporadic basis (the costs for these types of consultants are reported as "outside professional fees").

total employed support staff benefit cost: This consists of (1) employer's share of FICA payroll and unemployment insurance taxes; (2) employer's share of health, disability, life, and workers' compensation insurance; (3) employer payments to defined benefit and contribution, 401(k), 403(b), and nonqualified retirement plans; (4) deferred compensation paid or expensed during the year; (5) dues and memberships in professional organizations and state and local license fees; (6) allowances for education, professional meetings, travel, and automobile; and (7) entertainment, country and athletic club membership, and travel for spouse. This should not include (1) voluntary employee salary deductions used as contributions to 401(k) and 403(b) plans or (2) expense reimbursements.

total nonphysician provider FTE: A full-time nonphysician provider works whatever number of hours the practice considers to be the minimum for a normal work week, which could be 37.5, 40, 50 hours, or some other standard. To compute "total nonphysician provider," FTE, add the number of full-time (1.0 FTE) nonphysician providers to the FTE count for part-time nonphysician providers. To compute the FTE of a part-time nonphysician provider, divide the total hours worked by the number of hours that your practice considers to be a normal work week. A nonphysician provider working 30 hours compared to a normal work week of 40 hours would be 0.75 FTE (30 hours divided by 40 hours). A nonphysician provider working full-time for three months during a year would be 0.25 FTE (3 months divided by 12 months). A nonphysician provider cannot be counted as more than 1.0 FTE regardless of the number of hours worked.

total operating expense: Expenses incurred by the practice while earning medical revenue, consisting of employee salaries and fringe benefits (does not include physicians and mid-level providers), services and general expenses (e.g., office and administrative expenses, depreciation, pharmaceuticals, medical supplies, and occupancy costs such as rent and utilities), purchased services, and provider-related expenses (physician salaries, taxes, health insurance, licenses, and other costs associated with physician and mid-level provider compensation).

total physician benefit cost: Total benefits paid to physicians who comprise "total physician" FTE. This should include (1) employer's share of FICA payroll and unemployment insurance taxes; (2) employer's share of health, disability, life and workers' compensation insurance; (3) employer payments to defined benefit and contribution, 401(k), 403(b), and nonqualified retirement plans; (4) deferred compensation paid or expensed during the year; (5) dues and memberships in professional organizations and state and local license fees; (6) allowances for education, professional meetings, travel, and automobile; and (7) entertainment, country and athletic club membership, and travel for spouse. This should not include (1) voluntary employee salary deductions used as contributions to 401(k) and 403(b) plans or (2) expense reimbursements.

total physician compensation: Total compensation paid to physicians who comprise "total physician" FTE. This should include (1) compensation for shareholders and partners, salaried associates, employed physicians, contract physicians, locum tenens, residents, and fellows; (2) compensation for full-time and part-time physicians; (3) salaries, bonuses, incentive payments, research contract revenue, honoraria, and profit distributions; (4) voluntary employee salary deductions used as contributions to 401(k), 403(b), or Section 125 plans; and (5) compensation attributable to activities related to revenue in "nonmedical revenue." This should not include (1) amounts included in "provider consultant cost"; (2) amounts included in "total physician benefit cost"; or (3) expense reimbursements.

total RVUs: This consists of RVUs for: (1) "physician work RVUs," "malpractice RVUs," and "nonfacility practice expense RVUs"; (2) all professional medical and surgical services performed by physicians, nonphysician providers, and other physician extenders such as nurses and medical assistants; (3) the professional component of laboratory, radiology, medical diagnostic, and surgical procedures; (4) the technical components of laboratory, radiology, medical diagnostic, and surgical procedures; (5) all procedures performed by the medical practice (for procedures with either no listed CPT code or with an RVU value of zero, RVUs can be estimated by dividing the total gross charges for the unlisted or unvalued procedures by the practice's known average charge per RVU for all procedures that are listed and valued); (6) procedures for both fee-for-service and capitation patients; (7) all payers, not just Medicare; and (8) purchased procedures from external providers on behalf of the practice's fee-for-service patients. This should not include RVUs (1) for other scales such as McGraw-Hill and California; (2) for purchased procedures from external providers on behalf of the practice's capitation patients; (3) that have been weighted by a conversion factor (do not weigh the RVUs by a conversion factor); and (4) where the geographic practice cost index (GPCI) equals any value other than 1. The GPCI must be set to 1.000 (neutral).

U

university: Institution of higher learning with teaching and research facilities comprising undergraduate, graduate and professional schools.

V

validity: Meaningfulness within a generally accepted theoretical basis; that is, does the measure or metric mean what it's supposed to?

variance: Indicator of how large or small the difference is in the values (in non-statistical terms). Standard deviation, like variance, is a measure of variability or dispersion.

visit: See patient encounters.

W

workload: Generic term or measure for work that can be represented as visits, encounters, or RVUs.

workers' compensation: Fee-for-service gross charges, at the practice's undiscounted rates, for all services provided to patients covered by workers' compensation insurance. This should not include charges for (1) Medicare patients; (2) Medicaid patients; (3) charity or professional courtesy patients; or (4) self-pay patients.

Acronyms and Geographic Sections

A/R	accounts receivable
ASA	American Society of Anesthesiologists
CMS	Centers for Medicare & Medicaid Services
DIMS	document imaging and management systems
DO	Doctor of Osteopathy
EHR	electronic health record
FFS	fee-for-service
FTE	full-time-equivalent
HMO	Health Maintenance Organization
IBNR	incurred but not reported
IDS	integrated delivery system
MD	Doctor of Medicine
MGMA	Medical Group Management Association
MSO	Management Services Organization
NAPR	National Association of Physician Recruiters
NP	nurse practitioner
NPP	non-physician provider
OB/GYN	obstetrics/gynecology
PA	physician assistant
PhD	Doctor of Philosophy
PPMC	Physician Practice Management Company
RBRVS	Resource Based Relative Value Scale
RVU	relative value unit(s)
TC	technical component

Eastern Section	Midwest Section	Southern Section	Western Section
Connecticut	Illinois	Alabama	Alaska
Delaware	Indiana	Arkansas	Arizona
District of Columbia	Iowa	Florida	California
Maine	Michigan	Georgia	Colorado

Maryland	Minnesota	Kansas	Hawaii
Massachusetts	Nebraska	Kentucky	Idaho
New Hampshire	North Dakota	Louisiana	Montana
New Jersey	Ohio	Mississippi	Nevada
New York	South Dakota	Missouri	New Mexico
North Carolina	Wisconsin	Oklahoma	Oregon
Pennsylvania		South Carolina	Utah
Rhode Island		Tennessee	Washington
Vermont		Texas	Wyoming
Virginia			
West Virginia			

Physician Categories

Primary care physicians include:
Family practice: general
Family practice: sports medicine
Family practice: urgent care
Family practice: with obstetrics
Family practice: without obstetrics
Geriatrics
Internal medicine: general
Internal medicine: urgent care
Pediatrics: adolescent medicine
Pediatrics: general
Pediatrics: sports medicine

Nonsurgical specialty physicians include:
Allergy/immunology
Cardiology
Cardiology: electrophysiology
Cardiology: invasive
Cardiology: invasive/interventional
Cardiology: noninvasive
Critical care: intensivist
Dentistry
Dermatology
Emergency medicine
Endocrinology/metabolism
Gastroenterology
Gastroenterology: hepatology
Genetics
Hematology/oncology
Hospitalist
Infectious disease

Maternal and fetal medicine

Nephrology

Neurology

Nuclear medicine

Occupational medicine

Oncology (only)

Orthopedics: nonsurgical

Pathology: anatomic

Pathology: anatomic and clinical

Pathology: clinical

Pathology: general

Pediatrics: allergy and immunology

Pediatrics: cardiology

Pediatrics: child development

Pediatrics: clinical and lab immunology

Pediatrics: critical care intensivist

Pediatrics: emergency medicine

Pediatrics: endocrinology

Pediatrics: gastroenterology

Pediatrics: genetics

Pediatrics: hematology/oncology

Pediatrics: hospitalist

Pediatrics: infectious disease

Pediatrics: neonatal medicine

Pediatrics: nephrology

Pediatrics: neurology

Pediatrics: pulmonology

Pediatrics: rheumatology

Physical medicine and rehabilitation (physiatry)

Podiatry: general

Psychiatry: child and adolescent

Psychiatry: forensic

Psychiatry: general

Psychiatry: geriatric

Public health
Pulmonary medicine
Pulmonary medicine: critical care
Radiation oncology
Radiology: diagnostic-invasive
Radiology: diagnostic-noninvasive
Radiology: nuclear medicine
Reproductive endocrinology
Rheumatology

Surgical specialty physicians include:
Anesthesiology
Anesthesiology: pain management
Anesthesiology: pediatric
Dermatology: MOHS surgery
Gynecology (only)
Gynecological oncology
Obstetrics
Obstetrics/gynecology
Ophthalmology
Ophthalmology: pediatric
Ophthalmology: retina
Otorhinolaryngology
Otorhinolaryngology: pediatric
Podiatry: surgical foot and ankle
Podiatry: surgical forefoot only
Surgery: cardiovascular
Surgery: cardiovascular pediatric
Surgery: colon and rectal
Surgery: general
Surgery: neurological
Surgery: oncology
Surgery: oral

Surgery: orthopedic
Surgery: orthopedic (foot and ankle)
Surgery: orthopedic (hand)
Surgery: orthopedic (hip and joint)
Surgery: orthopedic (oncology)
Surgery: orthopedic (pediatric)
Surgery: orthopedic (spine)
Surgery: orthopedic (sports medicine)
Surgery: orthopedic (trauma)
Surgery: pediatric
Surgery: plastic and reconstruction

RESOURCES

I. Example Practice: Description, Reports, and Financial Statements

II. Predicting Demand

Article: Four Methodologies to Improve Healthcare Demand Forecasting, 2001
Full citation is: Cote, Murray J., and Stephen L. Tucker. "Four Methodologies to Improve Healthcare Forecasting." Hfm (Healthcare Financial Management) 55, no. 5 (May 2001): 54.
This item was published by the Healthcare Financial Management Association; and there is no longer a link to the item on the WWW. The abstract is available in the PubMed-Medline database at: https://www.ncbi.nlm.nih.gov/pubmed/11351811.

Hoders, Joshua, and William "Marty" Martin. "Population health management and the power of predictive analytics." MGMA Connection 17, no. 5 (July 2017): 38-40.

III. Patient satisfaction

MGMA Data Solutions. "Quality Is at the Heart of Patient Satisfaction: The Heart Center, Poughkeepsie, New York." In MGMA Performance and Practices of Successful Medical Groups: 2014 Report Based on 2013 Data. Englewood, CO: MGMA, 2014

MGMA Data Solutions. "Putting the Patient First Is Your Primary Goal: Canyon View Medical Group, Spanish Fork, Utah." In MGMA Performance and Practices of Successful Medical Groups: 2015 Report Based on 2014 Data. Englewood, CO: MGMA, 2015

Ross, Rebecca. "Determine Provider-Level Sample Sizes for Patient Satisfaction Surveys." MGMA Connection 16, no. 2 (March 2016): 29–31

IV. Advanced Access (open access)

Gans, David N. "Walking the Walk on Patient-Centered Care." MGMA Connexion 12, no. 8 (September 2012): 23–25

MGMA Data Solutions. "Once and Done — Today's Work Today: Hilltop Family Physicians, Parker, Colorado." In MGMA Performance and Practices of Successful Medical Groups: 2011 Report Based on 2010 Data. Englewood, CO: MGMA, 2011

Improving Patient Service with Open Access Scheduling, ACMPE Fellow Paper, By: Jennifer L. Souders, FACMPE, 2011

Centralizing Customer Calls—the Development and Operation of a Healthcare Call Center, ACMPE Fellow Paper, By: Clarice Bongiovanni, RN, FACMPE, 2013

V. Benchmarking guidance

Gans, David. "Benchmarking 301: Advanced Practice Metrics Provide Actionable Insight." MGMA Connection 14, no. 10 (December 11, 2014): 31–32

Gans, David N. "Benchmarking 501: Graduate Studies in Cost Allocation." MGMA Connection 15, no. 2 (March 2015): 16–18

VI. Value-Based Care

Davis-Jacobsen, Doral. "Becoming Risk-Capable: A Group's Transformation Story." MGMA Connection 15, no. 7 (September 2015): 28–32

Gans, David N. "To Understand New Payment Methods, Go Back to the Future." MGMA Connexion 13, no. 8 (September 2013): 35–38

Greene, Michelle A. "Three Financial Benefits of Measuring Quality." In Performance and Practices of Successful Medical Groups. 2014 Report Based on 2013 Data. Englewood, CO: MGMA, 2014

Wong, Meghan. "Switching to Value-Based Compensation Requires Data Benchmarks." MGMA Connection 16, no. 1 (February 1, 2016): 32–34

VII. Profitability and Operating Costs

Gans, David N. "Looking for Margin in All the Wrong Places." MGMA Connection 17, no. 3 (April 2017): 16–17.

Gans, David N. "An Administrator's Dilemma: Minimize Cost or Maximize Revenue." MGMA Connection 17, no. 1 (February 1, 2017): 18–19.

VIII. Productivity, Capacity, and Staffing

Gans, David N. "Cost-Efficiency with Medical Group Staffing." MGMA Connection 15, no. 8 (October 2015): 24–25.

Gans, David N. "Provider Compensation: Getting Your Money's Worth." MGMA Connection 15, no. 3 (April 2015): 30–32.

Gans, David N. "The Cost of Doing Business." MGMA Connection 16, no. 8 (October 2016): 22–23.

Gans, David N. "Threading the Needle: The Right Support for High Producing Medical Practices." MGMA Connection 17, no. 4 (May 2017): 13–15.

IX. A/R and Collections

Andes, Steven, and David N. Gans. "Getting More Bucks for the Bang." MGMA Connection 16, no. 3 (April 2016): 22–25

Fulcher, Annette, Marty Lambeth, Lauren Miller, and Amber Sullivan. "Reaching 95% Copay Collection Rate with Teamwork, Process Revamps." MGMA Connection 16, no. 4 (May 2016): 26–29.

Gans, David N. "Good Management Is Timeless." MGMA Connection 16, no. 6 (August 2016): 52–52.

MGMA Data Solutions. "The Cycle of Medical Practice Billing and Collections." In MGMA Performance and Practices of Successful Medical Groups: 2015 Report Based on 2014 Data. Englewood, CO: MGMA, 2015.

X. Operations

Gans, David N. "Creditworthy? How Lending Institutions Determine Who Qualifies for a Loan." MGMA Connection 14, no. 5 (June 5, 2014): 20–22.

Gans, David N. "Designing the Practice of the Future." MGMA Connection17, no. 2 (March 2017): 16–17.

Rezen, John. "The Building Blocks of a Data-Driven Organization." MGMA Connection 16, no. 5 (July 2016): 26–31. Glossary

INDEX

About the Authors

● ●

Gregory S. Feltenberger, PhD, MBA, FACMPE, FACHE, has over 23 years of operational health care experience and is the Chief Executive Officer at the Idaho Urologic Institute and the Surgery Center of Idaho. In addition, he is a retired Lieutenant Colonel and Medical Service Corps officer (health services administrator) after 21 years of actice duty from the United States Air Force. Previously, he was the Chief Operating Officer and Commander, 10th Medical Support Squadron at the Air Force Academy hospital and prior to that he was the Director of Managed Care/TRICARE Flight Commander at the Air Force Academy hospital. Before the Air Force Academy, he was the Chief of Performance Improvement Tool Development at the Office of the Air Force Surgeon General, Air Force Medical Support Agency, Data Modeling & Analysis Office in Falls Church, Virginia. And Greg has been a Chief Information Officer, Chief of Information Management, Group Practice Manager, and Medical Control Center Team Chief. In addition, Greg was competitively selected and completed a 10-month fellowship in Survey Development, Analysis, and Performance Measurement at the Medical Group Management Association (MGMA). Greg has extensive experience in the use of bivariate and multivariate statistics, sampling methodologies, quantitative and qualitative research methods, and statistical software. He received a PhD from Old Dominion University in Health Services Research. Also, Greg has a MBA in Information Systems from Kent State University, and a BA in Specialized Studies/Biomedical Equipment Technology (Summa Cum Laude). He is a Fellow in the American College of Medical Practice Executives (ACMPE), the standard-setting and certification body of the MGMA; a Fellow in the American College of Healthcare Executives; and a Certified Medical Practice Executive in the American College of Medical Practice Executives. Also, he was the President of the Idaho Medical Group Management Association (2016) and is a board member of the Saint Alphonsus Foundation. And finally, Greg has taught several online courses, authored several articles/ chapters and research posters, and he has presented at MGMA, ACHE, and Military Health System conferences.

David N. Gans, MHSA, FACMPE, is Vice President of Practice Management Resources at the Medical Group Management Association (MGMA) in Englewood, Colorado, where he is the MGMA staff expert on medical group practice management. He is an educational program speaker, author of a monthly column in MGMA Connexion, and he provides technical assistance to the association's staff and members on topic areas of benchmarking, use of survey data, financial management, cost efficiency, physician compensation and productivity, managerial compensation, the resource based relative value scale, employee staffing, cost accounting, medical group organization, and emergency preparedness. He is a retired Colonel in the United States Army Reserve. Dave earned an undergraduate degree in government at the University of Notre Dame, a master's degree in education from the University of Southern California, and a master's degree in health administration from the University of Colorado. He is a Fellow in the American College of Medical Practice Executives and a Certified Medical Practice Executive in the American College of Medical Practice Executives.

Gregory S. Feltenberger

Idaho Urologic Institute Association

Meridian, ID

gregory.feltenberger@yahoo.com

David N. Gans

Medical Group Management

Englewood, CO

dng@mgma.com

CPSIA information can be obtained
at www.ICGtesting.com
Printed in the USA
LVHW011937140622
721281LV00002B/147